Climate Change Finance and International Law

Since 2010, a significant quantity of international climate change finance has begun to reach developing countries. However, the transfer of finance under the international climate change regime – the legal and ethical obligations that underpin it, the constraints on its use, its intended outcomes, and its successes, failures, and future potential – constitutes a poorly understood topic.

Climate Change Finance and International Law fills this gap in the legal scholarship. The book analyses the legal obligations of developed countries to financially support qualifying developing countries to pursue globally significant mitigation and adaptation outcomes, as well as the obligations of the latter under the international regime of financial support. Through case studies of climate finance mechanisms and a multitude of other sources, this book delivers a rich legal and empirical understanding of the implementation of states' climate finance obligations to date.

The book will be of interest to scholars and students of international law and policy, international relations, and the maturing field of climate change law.

Alexander Zahar is Professor of Law at the Research Institute of Environmental Law, Wuhan University, China. He is the Editor-in-Chief of the journal *Climate Law* (Brill).

"This book gives an unprecedented and imaginative scholarly analysis of an important emerging field of international law, which is critical to advancing a solution to the problem of climate change."

Tianbao Qin, *Wuhan University, China*

"In the crowded field of climate law scholarship, Dr Zahar's book makes a significant breakthrough in our understanding of the legal context of financing solutions to global warming, especially in regard to multilateral funding mechanisms and support for developing countries. This excellent book will further cement his global reputation as one of the leading climate law scholars."

Benjamin J. Richardson, *University of Tasmania, Australia*

Routledge Advances in Climate Change Research

A full list of titles in this series is available at: https://www.routledge.com/
Routledge-Advances-in-Climate-Change-Research/book-series/RACCR. Recently
published titles:

Climate Change and the Anthropos
Planet, people and places
Linda Connor

Systemic Crises of Global Climate Change
Intersections of race, class and gender
Edited by Phoebe Godfrey and Denise Torres

Urban Poverty and Climate Change
Life in the slums of Asia, Africa and Latin America
Edited by Manoj Roy, Sally Cawood, Michaela Hordijk and David Hulme

Strategies for Rapid Climate Mitigation
Wartime mobilisation as a model for action?
Laurence L. Delina

Ethical Underpinnings of Climate Economics
Edited by Adrian Walsh, Säde Hormio and Duncan Purves

Responding to Climate Change in Asian Cities
Governance for a more resilient urban future
Edited by Diane Archer, Sarah Colenbrander and David Dodman

Climate Change Finance and International Law
Alexander Zahar

Urbanization and Climate Co-Benefits
Implementation of win–win interventions in cities
Edited by Christopher Hideo Doll and Jose Puppim de Oliveira

Climate Change Finance and International Law

Alexander Zahar

LONDON AND NEW YORK

from Routledge

First published 2017
by Routledge

2 Park Square, Milton Park, Abingdon, Oxfordshire OX14 4RN
711 Third Avenue, New York, NY 10017

Routledge is an imprint of the Taylor & Francis Group, an informa business

First issued in paperback 2018

© 2017 Alexander Zahar

The right of Alexander Zahar to be identified as author of this work
has been asserted by him in accordance with sections 77 and 78 of
the Copyright, Designs and Patents Act 1988.

All rights reserved. No part of this book may be reprinted or
reproduced or utilized in any form or by any electronic, mechanical,
or other means, now known or hereafter invented, including photocopying
and recording, or in any information storage or retrieval system,
without permission in writing from the publishers.

Trademark notice: Product or corporate names may be trademarks
or registered trademarks, and are used only for identification
and explanation without intent to infringe.

British Library Cataloguing-in-Publication Data
A catalogue record for this book is available from the British Library

Library of Congress Cataloging-in-Publication Data
Names: Zahar, Alexander, author.
Title: Climate change finance and international law / Alexander Zahar.
Description: Abingdon, Oxon ; New York, NY : Routledge, 2017. |
Series: Routledge advances in climate change research | "Earthscan." |
Includes bibliographical references.
Identifiers: LCCN 2016033827| ISBN 9780415708388 (hb) |
ISBN 9781315886008 (ebook)
Subjects: LCSH: Climatic changes – Law and legislation. | Environmental
law, International. | Climatic changes – Law and legislation – Economic
aspects.
Classification: LCC K3585.5 .Z345 2017 | DDC 344.04/633 – dc23
LC record available at https://lccn.loc.gov/2016033827

ISBN: 978-0-415-70838-8 (hbk)
ISBN: 978-1-138-61244-0 (pbk)

Typeset in Times New Roman
by Florence Production Ltd, Stoodleigh, Devon, UK

Contents

Abbreviations/glossary   xi

Introduction: argument summary and chapter overview   1

1   Climate finance: concepts and institutions   23

1.1   Introduction   23

1.2   Basic concepts of climate finance   23

     1.2.1   'New and additional' climate finance 25
     1.2.2   Incremental cost (or 'agreed full incremental costs') 26
     1.2.3   Adequacy and predictability of climate finance 28
     1.2.4   Burden-sharing of climate finance among states 29
     1.2.5   Which states contribute climate finance? 30
     1.2.6   Which states receive climate finance? 31
     1.2.7   Kinds of finance that qualify as state or regime finance 32
     1.2.8   The category of state-leveraged climate finance 33
     1.2.9   Development aid distinguished from climate finance 33
     1.2.10   'Access' to climate finance 34
     1.2.11   Ends to which climate finance may be applied (outcomes sought) and the split between mitigation and adaptation finance 35
     1.2.12   Emission pricing as a generator of climate finance 35
     1.2.13   'Innovative' sources of climate finance 36

1.3   Climate finance institutions and mechanisms   36

     1.3.1   Global Environment Facility 38
     1.3.2   Multilateral development banks and the World Bank 39
     1.3.3   Treaty mechanisms for mitigation finance: CDM and REDD 39
     1.3.4   Adaptation Fund and other adaptation-specific funds 40
     1.3.5   A new entry: the Green Climate Fund 41

1.4   Conclusion   41

viii   *Contents*

2   Climate finance in legal scholarship   51

2.1   Introduction   51
2.2   General scholarship on climate law with implications for
climate finance   51
2.3   Legal or broadly normative scholarship specifically on
climate finance   60
2.4   Conclusion   65

3   Legal obligations of states relating to climate finance   69

3.1   Introduction   69
3.2   Specific treaty rules on climate finance   70

    3.2.1   Substantive treaty rules 71
    3.2.2   Procedural treaty rules 74
    3.2.3   Summary of conventional sources 77

3.3   The relevance, if any, of principles of international law   78

    *3.3.1   Sovereignty over natural resources and prevention
of transboundary harm 78*
    3.3.2   Principle of precaution 79
    3.3.3   Sustainable development 80
    *3.3.4   Equity and the principle of common but
differentiated responsibility 84*
    *3.3.5   The polluter-pays principle and burden-sharing
among states 87*

3.4   Synthesis of treaty-based and other sources of law   90

4   State performance of obligations on climate finance   101

4.1   Introduction   101
4.2   'Need' for climate finance   102

    4.2.1   Assessments of need for mitigation finance 103
    4.2.2   Assessments of need for adaptation finance 105

4.3   Supply of climate finance   106

    4.3.1   Introduction and methodological issues 106
    4.3.2   Early climate finance, 1992–2009 108
    4.3.3   Fast-Start Finance period, 2010–2012 108
    4.3.4   Mid-term finance, 2013–2020 109
    4.3.5   Long-term finance under the Paris Agreement 110

4.4   Impact and effectiveness of climate finance   111
4.5   Conclusions on state 'compliance' with climate finance
obligations   112

Contents ix

5 The philosophy of the control of nature — 119

5.1 2°C as geoengineering — 119
5.2 Climate finance and the precarious control of nature — 121

    5.2.1 *Chance and self-delusion 122*
    5.2.2 *Inherent vice: fossil-fuel subsidies 124*
    5.2.3 *Negative social and environmental impacts of climate finance 125*
    5.2.4 *CDM finance and its compromises 126*

5.3 Conclusion — 130

Bibliography — 137
    A *General works* — 137
    B *Reports of FCCC-related bodies (including FCCC reporting guidelines)* — 154
    C *FCCC and Kyoto Protocol decisions* — 156
Index — 161

Abbreviations/glossary

$	All dollar amounts in this book are US dollars, unless otherwise indicated.
2°C warming limit	The upper limit of global mean temperature rise agreed to by the FCCC parties following the 2009 Copenhagen Accord.
1.5°C warming limit	A lower limit of 1.5°C referred to in the Copenhagen Accord and the Paris Agreement is merely aspirational and has no legal force.
Accord	See 'Copenhagen Accord'
ADB	Asian Development Bank
ADP	Ad Hoc Working Group on the Durban Platform for Enhanced Action (2011–2015).
Annex B (Kyoto Protocol)	List of emission-reduction obligations by Annex I parties to the Kyoto Protocol (in the form of a percentage increase/decrease from 1990 emissions) for the first commitment period under Protocol (2008–2012). For the second commitment period, an amended Annex B applies (see Decision 1/CMP.8).
Annex I party	A party listed in Annex I to the FCCC, consisting of industrialized countries and countries in transition to a market economy. This categorization was continued in the Kyoto Protocol but abandoned in the Paris Agreement.
Annex II party	A subgroup of the Annex I parties consisting of the group of OECD countries as it stood in 1992.
AWG-KP	Ad Hoc Working Group on Further Commitments for Annex I Parties under the Kyoto Protocol (2007–2012)
AWG-LCA	Ad Hoc Working Group on Long-term Cooperative Action under the Convention (2007–2012)
BAU	Baseline, or business as usual. That which would have been observed, e.g. in terms of greenhouse gas emissions or another variable, in the absence of some form of intervention, such as a government policy or private initiative; projection into the future of a historical trend.
BUR	Biennial Update Report

xii *Abbreviations/glossary*

CBDR	Common But Differentiated Responsibility (principle of)
CDM	Clean Development Mechanism, one of the three market mechanisms of the Kyoto Protocol.
CER	Certified Emission Reduction: an emission-reduction certificate issued pursuant to article 12 of the Kyoto Protocol, on the Clean Development Mechanism, and the provisions of Kyoto Protocol Decision 3/CMP.1.
CIF	Climate Investment Funds
CMP	Conference of the parties to the Kyoto Protocol.
CO_2 equivalent/ CO_2eq	A unit indicating that the global warming potential of a non-CO_2 greenhouse gas, or a mix of them (which may include CO_2), is expressed as the quantity of CO_2 that would have the same warming impact.
Compliance Committee of the Kyoto Protocol	The Committee makes determinations about state-party compliance with mandatory obligations on accounting and reporting of greenhouse gas emissions and meeting of emission targets. It is divided into the Facilitative Branch and the Enforcement Branch.
COP	Conference of the parties to the FCCC.
Copenhagen Accord	At COP 15 in 2009, informal negotiations in a group consisting of major economies and representatives of regional and other negotiating groups resulted in a political agreement called the Copenhagen Accord. Over objections from a minority of states, the COP took 'note' of the Accord without adopting it. At COP 16, many features of the Accord were adopted in a regular decision of the FCCC parties.
DAC	Development Assistance Committee, an OECD forum that consists of many of the largest funders of aid.
DFI	Development Finance Institution
DNA	Designated National Authority (CDM term)
DOE	Designated Operational Entity (CDM term)
EIT	Economy in Transition
ERT	Expert Review Team
EU ETS	European Union Emission Trading System
FCCC	United Nations Framework Convention on Climate Change. Opened for signature in 1992, entered into force on 21 March 1994.
FDI	foreign direct investment
FSF	Fast-Start Finance (covering the triennium 2010–2012)
GCF	Green Climate Fund, an operating entity of the FCCC's financial mechanism, created in 2010 by Decision 1/CP.16.
GDP	gross domestic product
GEF	Global Environment Facility, the first operating entity of the FCCC's financial mechanism.
GNI	gross national income

Abbreviations/glossary xiii

greenhouse gas	In the climate change regime, the term normally refers to the Kyoto Protocol's list of greenhouse gases in Annex A of the treaty. The list was extended in 2011 with the addition of nitrogen trifluoride (NF_3). The set of known greenhouse gases is larger than that controlled by the climate change regime. Some greenhouse gases are controlled by the Montreal Protocol to the Vienna Convention for the Protection of the Ozone Layer.
Gt	gigaton
GWP	Global Warming Potential
IAR	International Assessment and Review
ICA	International Consultation and Analysis
IEA	International Energy Agency
IFC	International Finance Corporation
ILA	International Law Association
IMF	International Monetary Fund
INDC	Intended Nationally Determined Contribution (term for an NDC put forth in the lead-up to the adoption of the Paris Agreement)
IPCC	Intergovernmental Panel on Climate Change
JI	Joint Implementation, one of the three market mechanisms of the Kyoto Protocol.
Kyoto Protocol	Kyoto Protocol to the FCCC. Opened for signature in 1997, entered into force on 16 February 2005.
leakage, in a CDM project	Greenhouse gas emissions unintentionally caused through the implementation of a CDM project.
leakage, specifically in forestry projects	Where protection of forest carbon in one location unintentionally causes carbon-emitting activities to shift to another location outside the project boundary.
LDC	Least Developed Country
LULUCF	land use, land-use change, and forestry
MDB	Multilateral Development Bank
Mt	megaton
NAMA	Nationally Appropriate Mitigation Action
NAPA	National Adaptation Programme of Action
NDC	Nationally Determined Contribution (under the Paris Agreement); see also 'INDC'.
ODA	Official Development Assistance, the technical term for 'aid', under some definitions must contain a grant equivalence of at least 25 per cent.
OECD	Organization of Economic Cooperation and Development
OOF	Other Official Flows, distinguished from ODA on the basis of their low grant equivalence or their essentially commercial ends.

xiv *Abbreviations/glossary*

Paris Agreement	Text of a treaty annexed to Decision 1/CP.21. The treaty text was opened for signature in April 2016 and is expected to come into force before 2020.
ppm	parts per million
REDD	Reducing Emissions from Deforestation and Forest Degradation in Developing Countries, a mitigation mechanism under the FCCC.
Rio markers	Indicators developed for use in the OECD's Creditor Reporting System for the monitoring of aid linked to environmental objectives.
SBI	Subsidiary Body for Implementation
SBSTA	Subsidiary Body for Scientific and Technological Advice
SIDS	Small-Island Developing States
TTE	Technical Team of Experts
UNEP	UN Environment Programme

Introduction
Argument summary and chapter overview

There is both continuity and change in the history of international climate finance. These two qualities are not always easily distinguishable in the source material. One reason for the difficulty in telling them apart is that important changes to international climate finance have been brought about indirectly, as a result of reforms elsewhere in the climate change regime. These implicit or knock-on changes have yet to be carefully traced by scholars.

The change with the greatest impact on climate finance happened at the Copenhagen conference of the parties (COP) to the FCCC (United Nations Framework Convention on Climate Change) in December 2009. This meeting led to a fundamental shift in climate law as a whole, and in climate finance law in particular. From the ad hoc platform of legal principles to which climate law clung since the Rio Summit in 1992, states in Copenhagen moved climate law – and with it climate finance – onto a new, more coherent, and rational basis. It was a fumbling and not fully self-aware change in legal direction, but once it was made there was no returning to the pre-Copenhagen law. A large part of this book is devoted to explaining the implications of the fresh start made in Copenhagen.

Before getting down to specifics, let us consider what the phrase 'international law on climate finance' might mean. A simple answer would be that it consists of the legal obligations of states with respect to climate finance. An obligation takes the general form of: 'State (in category A, or in general) is *required* to do B in circumstances C as entailed by legal source D.' There are several shades of 'required' in international law treaties; these are indicated by such terms as 'shall', 'shall to the extent possible', 'shall to the extent appropriate', 'will', 'should', etc. These create a spectrum of legal obligations suited to the complexity and context-dependency of an international treaty regime. Assuming we could identify and synthesize all legal obligations of states on climate finance, we would have described what international climate finance law is.

The simple answer produced by the method outlined above may be adequate for certain purposes – for example, if one had to undertake a verification or compliance process under the FCCC relating to climate finance, one would need to know what the relevant state obligations are. One would itemize the obligations, collect evidence of state conduct, align the latter with the former, and make an assessment. For the purposes of legal scholarship, however, more would be

2 *Introduction*

expected. Scholars are just as interested in questions such as the following: Are the obligations on climate finance ad hoc and fragmented, or do they make up a cohesive body of law? Do they promote or retard the objectives of the regime they are part of? (Climate finance is a component of climate change law *and* a component of the broader climate change regime, so conflict is possible at both of these levels.) To what extent are the obligations on climate finance consistent with pre-existing principles of international law? If the obligations do not yet form a body of law, are they evolving into one? Does it matter to us whether this developmental dynamic exists? (It *would* matter if, for example, it were a condition of success of the regime.)

These and other inquiries go well beyond the identification and listing of rules. They would need to be pursued to give a full scholarly answer to the question of 'What is international climate finance law?'. This book is the first extended treatment of international climate finance law. Despite the subject's obvious importance, it has barely been closely studied before.

I discuss the definition of 'climate finance' fully in Chapter 1. Briefly, climate finance is the FCCC-induced transfer of finance from richer to poorer countries for climate change action (mainly mitigation and adaptation). I say 'FCCC induced' because at the time of writing the Convention is the only comprehensive climate agreement in force.[1]

Climate finance law repays close study for the insights it provides into climate law as a whole. The usual way to approach climate law, however, has not been through climate finance. Scholars have preferred to understand climate law as constituted of general principles of international law (see Chapter 2). My method is different, as it relies primarily on a teleological analysis of the treaty law elaborated by the FCCC regime (as explained in Chapter 3). Thus, both the topic of climate finance law and the approach taken here have very little history behind them.

The international law scholar seeking evidence of an emerging law is not infrequently seeking a needle in a haystack. Fortunately, the current foundations of climate finance law are not so difficult to detect. At the domestic level, at least, the facilitation of environmental ends through finance is a familiar topic for lawyers. The control of pollution through the imposition of financial obligations (licences, fees, fines, etc.) are concepts related to each other through legal doctrine, as I will explain. Not only is international climate finance law relatively easily traceable, it is also a window onto the structure and logic of climate law as it has evolved to date.

At the same time, it is important to reiterate that the legal transition I referred to at the start, which began in Copenhagen in 2009, has not yet been completed. Climate law, and within it climate finance law, are both still unsettled, and their content and implications are sometimes deliberately obfuscated by states for political reasons. Nevertheless, there are enough visible elements of the emerging law to justify treating it as a distinct branch of international law. My aim in this book is to show through a synthesis of the law that the post-2009 developments have made state obligations around climate finance an integral part of climate law,

Introduction   3

so that it is impossible, and indeed undesirable, to discuss climate finance law separately from climate law as a whole.

In general, in the course of any survey of the state of the law, one must be careful to distinguish the law of the present, with all its imperfections, from a desired, more developed, and more binding law of the future; for in the process of trying to clarify the current law, it is all too easy to project onto it the elements that one would like to see in it. The temptation must of course be resisted. While law scholars can offer advice on what the law should be, only states can create international law. Even as climate law, and with it climate finance law, have been fundamentally and beneficially reconceptualized since the Copenhagen COP, there is no guarantee that states will stand by this development in the law and see it through to a coherent and rational, let alone fully implemented, conclusion. Thus we must accept that the imperfections in the law as it now stands may never be entirely overcome. We should not flinch from restating the law as it is, with all its imperfections (the lex lata distinguished from the lex ferenda). However, we are also entitled to make a case, where such a case can be made, that underneath the conflicting surface appearances of state practice lie rules, perhaps not always readily visible, that presently bind states. States may be the sole source of international law, but in their decisions and pronouncements they sometimes appear less than fully cognizant of what they have created and do not always rank legal consistency above other interests. A vital contribution of law scholars is to advance clear thinking about what the law is and the extent of state compliance with it.

Information on climate finance (the amounts involved, how they are raised and distributed, etc.) has become plentiful in recent years. However, even at this level of raw data on finance, climate finance lacks historical depth. It was not until the Fifth Assessment Report of 2013–2014 that the Intergovernmental Panel on Climate Change dedicated a whole chapter to climate finance.[2] This newfound regard for the topic reflects the states' conviction, made public in Copenhagen, that the problem of climate change will not be solved unless the FCCC parties manage to orchestrate a huge effort of financial support for low-/zero-emission development in poorer countries. While it was an important realization, it emerged from an analysis of facts and figures; in itself, it does not tell us anything about the state of the law then or now.

Having made several references already to the legal shift that happened in Copenhagen at COP 15, it is now time to consider what this means in more detail. I have described the shift as a fundamental one, because the decisions made at that conference changed climate law and brought it to rest on a new set of principles. So, what exactly changed in 2009? To answer this question, I will begin with an analysis of the Copenhagen Accord's main provisions on climate finance.

The Accord itself is a brief document. Its provisions on climate finance take up only a few lines. The Accord is not a treaty or a decision of the FCCC parties, but a political agreement, and thus is not the best source of international law. However, as an agreement widely subscribed to by states, it constitutes evidence of the law's development. (Readers may recall that the controversy that once

4 *Introduction*

surrounded the Accord had to do with the non-transparency of the process leading to its drafting and how this supposedly spelt the end of multilateralism. Its substance was not the issue.) The scheme prescribed by the Accord, including the one on climate finance, was absorbed into the corpus of FCCC commitments at the Cancun COP in 2010.[3]

I will divide the relevant text of the Accord into two parts and discuss them in turn. The Accord's first provision on climate finance reads:

> Scaled up, new and additional, predictable and adequate funding as well as improved access shall be provided to developing countries, in accordance with the relevant provisions of the Convention, to enable and support enhanced action on mitigation, including substantial finance to reduce emissions from deforestation and forest degradation (REDD-plus), adaptation, technology development and transfer and capacity-building, for enhanced implementation of the Convention.[4]

In accepting this obligation, developed countries (which are not explicitly mentioned in the quoted text but whose special role as contributors of climate finance is contextually implied) committed themselves to provide finance to developing countries to help them reduce their greenhouse gas emissions.[5] Perhaps more accurately, they *re*-committed themselves, because the obligation to bring about a mitigation of global emissions through a transfer of finance from the developed to the developing group of countries was not a new one: it can be traced back to the very origin of the climate change regime, namely to the text of the 1992 Framework Convention, where the obligation to contribute transnational finance (which is another term I will use for climate finance) was mostly shouldered by the parties listed in Annex II of that treaty. However, there is a perspective from which the Accord's wording created a novel obligation. To appreciate what changed between 1992 and 2009, we must attend to the detail of the language used.

The most significant insight into the quoted passage is that the obligation of developed countries to provide finance (or, to be exact, 'funding') is met with a corresponding obligation on the part of developing countries to receive the financial support extended to them and apply it to a specific end, namely measures that reduce their emissions (mitigation) from a business-as-usual (BAU) level. According to the Accord's text, the 'scaled-up' funding/finance to be contributed by the developed countries is to be used to unlock ('enable') mitigation action in countries of the developing group. In its overall amount, financial support for mitigation is to be scaled up ('enhanced'). In addition, developing-country 'access' to the transferred funds is to be 'improved' so that the enhanced transfer of climate finance may henceforth flow with fewer impediments. The important point to note is that, just as developed countries are given no option to opt out of this rule (for the Accord commits them through its use of 'shall' to supply mitigation finance), so developing countries also have no choice (for they must receive the finance and use it as intended). The 'shall' is threaded all the way through the logic of the quoted passage, forming a globally seamless mitigation task.

Introduction 5

In brief, mitigation is an obligation of all the signatories of the Accord, subject to the availability of climate finance. It was the first time such a model had been agreed to.

Some lesser elements in the quoted passage are also worth reflecting on. First, the word 'including', which follows the comma in the middle of the sentence, might suggest that everything coming after that point (i.e. after 'including substantial finance to . . .') is an aspect of *mitigation* finance. This reading runs into the difficulty that 'adaptation' finance, which is one of the items listed in the latter half of the sentence, is not normally considered a subset of mitigation finance. In fact, it is almost always treated as a separate 'pillar' of climate finance. (The number of such pillars is not fixed, although it is usually limited to three, with the third pillar standing for technology transfer or capacity-building or a combination of the two.[6]) Did the parties to the Accord actually intend adaptation finance to be subordinated to mitigation finance? From a logical point of view, mitigation finance *does* subordinate adaptation finance: the more that is spent on attenuating the causes of climate change, the less that will be needed to ameliorate its effects. Mitigation finance determines (and in vast-enough quantities could eliminate) the need for adaptation finance.[7] Adaptation costs, one might reasonably say, are withheld mitigation costs, multiplied by a variable that increases with time, because the postponement of mitigation measures multiplies the strength of the impacts already experienced and creates new ones, so that adaptation costs increase non-linearly.

Thus the concepts of mitigation and adaptation finance are conceptually more closely linked than the FCCC's image of distinct pillars would suggest.

However, it is also true that a significant amount of anthropogenic global warming is unavoidable. The current position of the FCCC state parties is that climate change expressed in warming of up to 2°C, and all the physical impacts that such warming entails, will, for lack of a better word, be *tolerated*. (The 2°C limit on what is a tolerable temperature change was adopted by the FCCC parties at the Cancun COP in 2010. There has been disquiet about the limit, a recent manifestation of which is seen in the Paris Agreement, article 2.1(a). However, the parties' dissembling does not change the fact that, for them, as matters stand, only a crossing of the 2°C threshold would constitute a breach of their collective commitment.) Accordingly, some adaptation costs are irreducible, and adaptation finance could never in practice be regarded as a component of mitigation finance. We are thus bound to think of it as a separate pillar of spending. Consequently, we are obliged to read the 'including' in the quoted passage as including only the REDD programme, finance for which is thereby conceptualized as being part of the mitigation pillar. This particular reading also means that 'substantial finance' applies to the REDD programme only – it does not extend past the next comma to 'adaptation', etc. However, just like mitigation action, adaptation action is covered by the word 'enhanced', and thus there is an obligation on developed countries to increase it too, although nowhere does the Accord say by how much in proportion to mitigation finance.

A second observation on the quoted passage is that the concept of 'enhancement' (enhancement of funding, enhancement of action) is here being given considerable weight by the parties to the Accord, for the word 'enhance' occurs twice in the

6   *Introduction*

one sentence: the scaled-up, new and additional, predictable, and adequate funding is for 'enhanced action on mitigation', as well as for 'enhanced implementation of the Convention'. Such enhancements were being sought in December 2009 because the FCCC parties were plainly aware, and had indeed begun to acknowledge, that global anthropogenic greenhouse gas emissions were increasing year by year, with most of the increase coming from developing countries. States had also come to accept the necessary implication that global warming could not be contained within the 2°C limit without strong mitigation action in developing countries, as well as developed ones. The quoted passage, with its emphasis on enhancement, seeks to elicit not only higher contributions from developed countries (i.e. more ambitious domestic mitigation targets as well as more generous transnational finance for mitigation in developing countries), but also, in a break with the past, an acceptance that developing countries must themselves come to have legally binding mitigation commitments. The Accord does not create such commitments; it goes only as far as to oblige developing countries to use all available climate finance to implement new mitigation measures. Yet it also indicates where the international regime must go next.

With these preliminary points in mind, we may proceed to the Accord's second key passage on climate finance:

> The collective commitment by developed countries is to provide new and additional resources, including forestry and investments through international institutions, approaching USD 30 billion for the period 2010–2012 with balanced allocation between adaptation and mitigation. Funding for adaptation will be prioritized for the most vulnerable developing countries, such as the least developed countries, small island developing States and Africa. In the context of meaningful mitigation actions and transparency on implementation, developed countries commit to a goal of mobilizing jointly USD 100 billion dollars a year by 2020 to address the needs of developing countries. This funding will come from a wide variety of sources, public and private, bilateral and multilateral, including alternative sources of finance.[8]

The most striking element in this passage, which accounts for the publicity it received at the conclusion of COP 15, is the quantification of the commitment of developed countries to transnational climate finance through to 2020, peaking, as the text says, at $100 billion in that year. I will soon discuss the dollar amounts and what they might mean. However, prior to examining the amounts of finance promised – a topic that has tended to overshadow other elements of the text – we must attend to the particular mitigation model promoted in this passage, especially with respect to the second of the two financing periods: 2013–2020.[9]

Similar to the first quoted passage, the Accord's mitigation model here is that substantial ('meaningful') mitigation actions are to be undertaken by *developing* countries, in exchange for which they will receive climate finance from the developed-country group. Thus the Accord reiterates the point about the need for a commitment of developing countries to mitigation action. It is portrayed as being every bit as important as the developed-state commitment to supply the needed finance. In the event that the promised finance is not supplied, implementation of the mitigation commitment of developing countries would be suspended; equally, however, FCCC state parties could not expect the 2°C limit to hold unless they were to implement the 'supported' mitigation commitment. The obligation to supply is inextricable from the obligation to receive, and the latter leads inexorably to an obligation to act. The model also implies that where a developing country no longer needs to be financially assisted for mitigation purposes – considering that 'the needs of developing countries' are bound to change over time, as some become wealthier faster than others – no more climate finance for domestic mitigation will be supplied to it by developed countries. Thus transnational finance in this model is only ever a temporary measure to increase mitigation ambition in countries that genuinely cannot self-fund stronger domestic measures.

While the Accord conditions climate finance on the three prerequisites of developing-country mitigation need, action, and transparency in implementation, the Accord's model presumes that the commitment of all signatories, irrespective of their stage of development, to reduce emissions, is not 'differentiated' in the 2010–2020 period.[10] This is to be contrasted with the model that prevailed up until the Copenhagen COP, which sliced the climate regime into two with a sharp concept of differentiation, differentiating states into Annex I parties, which had an obligation to mitigate, and non-Annex I parties, which had no such obligation.[11] Since Copenhagen, the focus has shifted, so that differentiation is now about the level of need for financial assistance for mitigation actions, not the obligation to mitigate, which is universal. This fundamental difference is often obscured, or even denied, in the pronouncements of states, especially developing states, which for political reasons want to maintain the myth that differentiation post-Copenhagen has not changed, but has remained true to its original expression in the Convention.[12]

As with the first quoted passage, the second also makes reference to funding for adaptation. The text prioritizes adaptation finance for the three subgroups of developing countries that are particularly poor or vulnerable (that is, LDCs (Least-Developed Countries), SIDS (Small-Island Developing States), and Africa, which includes several LDCs). It places no such restriction on mitigation finance. The latter is to be supplied to all developing countries where emission reductions can be made. The concept of adaptation finance is thus much narrower than that of mitigation finance, as it is directed primarily at climate change impacts (not further specified) manifested in a select group of countries. Put this way, the purpose of adaptation finance sounds relatively vague. Mitigation finance, by contrast, is directed at universal causes (greenhouse gas emissions) whose nature is well defined. Another difference is that adaptation finance, from an international law perspective, is necessarily a voluntary scheme as far as the participation of developing countries is concerned, for no country could sensibly be obliged to implement adaptation measures. Adaptation is a purely domestic concern, which must be supported internationally where appropriate, but which is induced by self-interest, not international legal obligation. The point is perhaps only a theoretical

8 *Introduction*

one, for in practice no poor country would turn down an offer of adaptation finance. However, there is a world of legal difference between the mitigation obligation, which post-Copenhagen is universal, and the adaptation 'obligation', which has never been more than an obligation to make finance available, not an obligation to receive it and put it to use. Pre-Copenhagen, when climate finance was still a stunted notion, no such distinction between mitigation and adaptation finance would be drawn; now, by contrast, the legal incongruity between mitigation and adaptation finance is in the open.

So how exactly does the Accord's mitigation model, which I have just presented in outline, contrast with the original mitigation model embodied in the 1992 Convention? It will be recalled that article 3.1 of the FCCC provides that states should protect the climate system 'on the basis of equity and in accordance with their common but differentiated responsibilities and respective capabilities'. 'Accordingly', the treaty declares, 'the developed country Parties should take the lead in combating climate change and the adverse effects thereof.' Taking the lead in this context was from the outset understood by the FCCC parties to mean that developed countries would be the first to commence intensive mitigation actions to reduce their emissions from past levels. The first target for developed countries was to return their emissions to 1990 levels by the year 2000.[13] In the meanwhile, emission growth in developing countries, i.e. *non*-mitigation, would remain the prerogative of non-Annex I parties. As affirmed in the FCCC's preamble, 'in order for developing countries to progress towards [the goal of sustainable social and economic development], their energy consumption will need to grow' – and, so too, by necessary implication, will their emissions. This, in a nutshell, is what I call the 'CBDR mitigation model', on account of its underlying legal principle of 'common but differentiated responsibility', specifically interpreted as the principle that wealthy countries are under an obligation to reduce their emissions whereas other countries are not. From 1992 until the Bali COP in 2007, where a dissenting coalition first surfaced and the seeds of the Copenhagen Accord were sown, the CBDR mitigation model held sway over the climate change regime.

Submitting to the direction set by the CBDR mitigation model, developed states proceeded to 'take the lead' in mitigation action, most notably with the operationalization of the Kyoto Protocol in 2005. This landmark in CBDR history further formalized the obligation of Annex I parties to act first on mitigation and affirmed the privilege of developing countries to be free of such responsibility.

Other, weaker, interpretations of the CBDR principle could have prevailed among the FCCC parties. However, as a matter of fact, other interpretations were left aside in favour of the strong thesis. In the wake of the Paris COP, where the pursuit of compromise generated a political spin that has muddied waters past and present, it is important to reiterate the point that the CBDR model has been understood for most of the period since 1992 to mean that developed states have mitigation obligations and must take on mitigation commitments under the Convention, whereas developing countries have no such obligations or commitments. The FCCC's mitigation model thus 'differentiated' states into those with mitigation obligations and those without any.

Introduction   9

It will be noted that it is entirely feasible, and indeed accurate, to discuss the CBDR mitigation model and its triumphant instantiation in the Kyoto Protocol, as I have done in these few paragraphs, without once mentioning *climate finance*. This is on account of the fact that climate finance is not conceptually central to the FCCC's original mitigation model, but is only a peripheral component of it. Under the strong CBDR thesis, wealthy countries are to undertake their own mitigation at their own expense; other countries need not undertake mitigation or incur any such expense. Some funding must indeed be made available by the former to the latter for the cost of voluntary mitigation actions and especially for adaptation; however, in this scheme, climate finance is little more than an afterthought.

It bears repeating that other beginnings were possible, had there been a political appetite for them at the time. Note in particular that article 4.1 of the FCCC is ambiguous about the strength of the CBDR model to be adopted, in so far as the text, which I will quote here in part, suggests that *all* states have mitigation obligations:

> All Parties, taking into account their common but differentiated responsibilities and their specific national and regional development priorities, objectives and circumstances, shall . . . implement . . . measures to mitigate climate change by addressing anthropogenic emissions by sources and removals by sinks of all greenhouse gases.

However, this apparent assertion of mitigation obligations for all states barely registers, even with the benefit of our post-Copenhagen hindsight, concealed as it is in the drawn-out paragraph of the original (which I have truncated). The idea trails off and is not revisited again in the Convention or in the elaborative decisions that followed. It would remain neglected until the Bali COP, which laid the groundwork for the eventual change in direction in Copenhagen–Cancun in 2009–2010. In the interim, the CBDR mitigation model reigned.

The continuity provided by the CBDR principle, first questioned in 2007 at the Bali COP, was finally interrupted in 2009 in Copenhagen. The Copenhagen Accord's mitigation model was incompatible with the original CBDR model. The change is evident less on the surface of the Accord, where little of a legal nature is revealed, as at a level implicit in that agreement. This brings me to address a preliminary methodological point, one related to the problem of 'narrative capture' that affects so much of the commentary on the climate change regime.

It is often not the purpose of compacts (such as the Accord, or even the Framework Convention) to *declare* the law, in the manner of an ordinary domestic statute. These instruments are not written in the expectation that their provisions will be fought over in a court of law. While some of their elements are declarative of the law, for the most part such instruments of international law are closer to 'conduct' than to 'sources' and must be mined for evidence about how they affect the state of the law. Additionally, nothing requires us to assume that states are always aware of the law they have created through their (non-declarative) conduct. We know for a fact that states have been eager to reach some kind of long-term

10 *Introduction*

agreement at the climate negotiations, to which end language, clarity, and logic may all suffer at different points in the resulting compromise. In these circumstances, a superficial continuity in language may accompany a radical change in policy logic. A black-and-white approach to legal obligation can be softened through a resort to modal qualifiers, and countries that did not before carry any obligations now find themselves implicitly, or under pressure, conceding that they do. States do not attend the climate negotiations for the purpose of developing textbook-perfect international law. For better or for worse, it falls to law scholars to clarify the law which those politically divided meetings develop. An instrument evidencing the law, such as the Copenhagen Accord, is of such a nature that everything from historical sensitivities to careless drafting carried out in the final minutes of a negotiating session can get in the way of its being an explicit and clear representation of the law. In such a context, an investigation into the state of the law does not necessarily lead to findings that are fully apparent from, or even consistent with, the surface features of every agreement or declaration of the FCCC parties.

If the CBDR principle is not at the foundation of the Copenhagen Accord's mitigation model, what is? By 2009, two propositions had become indisputable in the FCCC negotiations: (1) greenhouse gas emissions are a form of pollution; and (2) any substantial deviation for BAU emissions will be costly. Despite this realization, the Accord requires all states to engage in mitigation. A mitigation model that directs polluters to reduce their emissions, at a pecuniary cost to themselves, is an instance of the application of the polluter-pays principle. This principle, which has for many years found applications in domestic regulation, is widely accepted as expressing a legal norm, namely that the environment is not to be polluted without a cost to the polluter representing the polluter's gain or society's loss, if only symbolically. The polluter-pays principle works at the international level (where the subjects of law are states) just as well as it works with individuals or firms at the domestic level. Applied to a state, the principle obliges the state to incur a cost for polluting the global commons, whether for *any* amount of a given form of pollution, or for an excess above a set amount for that form of pollution, depending on the characteristics of the pollutant. The principle thus works at the state level by imposing a mitigation cost on the state, even where the state seeks to avoid the fee by controlling the pollutant, for an additional cost is generally associated with any deviation from BAU pollution. When the Copenhagen Accord extended the responsibility for mitigation action to all states, with transnational financial support to be provided where needed, it signified the incorporation of the polluter-pays principle into the climate change regime, albeit with certain modifications.[14]

What were the modifications? The mitigation model implicit in the passages I have quoted from the Accord does not require each state to bear the objective cost of its greenhouse gas pollution (whether for each unit of pollution or for pollution that exceeds a predetermined amount). Instead, the Accord's approach is to provide that, where a state cannot afford to reduce its emissions on its own because it is relatively underdeveloped or economically weak, yet harbours a

Introduction 11

tranche of current or projected emissions that could be reduced or avoided at a reasonable cost (compared with the cost of emission reductions elsewhere in the world), wealthier states are to assist it financially to achieve those reductions.

The rationale for the commitment to financial assistance in the implementation of the polluter-pays model at the state level to the problem of climate change is that some states are wealthier than others (and have money to spare for the common good), the marginal cost of abatement differs from one location to the next (and is generally lowest in developing countries[15]), the expected rapid expansion of the middle-class in developing countries, which is itself highly desirable, works against a reduction in global emissions unless finance for low-emission development pathways is available, and possibly also that wealthier countries have polluted more than others (per capita) in the past. Thus a principle of equity necessarily emerges to moderate the deployment of the polluter-pays principle in the Copenhagen Accord. The equity principle is to the effect that while every state must bear a cost for its emissions in order to achieve mitigation consistent with the 2°C limit, the cost per unit of pollution, and thus the burden of emission reduction to a state, should differ from state to state, and might even have to be nil for some states if equity requires that their mitigation costs are to be fully reimbursed. The mechanism by which pollution-unit costs and overall burdens for states are adjusted is, of course, climate finance.[16] By ensuring that mitigation funding is distributed around the world in accordance with opportunity and need, the legal principle that the polluter must pay can be applied to all states without 'differentiation' of states into categories with different legal obligations. The fact that some developing states may end up paying little or nothing at all does not make them any less bound by the (modified) polluter-pays principle. After all, if they can act, they must act.

I have suggested that the polluter-pays principle is implicit in the Accord. By this I mean that it is the legal imperative that best fits the Accord's logic. The logic is that greenhouse gas pollution is to be penalized no matter where it occurs in the world. Developing countries are not shielded from it. In the words of the Accord: 'Non-Annex I Parties to the Convention will implement mitigation actions.'[17] The legal norm that best explains this agreement and all subsequent resolutions of the FCCC parties, including the Paris Agreement, is the polluter-pays principle, moderated through the mechanism of international climate finance. The CBDR principle, which had been regarded as foundational to the climate change regime from the outset, was treated in Copenhagen as a misguided legal norm and was rejected. The 2009 shift in thinking constituted a significant development in the law, even if it was not trumpeted as such by states. As a legal development, it is of the kind that underlies state conduct without being fully visible. The reluctance of states to herald the abandonment of CBDR as the guiding principle of the regime may have something to do with its being regarded as a manifestation of the principle of equity. However, the polluter-pays principle is also a variety of the equitable principle: its inbuilt equitable dictum is that harm to the many for the gain of the few will not be tolerated. Emission-intensive lifestyles and production processes are a gain for the few, while the harm befalls

12   *Introduction*

all living things, in current and future generations. The polluter-pays principle abhors such exploitation. When I said above that a moderation in the application of the polluter-pays principle to the control of greenhouse gas emissions at the international level is necessary in the name of equity, it is a case of equity operating upon equity. The CBDR principle does not monopolize equity.

For the purpose of outlining my argument in this book, the important point is that the Copenhagen Accord ushered in a polluter-pays mitigation model, to be contrasted with the Convention's original CBDR model. In the years following Copenhagen, state adherence to the polluter-pays principle became more explicit in the language of the COP negotiations (more about this in Chapter 3). This change in foundational legal principle has enabled the development of a law on climate finance. The old mitigation model, whose purpose was to constrain the Annex I group only, had no conceptual space for climate finance. As a result, transnational finance for mitigation was only ever an appendage, involving essentially voluntary relations, out of which no law of climate finance could develop.[18] The new model, by contrast, has climate finance at its very core. To write about climate finance law post-Copenhagen is in fact to write about climate law itself, although from the vantage point of finance.

It is something of a puzzle that the polluter-pays principle did not find a foothold in the climate change regime prior to 2009.[19] Considering that global warming is essentially a pollution problem – a fact widely acknowledged already in 1992 – why did the legal imperative of 'no pollution without cost to the polluter' not find its way into the international legal response earlier? Consider also that there is a raw normative force to the polluter-pays principle, gained from its innumerable domestic applications to (non-greenhouse gas) pollution control. The CBDR principle's normativity, by contrast, seems at odds with the very problem at hand: instead of attacking the causes of climate change, it works to shield developing countries from the imperative of immediate mitigation action. We are led to presume that during the drafting of the FCCC there must have been an overwhelming *political* preference for the CBDR principle being recognized as the legal centrepiece of the climate change regime. Was it the price to be paid for the FCCC's global ratification? It seems like a politician's, not a lawyer's, response to an environmental problem. This political response might be easier to excuse when we also recall that, in 1992, the 2°C limit on warming had not yet been agreed to (and would not be agreed to for another 17 years). Without a warming limit, there could be no derivation of a global limit on greenhouse gas emissions still to be emitted (no global greenhouse gas 'budget'). Without that, the FCCC parties lacked an objective method by which to 'price' emissions to stay within the budget. Because an overall temperature/pollution limit had not yet been fixed, the idea that a target could be met through the imposition of appropriately calibrated pollution costs had nothing to link up with. Even if the idea was in circulation at the time,[20] it was spinning free of a mechanism. Perhaps by default, then, CBDR became the regime's controlling legal principle, and right away it yielded to a particular interpretation: that mitigation obligations would exist for a minority of states – the Annex I parties – only.

Introduction 13

To summarize my argument so far: in 2009, at the Copenhagen COP, and then in 2010 at the Cancun COP, where the Accord was absorbed into the corpus of FCCC decisions, the CBDR mitigation model, which had bound Annex I parties but had left all other states free to emit greenhouse gases without limit, ceded its position to the notion that all states have mitigation obligations and thus must bear the burden of cutting back their polluting activities. This legal imperative, already equitable in nature as it instantiated the polluter-pays principle, was further moderated by equitable considerations, becoming the imperative that developed countries are required to provide mitigation finance to developing countries (or, equivalently, are required to shoulder a higher cost per unit of domestic reduction) in order to offset some of the non-Annex I parties' abatement costs in light of their economic circumstances. This is what I have been calling the modified polluter-pays mitigation model. One could sift through the climate change treaties and itemize the rules that look like legal obligations, compiling them into a list called 'climate law'. However, at the foundation of today's climate law is a legal principle not mentioned by name in any of the treaties. The sifting method cannot identify the implicit dynamics that are a very real part of the law.

A mechanism to transfer climate finance around the world is an essential component of the modified polluter-pays model, as I have discussed. I have also noted the contrast on this point with the CBDR mitigation model, where there is no logical connection between it and climate finance. Because developing countries have no emission-reduction obligations under the strong thesis on CBDR, climate finance, to the extent that wealthier states make it available for international transfer, may be drawn upon by developing countries, voluntarily, for mitigation or adaptation projects, as they wish. It follows that the finance provided under the CBDR model cannot function as any kind of 'lever' by which to control global emissions and keep global warming from crossing an agreed limit. What still remains to be outlined in this overview is the place of climate finance within the modified polluter-pays model. How does this model determine overall (global) mitigation costs, and how are country-specific costs and appropriate financial transfers derived from the overall costs? The reader is well aware, of course, that no such things have been implemented in the real world. The question here is merely whether the model has the potential to be implemented.

The Copenhagen Accord was the first instrument under the COP to adopt the upper warming limit of 2°C: 'We agree that deep cuts in global emissions are required ... so as to hold the increase in global temperature below 2 degrees Celsius.'[21] The limit was confirmed in Cancun in 2010,[22] whereupon avoidance of 2°C of warming became the FCCC's specific objective.[23] (A lower limit of 1.5°C, although appearing in both the Copenhagen Accord and the Paris Agreement,[24] remains entirely aspirational.) Once set, the limit of 2°C made possible the application of the polluter-pays principle to the climate change problem in a non-arbitrary way, for now the amount of 'permitted' future emissions could be quantified[25] and emissions could in theory be priced so as to keep states from collectively exceeding the permitted global amount.

14 *Introduction*

International-level pricing now has the potential to operate as the control lever which has for so long eluded the regime. With the CBDR model removed as an obstacle to universal action, pollution reduction can in principle be pursued wherever it is most cost-effective.[26] (This includes cases where cost-effectiveness takes into account *projected* energy-consumption growth.[27]) The assessment of cost-effectiveness of mitigation opportunities could be carried out in several ways; for example, through sectoral analysis using industrial benchmarking information to identify areas where emissions per unit of output are relatively low.[28] The cost of investment-risk in the country and other costly circumstances will have to be factored in. Even so, not all countries with low-cost/high-yield abatement potential can be expected to deliver on their new mitigation obligations unassisted. Hence the obligation of transnational financial support. As may be gathered from the wording of the Copenhagen Accord, the necessary funding is to be delivered from wealthier states to developing countries, whether through an international fund or bilateral channels, according to need. Indeed, the Accord initiated the establishment of the Green Climate Fund for this purpose.[29] Under this model, while a global carbon price will be computable, from an individual-country perspective there is to be no fixed universal price for a unit of greenhouse gas abatement. Financial transfers through the FCCC's funding mechanisms are to ensure that the cost incurred per unit of abatement by a less affluent country is subsidized to a level that reflects what that country can fairly afford to do for mitigation, given the opportunities at hand.[30] Important details, such as burden-sharing agreements, would have to be worked out; but the framework and much of the knowledge for implementing such a system is already in place.

This, therefore, is the complex of legal norms behind the Copenhagen model: the polluter state must pay, but the burden must be adjusted by equity. The burden might still be enormous, because the 2°C threshold presents a monumental challenge – but in that case the burden should be felt as enormous by every state. Equity does not make the necessary actions any more palatable, only fair to all.

It is important to recognize the model's interconnected elements so as to be clear about the gamut of legal obligations that states have committed to, when switching direction and going down the Copenhagen path. Climate finance enables a universal mitigation obligation to be maintained without offending against equity. Mitigation and funding-for-mitigation under this legal regime are two sides of the same coin. Mitigation obligations are fully fungible. Again, this is something we have known for more than a decade (the Kyoto Protocol's three trading mechanisms already in 2005 launched the notion of fungible mitigation obligations) but the CBDR model has kept the idea marginalized.

Actual implementation of the modified polluter-pays model and its associated obligations is another matter entirely. Global emissions have been growing,[31] and are expected to continue to grow if no additional measures are taken.[32] Emissions have not been priced globally, of course, and there is no dedicated process currently underway to bring about such an outcome. No global emission budget, as such, has been agreed to by the FCCC parties, despite the fact that these same parties have elevated the non-crossing of the warming threshold of 2°C to

Introduction 15

essentially a legal commitment, and also despite the fact that the IPCC, for the benefit of the parties, regularly re-calculates the emission budget associated with the agreed threshold. It is another example of politics concealing legal obligations, that states will deny being committed to an emission budget even as they affirm being subject to a temperature limit. The COP decision adopting the Paris Agreement comes close to adopting a budget when saying that global emissions must fall to 40 Gt CO_2 eq by 2030, but does not further develop the point.[33] As for the Convention's financial mechanism, it continues to operate in a pre-Copenhagen, ad hoc fashion, both in raising climate finance and in spending it, with the spending part still reliant on voluntary (not legally necessitated) developing-country participation. The Paris Agreement delivers few improvements.[34] These facts do not affect my argument that the polluter-pays principle is now at the core of the legal regime created by the FCCC parties. States have reconstituted the law's foundation, and perhaps because some of this has been inadvertent and some of it politically sensitive, they have as yet made only half-hearted attempts to achieve compliance with their new legal obligations.[35]

In an earlier book,[36] I carried out an assessment of state compliance with international climate change law to the end of 2014. I found there that the law, when properly analysed, consisted of an identifiable set of rules, which existed at a certain level of abstraction – namely, less general than principles, but nowhere spelt out as such – which I named as follows: the accountable reporting rule; the specific mitigation rule; the general mitigation rule; and the good-faith/individualization rule. I found that significant shortcomings existed in the compliance of states with these requirements of the FCCC regime. It was again a case of states succeeding in developing the foundations of a rudimentary climate law, yet holding back from operationalizing it. States, I found, carried on, for the most part, in breach of their own law. It should come as no surprise that climate *finance* law is in the same situation.

In that earlier book I also considered whether international climate law entails a bottom-up or a top-down approach to mitigation. These terms have been the cause of a certain amount of confusion. It is common for scholars to claim that, since around 2013, states have entered an era of bottom-up mitigation, and that the FCCC parties have all but abandoned the top-down approach.[37] What these scholars seem to mean is that mitigation targets are no longer set from 'above', as in the Kyoto Protocol; they are determined from 'below', as in the Paris Agreement's Nationally Determined Contributions (NDCs). But this is inaccurate. Legally, the contrary is true. Up until 2009, climate law had at its core the CBDR principle, which led to wholly bottom-up applications. The Kyoto Protocol, despite what some say about it, is an entirely bottom-up approach to mitigation.[38] It does no more than formalize the emission-reduction commitments volunteered by a handful of states. The 2009/2010 adoption by the FCCC parties of an upper limit on global warming, which happened in response to the realization that there would be no steep decline in global emissions without a radical restructuring of the climate change regime, led to the demise of the CBDR mitigation model, as I outlined above. Afflicted by a bottom-up logic, that model contained no

16   *Introduction*

mechanism (no control lever) for the long-term modulation of global emissions. As of 2009, states have rebuilt their mitigation model, and thus international climate law, on the polluter-pays principle, whose logic is top-down: the price of pollution is to be derived from a global emission budget, which in turn is to be derived from a global temperature limit. The ultimate burdens are to be decided with reference to a general principle of equity. The scheme that the FCCC parties have led themselves to could not be more top-down.

A step-by-step comparison laid out in Table I.1 highlights the bottom-up/top-down difference in logic between the two approaches.

The methodological point bears reiterating that the direction in which climate law is evolving, on the one hand, and the statements that FCCC parties make about the state of the law, on the other, are not always consistent. The Copenhagen Accord, subsequent decisions of the FCCC parties, and even the Paris Agreement, contain language suggesting that the CBDR principle is alive and well in the post-2009 regime.[39] However, a substantive analysis reveals the opposite: not legal continuity but change. Another point I develop in this book (Chapter 3) also goes

Table I.1 Bottom-up vs top-down differences between mitigation models

Mitigation model 1992–2009	*Mitigation model post-2009*
Legal basis: CBDR principle	Legal basis: polluter-pays principle
Bottom-up logic	Top-down logic
1 Some states must act before other states (due to their wealth or past conduct).	1 Every state is responsible for its polluting activities and must pay a pollution price.
2 These states are to pledge emission reductions (as in the Kyoto Protocol) against an ad-hoc baseline (i.e. 1992).	2 Reduction, globally, of x Gt CO_2 eq over y years is needed to stay below the agreed 2°C warming limit.
3 At follow-up negotiation rounds, more states can join in pledging reductions. (In the case of the Protocol, fewer did, in fact.)	3 Reduction burdens are allocated to individual states on the basis of least-cost abatement (economic efficiency principle).
4 Finance is pledged by affluent states to help developing countries engage in mitigation, but the amounts are ad hoc and the uptake of finance is voluntary.	4 The capacity of states to pay for their allocated reductions is assessed in a negotiation forum or through an agreed formula aiming at an equitable burden.
5 Because only a minority of states commit to emission reductions, it is not possible to work towards a global target of emissions and a corresponding temperature target.	5 State compliance costs are adjusted through international climate finance (some states must contribute to it whereas others must receive it and expend it on mitigation).
6 Emission reductions and climate finance are not mutually coordinated, as they are not referenced to a common target.	6 Climate finance is coordinated with state emission-reduction commitments to achieve compliance with the 2°C limit.

Introduction 17

against the current scholarly mainstream; it is that not all environmental law principles are simultaneously applicable to the problem of climate change, such that they form a ready-made body of legal principle capable of regulating state conduct on the problem of global warming, as several scholars have assumed. A pertinent example of the incompatibility between certain environmental law principles when applied to the new problem of climate change is that the CBDR principle managed to keep the polluter-pays principle at bay for almost two decades, until it was suddenly displaced by it. Other cases of incompatibility are discussed in Chapter 3. It is easily demonstrated that principles optimistically presumed to belong organically to the body of climate law – which is itself viewed, incorrectly, as being part of environmental law – offer no relevant guidance, in fact, when brought to bear on the problem of climate change. These reflections count as reflections on the nature of climate law, which the legal literature has not done enough to clarify.

To conclude this introductory section, I return to consider the provision of the Copenhagen Accord, quoted earlier, which purports to quantify the climate finance to be raised through to 2020. The two targets mentioned therein – $30 billion for the 2010–2012 period and $100 billion per year by 2020 – seemed, at the time of their announcement, impressive. They are indeed vast sums by any measure. Yet vast sums are expected in connection with a vast underlying problem. More interesting is whether they are implied by – and thus linked somehow with – the problem's solution. Close attention to the language of the Accord evidences the absence of any such link. Throughout the history of the climate change regime there has been a remarkable reluctance by FCCC parties to aim for full compliance with whatever legal scheme is current. It is the same with the Accord, which despite having called for the containment of warming to below 2°C, gives no indication that the dollar amounts are anything but arbitrary figures. Thus the amount for the triennium ($10 billion per year over three years) was chosen presumably for being achievable in the short run. The second amount ($100 billion per year by 2020) was arrived at, it seems, by multiplying the annualized allocation for the first period by ten. Far from being mathematically linked to compliance with the 2°C limit, the quantification of climate finance under the Accord is a simplistic exercise in round numbers. The promised amounts are a continuation of the earlier model of climate finance, under which ad hoc pots of money for mitigation and adaptation were offered to developing countries willing to avail themselves of them. Even though the Accord made the modified polluter-pays model central to international climate law, it resiled from utilizing it to quantify climate finance. It also made no attempt to analyse the quantified totals into contributions and receipts at the state level – and thus to even begin a conversation about burden-sharing. The Accord's targets for finance, which soon became the FCCC's own targets, and which even after the 2015 Paris COP remain the targets through to 2020, lack a legal rationale. They made headlines because the announced per-annum amounts were larger than any FCCC finance that had been raised or promised before.

The absence of a legal rationale is one of several problems with the Accord's provisions on climate finance. Here are some others. First, developed countries

18   *Introduction*

committed themselves to 'providing' $30 billion by 2012. For the period from 2013 onward, by contrast, the commitment was only 'to a goal of mobilizing jointly' – and therefore to a *process*, not to a specific amount, even though a specific amount is mentioned for the year 2020 (only). Second, the Accord's finance is required to be 'new and additional', yet the text of the agreement gives no indication of a baseline for newness or additionality (leaving open the possibility that finance committed already prior to COP 15 to the period 2010-and-following is to be counted), rendering this requirement indeterminate. Third, the finance for the second period (2013–2020) is to come, in the Accord's words, not exclusively from governments but from 'a wide variety of sources, public and private, bilateral and multilateral, including alternative sources of finance'. Finance from some of these sources is not the states' finance to control; thus here again only a process is being promised, not a specific amount. Fourth, there is no indication of how 'The collective commitment by developed countries' to raise the promised finance (or carry out the promised process to raise it) is to be converted to a state-level obligation. The provision creates a collective responsibility for developed-country parties; it says nothing about an individual state responsibility for the promised amounts. A developed state thus only knows that it is required to raise climate finance, not how much it is required to raise. Fifth, the provision does not explain how 'meaningful mitigation actions' or 'transparency on implementation' by developing countries (both named as conditions for the receipt of climate finance) will be assessed as such. Nor does the Accord contain any indication of what a 'balanced allocation between adaptation and mitigation' means. (Is a 50–50 split balanced, or is a 90 per cent allocation to mitigation balanced because it reduces future adaptation costs?)

If we were to try to express the essence of these parts of the Copenhagen Accord, we might settle on the following proposition: *An ad hoc amount of climate finance should be raised internationally for mitigation and adaptation in developing countries over the coming years.* The proposition would suggest a complete lack of progress in the 17 years since the 1992 Convention. It would be a bleak picture indeed of the condition of international climate finance law.

The true story is a fraction more positive than this, at least from a legal point of view. An important advance in climate law as a whole has been assured by the developments at the COP meetings in 2009–2010. A standard is now available against which subsequent state conduct on climate finance may be judged. Whereas under the CBDR mitigation model an ad-hoc approach to climate finance was inevitable, under the modified polluter-pays model, ad hocness is logically excluded. Already prior to the Accord, developed countries had a legal obligation to provide climate finance; however, because the 2°C limit was not set until 2009, and mitigation action had not, prior to that point, been made a universal obligation, states had no responsibility, whether individually or collectively, to contribute any particular amount of climate finance. There was thus no foothold for a compliance narrative on climate finance. In the period following the Accord, the context changed: the amount required to be provided under international climate law could, in principle, be calculated. An ongoing ad-hoc approach by states to climate finance can now be characterized as a breach of their legal obligations. Strangely enough, from a legal perspective, this represents a kind of advance. For it is better to have created a law that potentially solves a problem, yet is left in limbo (and condemns states to be in breach of it for as long as the limbo lasts), than to be in non-breach of laws that do nothing but make the problem worse. From a climatic perspective, it probably makes no difference; from a legal perspective, it makes a huge difference.

Post-Copenhagen, the climate finance obligation under the Convention is simply an aspect of the general mitigation obligation that requires all states to work towards the avoidance of 2°C of warming. Any shortcomings in states' implementation of their obligations on climate finance will undermine their mitigation obligation as a whole. Thus it is important to attempt to understand, as this book sets out to do, whether the climate finance obligation has been advanced at all since the 2009 Accord, not just in theory or design but in the acts of raising, distributing, and expending climate finance. In order to answer this question, it will be necessary to consider actual information on the states' provision and use of climate finance (Chapter 4).

The book's chapters are laid out in a line of argument: background; law; state practice; and assessment. In Chapter 1, I define climate finance and its key component concepts, several of which are legally significant. I also briefly describe the international institutional architecture of climate finance and the methods of its generation and distribution. In Chapter 2, I review the legal literature on climate law and climate finance to reach an understanding of how climate finance is perceived in the legal discipline. The standard fare of legal writing on climate finance turns out to be a cataloguing of state actions, or insufficient state actions, or trumped-up or idealized state obligations. In Chapter 3, I present the law of climate finance as it has evolved to date. This involves the consideration of conventional and customary sources. Several established legal principles are potentially relevant to the regulation of climate finance, but none, I argue, compare in importance with the polluter-pays principle. It is this principle that was incorporated in modified form into climate law in 2009. In the same chapter I also show that there has developed a procedural law on climate finance, which pertains primarily to state reporting and its quality control. In Chapter 4, I generally limit my discussion of actual state provision and use of climate finance to the years 2010–2016, namely the period immediately following the Copenhagen COP, through to the time of writing. I also discuss the impacts of climate finance during the period 2010–2016 – what we can and cannot know about them. Finally, in Chapter 5, I present an assessment of the practice of states on climate finance against the applicable legal standards. Lest it be thought that I am suggesting that the modified polluter-pays model is without its own difficulties, in this last chapter I develop an argument that the newly ascendant model represents the culmination of an idea that nature can be controlled through the fine-tuning of state policy. It is a fanciful conception! It is also dangerous, for it has the potential to lull us into thinking that we can determine the planetary outcomes of our own actions.

20 *Introduction*

Notes

1 My definition is to be contrasted with extremely broad alternatives, such as the OECD's (see Organization for Economic Cooperation and Development and Climate Policy Initiative (2015), *Climate Finance in 2013–14 and the USD 100 Billion Goal*, Paris: OECD and CPI, p. 10: 'definition [used in] this report considers climate finance to include all finance that specifically targets low-carbon or climate-resilient development'), which do not facilitate an investigation of the FCCC regime itself.

2 See Intergovernmental Panel on Climate Change (2014b), *Climate Change 2014: Mitigation of Climate Change: Contribution of Working Group III to the Fifth Assessment Report of the Intergovernmental Panel on Climate Change*, New York: Cambridge University Press, ch. 16.

3 See FCCC (2010), *Decision 1/CP.16, The Cancun Agreements: Outcome of the Work of the Ad Hoc Working Group on Long-Term Cooperative Action Under the Convention*, FCCC/CP/2010/7/Add.1.

4 FCCC, *Decision 2/CP.15 (2009), Copenhagen Accord*, FCCC/CP/2009/11/Add.1, para. 8.

5 On the definition of 'developed' and 'developing' countries, see Chapter 1.

6 Technology transfer and capacity building come at a cost, and may therefore be categorized as special cases of climate finance. In this book, whenever I refer to climate finance for mitigation or adaptation, I mean to include any associated costs of technology transfer or capacity building. I see no reason to classify the latter as an additional, third, category of climate finance.

7 This tension is newly acknowledged in the Paris Agreement: 'Parties recognize that the current need for adaptation is significant and that greater levels of mitigation can reduce the need for additional adaptation efforts' (FCCC (2015), *Paris Agreement (Annex to Decision 1/CP.21)*, FCCC/CP/2015/10/Add.1, article 7.4).

8 *Copenhagen Accord*, para. 8. Note that both 'funding' and 'finance' are again used, in this second of the two quoted passages, apparently interchangeably.

9 The first period, 2010–2012, is called the Fast-Start Finance period.

10 An exception was made for 'Least developed countries and small island developing States [which] may undertake [mitigation] actions voluntarily'; *Copenhagen Accord*, para. 5. This exception itself implies that, for other developing countries, mitigation is no longer simply voluntary.

11 'Differentiated' can mean differentiation of states into two categories, one with, and one without, mitigation obligations. It can also mean what it has come to mean post-Copenhagen, namely that states have 'different' mitigation obligations (i.e. along a spectrum). The difference lies not in having or not having the obligation, but in whether mitigation action will be internationally 'supported' or not. We can think of these two theses on 'differentiation' as constituting the strong and weak theses, respectively. From a legal point of view, the difference between obligations for a few states (strong differentiation) and obligations for all states (weak differentiation) is a fundamental one, because the discussion thereby ceases to be about who has the obligation and begins to be about whether a state has complied with its obligations and whether the community of states together is meeting the objectives of its treaty regime.

12 United States Secretary of State John Kerry is quoted as having said during COP 21 (Paris, 2015) that NDCs are a 'monument to differentiation' (International Institute for Sustainable Development (2015), 'Summary of the Paris Climate Change Conference: 29 November–13 December 2015', 12 (663) *Earth Negotiations Bulletin* 1, p. 43). This remark – gladly received by those who prefer to see continuity instead of change – misses the point that what is now left of differentiation is limited to the question of indigenous capacity to act on mitigation in the absence of external support. There is no question any more that a developing country which *can* act, *must* act, or that if it needs support to act, and the support is made available, it must take it and act on mitigation.

Introduction   21

13   See FCCC, article 4.2.a.

14   I am not the first to make this observation; see Lin Feng and Jason Buhi (2010–2011), 'The Copenhagen Accord and the Silent Incorporation of the Polluter Pays Principle in International Climate Law: An Analysis of Sino-American Diplomacy at Copenhagen and Beyond', 18 *Buffalo Environmental Law Journal* 1, p. 3 (the 'Copenhagen Accord . . . represents a fundamental shift in the balance between the environmental law maxims of "common but differentiated responsibilities" (paramount in the Kyoto Protocol order) and the "polluter pays" principle, now silently incorporated'). However, while Feng and Buhi's conclusion about the shift in foundational principles is similar to my own, the two authors do not explain how they reached their conclusion. In their article, their thesis is a bare assertion.

15   Jessica F. Green, Thomas Sterner, and Gernot Wagner (2014), 'A Balance of Bottom-up and Top-Down in Linking Climate Policies', 4 *Nature Climate Change* 1064, p. 1065 ('marginal costs of abatement are often thought to be lower in the developing world').

16   Milan Brahmbhatt and Andrew Steer (2013), 'Mobilizing Climate Finance', in *International Climate Finance*, edited by Erik Haites, Abingdon: Routledge, p. 135 ('By separating who finances climate action from where it occurs, flows of climate finance from developed to developing countries are a key way to reconcile economic efficiency with equity').

17   Copenhagen Accord, para. 5.

18   Cf. FCCC, article 12.4: 'Developing country Parties may, on a voluntary basis, propose projects for financing.' This 'voluntarism' still pervades the climate change regime, as I explain in Chapter 3.

19   Cf. Feng and Buhi, 'Copenhagen Accord', p. 13: 'Unlike CBDR, this [polluter pays] principle was not explicitly incorporated into the UNFCCC.' Having made this observation, Feng and Buhi simply move on, making no attempt to explain such a peculiar fact.

20   Economists, of course, have always been aware of the availability and benefits of pollution pricing. Politicians, loath to be seen as causing price hikes, have for many years ignored their advice. See Chapter 3 for more on this point.

21   Copenhagen Accord, para. 2.

22   FCCC (2010), *Decision 1/CP.16*, para. 4.

23   The 2°C limit is arguably not arbitrary but has a basis in science; see Nathan Rive *et al.* (2007), 'To What Extent Can a Long-Term Temperature Target Guide Near-Term Climate Change Commitments?', 82 (3–4) *Climatic Change* 373, pp. 376–377.

24   Copenhagen Accord, article 12; Paris Agreement, article 2.

25   UN Environment Programme (2014), *The Emissions Gap Report 2014: A UNEP Synthesis Report*, Nairobi: UNEP, p. 7 ('the [IPCC's] important conclusion that there is a maximum amount of carbon dioxide emissions, or budget that can be discharged to the atmosphere over time if society wishes to stay within a 2°C or other global warming limit').

26   Cost-effective mitigation is a requirement under article 3.3 of the FCCC: 'Policies and measures to deal with climate change should be cost-effective so as to ensure global benefits at the lowest possible cost.'

27   A spectacular growth in energy demand in countries such as India is expected in the years to come: '600 million new electricity consumers will be added in the country by 2040, requiring more than \$140 billion in energy supply and energy efficiency investments annually': IEA (2015), *India Energy Outlook 2015*, Paris: IEA p. 13.

28   Low-cost mitigation could also be considered more crudely as any mitigation project costing less than, say, \$25/t CO_2 eq avoided or sequestered: Susanne Olbrisch *et al.* (2013), 'Estimates of Incremental Investment for, and Cost of, Mitigation Measures in Developing Countries', in *International Climate Finance*, edited by Erik Haites, Abingdon: Routledge, p. 39.

22 *Introduction*

29 *Copenhagen Accord*, para. 10. On the GCF, see Chapter 1.

30 Several available methods could achieve this result. See, for example, Lasse Ringius, Asbjørn Torvanger, and Arild Underdal (2002), 'Burden Sharing and Fairness Principles in International Climate Policy', 2 *International Environmental Agreements* 1, p. 14 (e.g. 'GDP per capita can be interpreted as a proxy variable for ability to pay'). This question is considered in more detail in Chapter 3.

31 UNEP, *Emissions Gap Report 2014*, p. 3 ('global emissions grew by an average of 3 per cent per year, to 53 and 54 Gt CO_2e in 2011 and 2012, respectively').

32 Ibid., p. 6 (where UNEP notes that, according to an ensemble of 191 scenarios, 'in the absence of additional policies to reduce greenhouse gases, global emissions are projected to rise to 59 Gt CO_2e per year (range 57–61 Gt CO_2e/yr) by 2020. They are likely to continue climbing to 87 Gt CO_2e per year (75–92 Gt CO_2e/yr) by 2050 . . . consistent with global average temperature levels that are around 4°C warmer in the year 2100 than the period 1850–1900').

33 FCCC (2015), *Decision 1/CP.21, Adoption of the Paris Agreement*, FCCC/CP/2015/10/Add.1, para. 17.

34 For a summary, see Alexander Zahar (2016), 'The Paris Agreement and the Gradual Development of a Law on Climate Finance', 6 (1–2) *Climate Law* 75.

35 State procrastination is probably due to the political calculation that, as UNEP put it, 'Scenarios with later action have lower mitigation costs in the near term and this implies a lower burden on current economic growth': UNEP, *Emissions Gap Report 2014*, p. 19. Delaying mitigation action to reap short-term political/economic benefits implies a higher future need for transnational finance and higher overall mitigation costs. The short horizons of politics would tend to underplay this fact. Another likely difficulty is that while non-Annex I emissions are growing strongly, Annex I emissions have been coming down: 'Over the last decade, per person emissions . . . increased in non-OECD G20 countries and decreased in OECD Europe and OECD North America' (ibid., p. 3). Electorates of Annex I countries would have to be persuaded to foot part of the bill for turning around the economies of non-Annex I countries, when their own economies have already been turned around and when many of those non-Annex I countries are economic competitors.

36 Alexander Zahar (2015a), *International Climate Change Law and State Compliance*, Abingdon: Routledge.

37 E.g. Harro van Asselt, Michael Mehling, and Clarisse Kehler Siebert (2015), 'The Changing Architecture of International Climate Change Law', in *Research Handbook on Climate Change Mitigation Law*, edited by Geert van Calster, Wim Vandenberghe, and Leonie Reins, Cheltenham: Edward Elgar, p. 14 ('The climate change regime has witnessed a gradual shift towards . . . a bottom-up approach'); Meinhard Doelle (2016), 'The Paris Agreement: Historic Breakthrough or High Stakes Experiment?', 6 (1–2) *Climate Law* 1, p. 10; and Christina Voigt and Felipe Ferreira (2016), 'Differentiation in the Paris Agreement', 6 (1–2) *Climate Law* 58, p. 63.

38 This has been noted by, among others, Nicholas Stern (2007), *Stern Review Report on the Economics of Climate Change*, UK Treasury, p. 478.

39 The Durban Platform decision launching the process which resulted in the Paris Agreement does not contain a reference to CBDR; see FCCC (2011), *Decision 1/CP.17, Establishment of an Ad Hoc Working Group on the Durban Platform for Enhanced Action*. Nevertheless, CBDR is upheld in the Copenhagen Accord ('We emphasise our strong political will to urgently combat climate change in accordance with the principle of common but differentiated responsibilities and respective capabilities'), as well as in the Paris Agreement, although in the latter case it is further watered down by the addition of 'in the light of national circumstances' after the already-unwieldy CBDR-RC formulation.

1 Climate finance

Concepts and institutions

1.1 Introduction

The concept of climate finance is relatively new.[1] Because the FCCC brought the concept into existence, it is still useful to define it with reference to the FCCC itself and its objectives. At the same time, the terminology of climate finance draws heavily on that of international development finance[2] and deploys a handful of other technical terms whose meaning may not be immediately apparent. Many of the institutions that the FCCC relies on to deliver climate finance pre-existed the Convention and so did not have the delivery of climate finance as their primary purpose.

This chapter provides an introduction to the key concepts of climate finance. Not all of them have clear or uncontested definitions; few of them are recognizably *legal* concepts. Yet all of the concepts I discuss here are relevant to a legal analysis of climate finance because they constitute the components of legal obligations created through the FCCC and its elaborations. Towards the end of the chapter I review the 'decentralized governance structure'[3] that has characterized climate finance to date. The main financial institutions facilitating the movement of climate finance between states will be familiar to most readers of this book and are therefore only briefly discussed.

1.2 Basic concepts of climate finance

I define 'climate finance' as consisting of (1) the finance raised by states pursuant to their international obligations under the FCCC and its elaborations in decisions of the state parties (which finance I will refer to as 'state finance'); and (2) finance raised through the deployment of state finance, and in particular the finance recruited to the purposes of the FCCC through the leveraging of non-state finance. I will refer to the latter as 'state-leveraged finance', which, being by definition non-state finance, may also be thought of as 'private' finance. Involvement of the FCCC state parties is essential to both concepts, with the consequence that finance that is independent of state involvement is not climate finance, under this two-part definition.

The notion of climate finance constituted of state finance and finance leveraged with state finance is neither so narrow that it fails to incorporate the main sources

24   *Concepts and institutions*

of climate finance, nor so broad that it makes it impossible to isolate and study the empirical aspects of the topic.[4] If we are to maintain that international law creates state obligations on climate finance – as it surely does – it must be possible to distinguish climate finance, for which states are responsible, from other finance that is not their responsibility and occurs independently of them. Only then could we assess whether states are meeting their climate finance obligations. I will therefore at times also refer to climate finance (consisting of the two elements of state finance and state-leveraged finance) as 'regime' or 'treaty' finance, to emphasize the dependence of the concept of climate finance not only on state involvement in its production or generation, but also on the very existence of the FCCC and the international 'climate change regime' that has formed around it.

Thus regime or treaty finance is to be distinguished from other finance that in one way or another (and in particular through private initiative) responds to the problem of climate change without instigation by the climate change regime of the FCCC. The distinction is of course artificial, although no more artificial than other distinctions made for legal reasons. The main difficulty is with the element of state-leveraged finance and the role it plays in the compliance rhetoric of states. For while it is true that state finance can 'unlock' private finance and that some private finance would remain indefinitely 'locked up' without state finance, it is less clear that state-leveraged finance should always be counted as new climate finance, or that a state should be allowed to claim the whole amount of leveraged private finance as its own contribution to climate finance for FCCC purposes.

In practice, when considering the amounts of climate finance contributed, it is tempting to retreat to the notion of state finance as a measure of state performance. The estimation of state finance is hardly free of methodological difficulty, but the estimation difficulties are much greater for state-leveraged finance.[5]

Let us consider other definitions of climate finance in circulation. Buchner *et al.* define 'climate-specific finance' as 'capital flows targeting low-carbon and climate-resilient development with direct or indirect greenhouse gas mitigation or adaptation objectives/outcomes'.[6] The work in which this appears is a report of the Climate Policy Initiative. It is not a legal analysis. Nothing, therefore, prevents Buchner *et al.* from settling on a very broad definition. The report's authors do not require a link between 'climate-specific finance', on the one hand, and the FCCC (or another state-level source of legal responsibility), on the other. A different definition is offered in another non-legal work, by Nakhooda *et al.*: 'Climate finance refers to the financial resources mobilised to help developing countries mitigate and adapt to the impacts of climate change.'[7] This narrows climate finance to that which is earmarked for mitigation and adaptation in developing countries. However, it does not indicate who is responsible for mobilizing the finance, so this definition, too, is formulated more broadly than my own.

The Intergovernmental Panel on Climate Change has noted that climate finance under the FCCC is not well defined.[8] However, it has not offered its own definition, merely observing that, as a matter of fact, 'The term "climate finance" is applied both to the financial resources devoted to addressing climate change globally and to financial flows to developing countries to assist them in addressing climate change.'[9] This summary is too broad to serve as a definition in a legally oriented discussion.

The Paris Agreement contains an indirect definition of climate finance at article 9(7): climate finance means 'support for developing country Parties provided and mobilized [by developed-country parties] through public interventions'. This becomes similar to my own definition, if we read into article 9(7) the words 'pursuant to the Paris Agreement'.

I will now proceed to consider the main concepts relevant to the law on climate finance, in the sense of regime or treaty finance. I begin with four concepts that occur together in article 4.3 of the FCCC:

> The developed country Parties and other developed Parties [namely the European Union] included in Annex II shall provide *new and additional financial resources* . . . including for the transfer of technology, needed by the developing country Parties to meet the agreed *full incremental costs* of implementing measures that are covered by [article 4.1]. The implementation of these commitments shall take into account the need for *adequacy and predictability in the flow of funds* and the importance of appropriate *burden sharing* among the developed country Parties.

Following a discussion on each of the four highlighted concepts, I will proceed to discuss several other relevant concepts which occur in the FCCC itself and in other texts of the international climate change regime.

1.2.1 *'New and additional' climate finance*

The requirement that climate finance under the FCCC must be new and additional is far from straightforward. As both physical science and law, the study of climate change and the human response to it is partly about understanding the past and partly about foreseeing the future. Understanding the past is hard enough, of course. Even understanding a country's recent anthropogenic emissions can be a challenge, and in fact in most cases such estimates are highly uncertain, if they are available at all. (At this writing, China announced that it may have underestimated its emissions from coal combustion by as much as 1Gt CO_2 per year, an error that is more than twice Australia's annual output of CO_2 from all sectors.[10]) Foreseeing the future is even more difficult, because it necessitates a host of assumptions, many of which lose plausibility very quickly.

The concept of 'new and additional' straddles both past and future. 'New' in this context means new amounts of money, as opposed to funding taken from another development- or environmental-aid programme and renamed 'climate finance'. 'New' therefore represents not only growth in a specific budget-line item but growth across the whole of the relevant budget – e.g. growth across the whole of official development assistance (ODA).[11] A contrasting example would be money taken out of a subsidy programme for petroleum exploration and used for climate finance – this would count as new money, even though it is a reallocation of existing government expenditure.

26   Concepts and institutions

'Additional' means additional to what a government would have allocated anyway – e.g. because it had planned to do so in an earlier state budget – were it not for the new commitment. 'What a government would have given anyway' forms the 'baseline' – an essential concept in the language of additionality. Additionality is mostly about a hypothetical future – about what would *not* have happened in the future in terms of growth in financial support (or lack thereof) but for the government acting on its new commitment. To continue the previous example, the petroleum subsidy money reallocated to climate finance would not only be new, but also additional, had the government had no intention to make such a reallocation prior to the new commitment.

Even this relatively simple example, though, is not free of complexity. Because climate change law is about getting states to do their fair share, measured in terms of what would otherwise *probably* not have been done, the difficulties signalled by 'new and additional' are ever-present and inescapable.

The assessment of newness and additionality could be simplified by deeming a calculation that uses readily available data to be sufficient proof of the FCCC's required condition for climate finance. For example, total ODA[12] expressed as a percentage of gross domestic product (GDP),[13] when plotted out year by year, could be a rough measure of growth (or decrease) in climate finance, as well as, possibly, additionality. This is because ODA normally includes support for activities that count as climate change adaptation or mitigation. An actually occurring variation on this simple method is to require that ODA must first cross the threshold of 0.7 per cent of gross national income (GNI) before a state could be said to be providing new and additional climate finance. The 0.7 per cent figure, which originates in a loose agreement on development aid dating to 1970,[14] would serve as a permanent reference level or baseline. The 0.7 per cent threshold is still relevant after all these years, because only about five developed states have managed to cross it.

A few countries do use such simplified tests[15] to account for newness and additionality.[16] However, the climate change regime offers no guidance on which test to use. While the 0.7 per cent measure is promoted by developing countries, it is resisted by most developed countries.[17] No other baseline has received even general acceptance by other states.[18] But even the 0.7 per cent figure is hardly fine-grained or precise enough to be a guide on how states are meeting their legal obligations from year to year.

1.2.2 Incremental cost (or 'agreed full incremental costs')

The FCCC's term 'incremental costs' depends for its meaning on a distinction between, on the one hand, domestic actions that produce environmental benefits that go to the community of states, and, on the other, actions whose benefits (not necessarily environmental) are merely local to the state implementing them.[19] The term is also related to the concept of developmental pathways. A developing country may prefer a conventional developmental pathway, which it knows from experience will deliver national economic benefits quickly and reliably, over a less conventional pathway which potentially delivers comparable economic benefits as well as global environmental goods, yet is more expensive to implement and causes disruption to traditional, familiar, ways of life.

Where a programme or project delivers no real local benefits but only global environmental benefits (e.g. the reporting of state policies and measures to an international treaty secretariat, in which case the international benefit is an increase in knowledge for the international community), the incremental cost of the project is the same as its total cost, because there is essentially no benefit for the implementing country.[20] Where, at the other extreme, there is no *global* environmental interest in the project, but only a local benefit, the concept of incremental cost does not apply. In cases in-between, the incremental cost is the difference in cost between technologically traditional, globally harmful, development, and technologically advanced, less globally harmful, development. Climate finance, according to the Convention, is to be limited to covering this difference in cost.

Action to reduce greenhouse gas emissions always, by definition, delivers a global good. Therefore, every emission-reduction project (in a developing country) has an associated incremental cost, but only if the government of that country is unlikely to pursue it because it can derive the same local benefit (e.g. more electricity) from a more affordable, but more emission-intensive, project, and the government cannot reasonably afford to pay for the lower-emission project from its own resources. If the government can reasonably afford to pay for the cleaner project itself, then of course it should not be seeking climate finance for it, and where this holds, the concept of incremental cost does not apply.

If the concept of incremental cost is less convoluted than 'new and additional', it has its own share of difficulty. An immediately apparent problem is its application to finance for adaptation. In contrast with mitigation, which is always globally beneficial, adaptation is only locally beneficial, and does not, in any ordinary sense, ever deliver a global environmental benefit. It follows that the concept of incremental cost does not apply to adaptation projects, and therefore that when states are directed to provide incremental-cost funding, the implied purpose is to support mitigation.[21] However, for political reasons, states never draw that conclusion.[22]

Another obvious difficulty in applying the concept of incremental cost has to do with what the government of a developing country 'cannot reasonably afford to do'. Since not every emission-reduction measure beyond BAU will be unaffordable to the country,[23] how is one to decide which is? Contributing and recipient countries must consider the merits of each project, case-by-case.[24] Nevertheless, there are no rules common to the process of determining incremental cost for climate finance.[25] Olbrisch *et al.* call the basic methodology of incremental costs 'simple',[26] but its actual implementation is far from simple.

There is, in particular, the following additional complexity. The incremental cost of a project equals its incremental capital cost (or 'incremental investment') *plus* its incremental operating cost (or 'incremental running cost', which will be negative if it is a saving).[27] The calculation of the incremental running cost is much more complex than that of the incremental investment.[28] Yet, information on the

28 *Concepts and institutions*

running cost is vital, because, for example, renewable-energy projects typically have a high capital cost but a low operating cost compared with the fossil-fuel sources they replace.[29] This means that their incremental cost is lower than it would seem if, due to ease of calculation, only the incremental investment for the two types of project were taken into account.

Article 4.3 of the Convention further specifies that the incremental cost of a project paid to a developing country is to be the 'full' incremental cost. Yamin and Depledge explain what this means: ' "full" means that all significant costs are to be identified and that [climate finance] is not to be reduced by subtracting either any additional domestic benefit or share of the global benefit the recipient country will enjoy'.[30]

A variation of the concept of incremental cost is used in the Clean Development Mechanism, whose projects always set out to reduce emissions and therefore always entail global environmental benefits. It could be argued that, in the CDM context, the requirement of 'financial additionality' is conceptually closest to that of incremental cost: the proposed CDM project must not be affordable in the host country in the normal course of events (i.e. without the CDM subsidy).[31] In general, however, additionality in the CDM leaves much room for interpretation.[32]

To what extent does state reporting on climate finance utilize the concept of incremental cost? The FCCC process of Biennial Reports, which is the most demanding type of reporting on climate finance that states must currently comply with (which is not to say that it is very demanding), requires each state to demonstrate that the climate finance provided is new and additional, but it does not say anything about meeting full incremental costs.[33] This is because most state reporting is still limited to presenting information on the *provision* of climate finance rather than its expenditure.[34] To answer the question of whether developed countries are meeting their legal obligations on incremental cost, reporting on climate finance would have to operate on the level where provision meets need – which it does not do at present.

Other kinds of reporting (i.e. non-state reporting) also usually do not attempt to isolate the element of incremental cost in climate finance. For example, the Climate Policy Initiative's *Global Landscape* studies 'look at total, not incremental, investment costs because [they] track the progress of current total climate mitigation and adaptation investment, not investment above a hypothetical higher carbon alternative'.[35]

The notion of incremental cost is also related to that of the 'financing gap' – on which, see the next section below.

1.2.3 Adequacy and predictability of climate finance

Developed-country parties to the FCCC must 'take into account the need for' adequacy and predictability in the flow of climate finance. This formulation, in article 4.3 of the Convention, seems designed to avoid committing developed countries to the provision of adequate climate finance in a predictable manner – for this, in fact, is the effect of 'take into account'. The obligation is procedural,

Concepts and institutions 29

not substantive, but even procedurally it is not clear what it entails for contributing states. One possibility is that it concerns only the programme/project level, so that once a developed country has agreed to support an initiative on mitigation or adaptation in a developing country, it should provide the full support without delay, so that the developing country can move ahead efficiently with the project in the secure knowledge of continued funding.[36]

Another possibility is that the procedural obligation does actually concern global climate finance flows, and that it is saying that they should be adequate and predictable, if not now, then in the future. It would certainly be beneficial if global climate finance had these qualities, because private-sector investment in clean or resilient development might then itself become adequate and predictable.[37] The stronger (global) interpretation of the requirement is thus more supportive of the objective of the Convention.[38]

In a related provision, the Convention also calls on the COP and the operating entities of the FCCC's financial mechanism to agree on arrangements for the 'Determination in a predictable and identifiable manner of the amount of funding necessary and available for the implementation of this Convention and the conditions under which that amount shall be periodically reviewed' (article 11.3). The wording here could be read as supporting the stronger interpretation of adequacy and predictability (namely that global 'need' should be determined and then matched by 'supply'); however, the expression 'and available' cuts down the force of 'necessary', and when the two are averaged out, they probably mean no more than 'adequate'. There is no guidance in the Convention itself on how such adequate (let alone necessary) funding should be calculated.

If the global need for climate finance could be estimated and the supply of climate finance known, a new concept would come into play: 'the difference between needs assessments, and available finance, [is] the climate financing gap'.[39] The concept of the climate financing gap is a deliberate echo of UNEP's 'emissions gap'. The closing of these two gaps is, logically, a single exercise guided by the FCCC's objective. Several institutions, non-governmental organizations, and scholars have tried at various times to measure climate finance need and supply. This work is discussed in Chapter 4. There is still no authoritative source on the amounts of climate finance needed and supplied, as there is, for example, on CO_2 concentrations in the atmosphere or the greenhouse gas emissions of Annex I parties. While the FCCC treaty called for adequacy and predictability in climate finance, it has never managed to operationalize or give practical meaning to either of these concepts.

1.2.4 Burden-sharing of climate finance among states

We have seen that article 4.3 of the FCCC calls for 'appropriate burden sharing [of climate finance] among the developed country Parties'. While burden-sharing is not mentioned again in the Convention, the treaty as a whole in essence sets out to achieve a kind of burden-sharing among states with respect to the problem of climate change as a whole. The burden-sharing of climate finance, which is

30 *Concepts and institutions*

specifically called for in article 4.3, is a logical component of the FCCC's call to states to burden-share mitigation action, with a view to achieving the FCCC's objective.

The conceptual difficulty with the requirement to share the burden of climate finance lies less with burden-sharing, per se, than with the notion of 'appropriate' burden-sharing, which is unlike any of the qualifications we have considered so far. Other requirements set out in article 4.3 are amenable to technical definitions. By contrast, the equitable solution alluded to by the phrase 'appropriate burden-sharing' invites states to negotiate and determine an equitable distribution among themselves, and to keep the distribution equitable over time. This is no mere technical matter. Whereas the amount of necessary mitigation could be calculated and the incremental cost of candidate projects agreed to, and whereas developed states could raise new finance without raiding existing aid programmes as well as ensure that the flow of finance to each project is adequate and predictable, such action will not be scaled up unless states can agree on what a fair share of effort is.

Article 4.3 hands the burden-sharing problem to developed countries to solve. However, a corresponding burden-sharing challenge is necessarily put before developing countries as well: How will effort be distributed fairly among developing countries, so that full and effective use is made of the mitigation and adaptation finance that is made available by the group of developed countries? Implicitly, the Convention demands an answer on this point, too.

1.2.5 Which states contribute climate finance?

The Convention assigns the climate finance obligation to Annex II parties. (It is this group of countries that 'shall' carry out the requirements of article 4.3.) Other elements of the treaty, as well as subsequent state practice, would suggest that the obligation extends to all, or most, of the parties of the *Annex I* group.

For example, article 11.5 states that 'The developed country Parties may . . . provide and developing country Parties avail themselves of, financial resources related to the implementation of the Convention through bilateral, regional and other multilateral channels'. In this instance, the contributors to climate finance are all the developed-country parties (a class larger even than the Annex I parties[40]), with the degree of obligation diminished to a 'may'. In state practice, the modal 'may' (which suggests a low degree of legal obligation) has consistently been overlooked, such that increasingly since 1992 'developed countries' have been directed by the COP to supply climate finance in a modal voice closer to that of 'shall'.[41]

Indeed, more than a decade ago, Yamin and Depledge observed that, 'In practice . . . contributions to the Convention's financial mechanism are provided by a broader range of countries than those included in Annex II'; moreover, in Global Environment Facility replenishments, many countries not listed in Annex II have regularly pledged contributions.[42] At the Copenhagen COP in 2009, even Brazil vowed to contribute climate finance, becoming the first developing country to do so.[43] The Paris Agreement, which has done away with the 'Annex' language, formally shifts the supply obligation onto all 'developed countries',[44] without seeking to define which countries belong to this group. While a narrow reading of the climate finance obligation under the FCCC would still have it limited to Annex II parties, repeated state practice since 1992 has rendered the narrow reading increasingly unconvincing.

So, to answer the question posed by this section's title, the category of states providing climate finance is changing. It used to be that only Annex II parties had that responsibility. In a formalistic sense, this is still the case (e.g. only Annex II parties are obliged to report on their provision of climate finance in the Biennial Reports,[45] although all Annex I parties 'may' do so). In practice, most Annex I countries, as well as several economically advanced 'developing' countries, conduct themselves as if the supply obligation extends to them too.[46] The obligation to provide climate finance seems indeed to have become one of 'any country in a position to do so'.[47] Countries are thus regrouping and rearranging their obligations, while the written 'law of the Annexes' stays frozen in time. This change should be understood in the context of what I said in the introduction to this book about the post-2009 reconstruction of the international climate change regime on the foundation of the polluter-pays principle.

1.2.6 Which states receive climate finance?

Article 11.5 of the FCCC provides that developing-country parties 'may . . . avail themselves of' climate finance. While it is true that all non-Annex I parties are eligible in treaty law to receive climate finance,[48] in practice the wealthier non-Annex I parties do not seek it. Even China, which historically has received large amounts of mitigation finance, in recent years has sought relatively modest amounts of it.[49]

According to the IPCC, 'Recipient countries include developing countries and 13 European Union member states.'[50] This type of statement can be misleading because it conflates 'climate finance' in the FCCC's sense with a broader notion of finance that includes all state-to-state finance for mitigation and adaptation activities. To illustrate the confusion through a Kyoto Protocol example, it would be like treating 'climate finance' as the sum of CDM, Joint Implementation, and state-level emission-trading finance, instead of limiting the notion of climate finance to CDM finance – clearly, the other two categories do not qualify for inclusion.

When talking about climate finance in the FCCC's sense, developed countries tend to emphasize that the climate finance they contribute is channelled to countries that are 'particularly vulnerable' to climate change.[51] There are two problems with this emphasis. First, the notion of vulnerability implies that the finance concerned is adaptation finance, whereas in fact the bulk of climate finance (see Chapter 4) is for mitigation purposes. The proportion of climate finance earmarked for mitigation is likely only to grow as the pressure for more ambitious action against climate change itself grows. If developing countries that are 'particularly vulnerable' have a stronger legal claim to climate finance than other developing countries, it is only to the adaptation component of it.

32   *Concepts and institutions*

Second, as Norway has pointed out in one of its National Communications,

> There is no internationally agreed definition of which developing country parties are 'particularly vulnerable', nor is there any likelihood that such a definition will be agreed in the foreseeable future. . . . Hence, the definition of which countries are most vulnerable is up to each [contributing] country.[52]

1.2.7 *Kinds of finance that qualify as state or regime finance*

As discussed in earlier sections, climate finance is to cover the increment that makes non-BAU low-emission-investment decisions in developing countries unaffordable – on some reasonable analysis of affordability – to those countries. (The non-BAU condition implies that the proposition is of no interest to the private sector.) Because climate finance must also be new and additional, to be characterized as state finance it must involve a net cost to contributing states. By definition, then, climate finance in the relevant sense is a form of 'public' finance. Contributing states raise it through general taxation, pollution-licensing, or another mechanism.[53] It is 'public' not only because states themselves raise it, but also because, in principle, it could be directed to any other government programme; instead, it is accounted for as ODA (generally speaking) and sent to a developing country as climate finance.

As also discussed, for state finance to count as regime finance it must have a demonstrable link to the FCCC. When contributing states report on their climate finance they often make the required link by describing the mitigation or adaptation outcomes that particular contributions are intended to deliver. Finance that passes through the Convention's financial mechanism is by definition state/regime finance. The mechanism was set up by article 11.1 of the Convention. It now consists of two funds, the GEF and the GCF (Green Climate Fund). In fact, the largest amount of climate finance is distributed not through these funds but through bilateral mechanisms and through the multilateral development banks (MDBs).[54] The link with the FCCC in this case may be more difficult to demonstrate. Contributing states must resort to a description of the intended outcomes of the finance to make the link.

Article 11.1 also specifies that climate finance is to be provided 'on a grant or concessional basis'. While state finance does not have to pass (and for the most part does not pass) through the article 11 mechanism, the FCCC appears to lay down a general requirement that all of it must be provided 'grant-like' or concessionally. This makes perfect sense, for otherwise climate finance would not involve a net cost to contributing states. As a matter of fact, grants and concessional loans are the better understood and most common forms of climate finance.[55] Developing countries would very much like to see state finance limited to these two forms.[56] But some developed countries emphasize that their climate finance is made up of other elements as well.[57] The larger the number of elements, the easier it is to argue that any promised amounts have been delivered. However, such a redefinition through the inclusion of alternative sources tends to weaken the link with the FCCC, making it harder to assess compliance.

In sum, the kind of funding that qualifies as state or regime finance is not fully settled.[58]

1.2.8 The category of state-leveraged climate finance

It will be clear by now that the definition of climate finance has an aspect to it that is inescapably political. Developed countries will seek to define the concept broadly so that their responsibility as suppliers is lessened or is harder to determine; while developing countries will seek to define it narrowly so that the amounts supplied are more easily identified and the responsibility of developed countries is more easily checked. This political contest could be eliminated if climate finance came to be understood as an aspect of global mitigation consistent with the 2°C threshold. The narrative would change from a contest about inputs to a debate about the adequacy of outputs. However, the current narrative is still the old input-narrative which turns on the promise of an amount of climate finance and whether it has been delivered. Hence states squabble over whether leveraged finance should be counted.

It has been argued that the role of public funds is now a catalyst for mitigation funding, rather than its main source.[59] This is a very different role for public funds than that envisaged under the FCCC. Or is it?

If governments were to act decisively on climate change, namely with unity and with ambition, the private sector would respond by directing new investment into newly profitable forms of production.[60] The private sector can mobilize far more finance than the public sector could hope to do.[61] This widely accepted thesis[62] implies that, in an important sense, leveraging private finance is exactly what (state) climate finance is about. Thus developed (supplier) countries have a point when they try to have it included in their accounting.[63] The thesis on private-sector engagement also implies that government action must be modulated over time, depending on the strength of the private-sector response, which cannot be fully anticipated. Because state finance tops up what the private sector will not provide, regular reassessment of the level of state finance is necessary. The same is true of government-driven domestic mitigation measures, since they do the same work as transnational finance. Another reason for the need for periodic reassessment of international mitigation commitments (if ever they were to be made) is that the remaining emission budget needs to be scientifically updated. Frequent renegotiation of state-government burdens is central to the post-Copenhagen logic. Of course, states have not yet followed through with it.

1.2.9 Development aid distinguished from climate finance

Development aid, which has pre-existed climate finance by many decades, is also a form of state finance or state-leveraged finance. Since 1992, the objectives of international aid for developing countries have overlapped with those of climate finance so that it is sometimes difficult, or impossible, to tell them apart. The main exception is aid of a purely humanitarian kind, such as that provided after a storm

34 *Concepts and institutions*

or flood, which is easily distinguishable from both development aid and climate finance, which have more distant horizons, aiming as they do to build or renovate infrastructure and modernize and clean up economic production.[64]

Development aid, or ODA,[65] is to 'provide assistance to poor countries and vulnerable populations, with the objective of fighting extreme poverty . . . and supporting long-term development'.[66] However, elements of it also seek to produce global public goods, such as the protection of native forests. Climate finance, most of which is classified as ODA,[67] might thus seem to be a species of development aid,[68] whereupon the challenge becomes one of differentiating it from aid that does not primarily promote the FCCC's objectives.

There is an alternative view, namely that climate finance is a response to a global pollution problem that affects developed countries as much as any other group of countries.[69] Its objective is not development, but the reduction of a particular type of pollution produced in vast quantities in all countries.[70] Even if the types of project supported with climate finance overlap with the types supported with development aid, for climate finance such projects represent a means to an end (reduction in greenhouse pollution), not – as in development aid – the end itself (e.g. economic and health benefits). From this view, the conception of climate finance as a species of development aid is a confusion, or even a political obfuscation to bring climate finance under the control of development aid.

The difference in the two perspectives largely corresponds to the difference between adaptation finance and mitigation finance. Once again we are forced to make this distinction to avoid confusion. All adaptation spending could be thought of as a refocused type of development spending:[71] the new focus is necessitated by new knowledge about worsening climatic conditions and sea-level rise. It is a response to natural changes that are sure to happen; mitigation spending, by contrast, is not the continuation of an old funding stream adjusted in response to new information. It is a new funding stream to fight a newly emergent problem. This distinction between development aid and climate finance is an argument for accepting the reduction in the meaning of climate finance to that of mitigation finance. However, for reasons given already,[72] this cannot and should not happen, and the FCCC must retain responsibility for adaptation finance.[73]

1.2.10 'Access' to climate finance

Once climate finance is 'supplied' by developed states to the FCCC's financial mechanism, who controls access to it? The question of access is closely related to that of control, which has turned into a political issue primarily – less so a legal one. Developing countries argue that they should be at least equally represented in international organizations that make decisions on access to climate finance.[74] Access is briefly mentioned in the Convention (article 4.5), and only slightly more expansively in COP decisions[75] and the Paris Agreement.[76] It is not an issue in bilateral finance, where the assistance is transmitted directly from one country to another. The contributing country's full control of access in the case of bilateral finance probably explains why most climate finance is provided through this route.

Concepts and institutions 35

In multilateral finance, where the assistance is deposited with an international institution, e.g. the GEF, the access issue continues to be heard. However, the GCF's access arrangements have addressed developing-country concerns, so that debates over access have died down within the FCCC regime since the advent of the new climate fund.[77]

1.2.11 Ends to which climate finance may be applied (outcomes sought) and the split between mitigation and adaptation finance

The FCCC does not define the outputs of climate finance except in the most general terms. The regime is almost entirely input-oriented on the subject of climate finance. Thus the clichéd expression that climate finance must be 'balanced'[78] as between mitigation and adaptation – repeated most recently in the Paris Agreement[79] – is an input rule. It is true that the same Agreement has made a general, tentative link between climate finance and the 2°C warming limit,[80] thus potentially reorienting it to the achievement of this outcome. Yet apart from such abstractions (mitigation, adaptation, 2°C limit) the regime does not further specify or restrict the ends to which climate finance may be applied.[81]

From a legal point of view, then, the most that could be said about the ends of climate finance is that it must be applied to mitigation and adaptation in developing countries. The FCCC creates no explicit obligation on states to determine or report on the actual outcomes of climate finance, nor does it spell out incidental outcomes that must be avoided. The actual split between mitigation and adaptation finance, as well as the extent of our knowledge about the outcomes obtained with climate finance, are matters considered in Chapter 4.

1.2.12 Emission pricing as a generator of climate finance

This topic, more than a concept, is about the options that governments have to raise climate finance domestically by making individuals or corporations pay for their greenhouse gas emissions. A government may tax emissions at a fixed price per unit; or it may limit permitted emissions to a certain quantity, issuing permits that must be purchased, ultimately, from the government.[82] Either way, the government can exercise some control over domestic emission levels and create a significant stream of revenue in the process. The new income would represent the cost that the country attributes to greenhouse gas pollution, in the limited sense that this is the total amount that the polluters at large in the country must pay. (Whether it corresponds to a broader notion of 'cost of pollution' is another matter, much more difficult or maybe impossible to determine.) The revenue can be used in any number of ways – e.g. tax-breaks for low-income households,[83] technology research, or, of course, climate finance earmarked for bilateral transfer or for deposit in multilateral institutions.[84]

International emission pricing would generate transnational flows directly. While international pricing has never been instituted, the CDM at its high point was a microcosm of it. Prior to the collapse in demand for CERs, the CDM kept

36 Concepts and institutions

up a strong flow of finance from the European Union (primarily) to developing countries. Was this really climate finance?[85] I reiterate that there is no simple answer. Because the CDM is an offset mechanism whose purpose is to assist countries to meet existing mitigation commitments, arguably it is incapable of generating climate finance, because the reductions it finances do not represent 'additional' effort.[86] The counterargument is that the original commitments under the Kyoto Protocol, e.g. those of the European Union, would have been less ambitious had it not been for the CDM. By enabling cheaper emission reductions, the CDM led to additional mitigation, and thus additional finance, even if it cannot be said that every CER traded represents additional effort.

The key point of this section is that international emission pricing, if it happened, would be a by-product of the imposition of national emission limits within a framework of international emission trading. (The alternative would be an international mechanism for the pricing of emissions similar to the domestic pricing of emissions through taxation.[87]) The Paris Agreement has laid the foundation for future emission pricing by imposing emission-reducing NDCs on countries, and allowing countries to trade emission reductions.[88] In time, this will create a flow of finance to countries with cost-effective mitigation opportunities.[89] Much of this will be offset finance (like the CDM), but some of it will represent additional effort and thus count as climate finance.

1.2.13 'Innovative' sources of climate finance

The term 'innovative sources of finance' attained currency after the Copenhagen COP, when it became clear that it was necessary to ramp up climate finance quickly to engage developing countries, but that conventional sources of finance – namely public finance through ODA – would not keep pace.[90]

'*Alternative* sources of finance' was the term used in the Copenhagen Accord.[91] It later changed to 'innovative'.[92] It is commonly used to mean novel or unconventional sources, not widely tried before. It can also signify finance that has been (or could be) derived from economic activity particularly closely linked to the causes of climate change (e.g. levies on bunker fuels or international aviation). Sometimes it is also used to mean a radically new potential source that has never been tapped before, which may even be an economic activity that does not directly contribute to climate change (e.g. taxing international financial transactions).[93] Unlike the leveraging of private sources of finance, innovative sources do not face the problem of not qualifying as state or regime finance. All the innovative options involve state governments taking money out of targeted sectors and redirecting it to climate finance.

1.3 Climate finance institutions and mechanisms

Article 11 of the FCCC set up a 'mechanism for the provision of financial resources on a grant or concessional basis' to function under the guidance of the COP, whose operation 'shall be entrusted to one or more existing international

Concepts and institutions 37

entities'. The mechanism was thus limited at first to the provision of grants and concessional loans by one or more existing international entities.[94] The COP controlled the financial mechanism it had created, but not the (pre-)existing international entity which was made the first operating entity of the financial mechanism, namely the GEF. To the GEF, the FCCC could offer only guidance.[95]

The Convention also encouraged a flow of climate finance through channels separate from its financial mechanism: 'The developed country Parties may also provide and developing country Parties avail themselves of' climate finance through bilateral and multilateral channels.[96] As mentioned earlier, these two channels saw strong growth and now dominate the provision of climate finance.

Institutions of climate finance have multiplied since 1992. At first, the FCCC made no effort to set up a streamlined system for the distribution of climate finance. Not until Copenhagen, in 2009, was a dedicated, fully FCCC-controlled institution for the allocation of regime finance promised, and soon enough established, to try to wrest control of climate finance from the multiplicity of institutions that had in the meantime come to engage in its administration. The complex institutional landscape persists despite the establishment of the Green Climate Fund. Bilateral development-assistance institutions serving the purposes of the FCCC have been set up by several developed countries to channel climate finance directly to favoured initiatives.

Financial instruments used by the various institutions include grants, concessional loans, and guarantees, which are clear cases of state finance, but many other approaches (private equity, export credit, etc.) are also used. Some developing countries have set up dedicated national institutions to receive climate finance, and these too form part of the complex landscape. The situation creates risks of inefficiency (e.g. coordination failure), lack of transparency, data gaps and reporting inconsistencies, duplication of effort, higher transaction costs, and conflicting objectives.[97]

A country profile may serve to illustrate the present institutional situation for climate finance. I will use the United States as an example. The example's standpoint is not a neutral one, but represents the United States' own view of climate finance and what it is doing about it. US climate finance is provided as bilateral climate finance, multilateral climate finance, development finance, and export credit.[98] The United States contributes to the GEF as well as to MDBs, which are not under the FCCC mechanism (and which also receive a share of the United States' development finance).[99] US bilateral climate finance to developing countries is provided in one of three forms: congressionally appropriated, grant-based climate assistance, mainly administered by USAID; development finance, primarily through the Overseas Private Investment Corporation (OPIC), which provides 'standard debt products', secured loans to private equity funds, and political-risk insurance to project lenders and equity investors; and export credit through the Export-Import Bank of the United States.[100] Besides the GEF, the multilateral channels which the United States has contributed to in the recent past include the Clean Technology Fund, Forest Investment Program, Initiative for Sustainable Forest Landscapes, LDC Fund, Pilot Program for Climate Resilience, Scaling-Up Renewable Energy

38 Concepts and institutions

Table 1.1 Mapping types of public climate finance onto institutional delivery channels.[102]

Type of public finance		Form of public financial support	
		International to national, including bilateral[103]	International to project
Contribution to investment or operation (grants)[104]	Upfront grant	ODA, including Carbon	GEF and GCF grants, MDBs
	Funding during operation	Investment Funds Grant linked to continuous delivery[105]	CDM
Facilitation of access to finance	Provision of loans,credit lines	World Bank loans	MDBs
	Risk coverage insurance or guarantee products)[106]	World Bank partial guarantees,[107] guarantees by state export-credit agencies[108]	

Program in Low Income Countries, and Special Climate Change Fund. The United States also contributed to the capital resources of the MDBs.

Because contributions to MDBs are not earmarked for specific purposes, it is not possible to specify what proportion of the contributed finance to MDBs ultimately supports climate change activities in developing countries. Despite this fact, MDB finance for climate activities is included in the estimations of the Copenhagen Accord's promise of $100 billion per year by 2020.[101]

Below, I briefly review the various institutions of climate finance, including the GEF.

1.3.1 Global Environment Facility

The GEF is one of the two institutions, along with the GCF, assigned to the operation of the FCCC's financial mechanism. The GEF's mandate is to provide developing countries with new and additional grant and concessional funding to meet the agreed incremental cost of projects with global environmental benefits.[109] (The GEF in fact acknowledges that finance for climate adaptation does not deliver *global* environmental benefits;[110] nevertheless, it provides such funding anyway.[111])

Streck, writing in 2001, praised the GEF for 'answer[ing] new challenges of international public policy with a new type of international institution'.[112] However, from a present perspective, the GEF model of climate finance is embedded in pre-Copenhagen thinking. Consider the model's salient features: in the course of periodic replenishments, developed countries contribute money to the GEF; developing countries then apply to make use of it in environmental initiatives;

the GEF's allocation decisions are notionally related to the original objective of the FCCC; however, they are not at all related to the later 2°C limit. Moreover, the fund is not exclusive to the climate change regime. It has other, potentially conflicting, objectives under other international treaties. There is no obligation on the GEF to ensure that all of its funding is spent on projects that produce results consistent with the FCCC's objective.[113] Not all environmental projects with global benefits necessarily deliver greenhouse *mitigation* benefits. Due to the GEF's institutional independence from the FCCC, the climate change finance that passes through the GEF is not controlled by the Convention's COP.[114] All in all, the GEF is set up as a programme of environmental aid for piecemeal improvements in poorer countries, not as a mechanism through which to coordinate global mitigation action and keep global warming from crossing 2°C. It reflects the original conception of climate finance under the CBDR principle, which held it to the level of a side-issue in the climate change regime: mitigation would happen in Annex I countries, whereas non-Annex I countries would focus on economic development, local environmental protection, and adaptation.

1.3.2 Multilateral development banks and the World Bank

Since 1992, MDBs have come to play a key role in the distribution of climate finance.[115] If the GEF's objectives on climate finance appear muddled, MDB finance is even harder to categorize, with some programmes designed to have impacts deliberately indistinguishable from general development assistance.[116] Three banks in particular – the World Bank, the Asian Development Bank, and the Inter-American Development Bank – dominate the sector.[117] On the strength of their paid-in capital and guarantees of their member countries, MDBs can borrow from capital markets at lower rates than those available to many developing countries. The concessional loans thus enabled are directed to projects with the required benefits and have a grant-equivalent value.[118]

The World Bank also manages dedicated multilateral climate funds, the most important of which are the Climate Investment Funds (CIF). Created in 2007, they are a pooled multi-donor trust fund jointly implemented by MDBs and managed by the World Bank. They consist of the Clean Technology Fund and the Strategic Climate Fund (composed of the Pilot Program for Climate Resilience, the Forest Investment Program, and the Scaling-Up Renewable Energy Program for Low Income Countries). Funds disbursed through the CIF are in the form of grants or concessional loans.[119] The Clean Technology Fund is the largest multilateral mitigation fund, with a cumulative capitalization of $5.5 billion.[120]

1.3.3 Treaty mechanisms for mitigation finance: CDM and REDD

At its height around 2010, the CDM arguably achieved the status of an international institution of climate finance, moving significant amounts of money from Annex I parties to dozens of developing countries. While the CDM operated

40 *Concepts and institutions*

outside the framework of the financial mechanism of the Convention,[121] CDM-supported projects touched many thousands of people, and the CDM Executive Board's stature grew in proportion to its influence on the ground. There was even talk of the CDM surviving the Kyoto Protocol and becoming a permanent fixture of the new regime that was then under negotiation in the AWG-LCA (Ad Hoc Working Group on Long-term Cooperative Action). As we now know, this would not happen: the Paris Agreement discontinued the model of 'assigned amounts' for Annex I countries and makes only the most general reference to the creation of a replacement international offset mechanism,[122] whose design is to take account of past experiences with such mechanisms (by implication, the CDM). Thus we may speak of the rise and fall of the CDM, the first institution of climate finance (and not just of offset trading) to have completed this cycle.

Assuming, of course, that the CDM is accurately characterized as an institution of climate finance,[123] it is a greater stretch to apply the same term to REDD.[124] The latter has the potential to create much larger financial flows than the CDM.[125] Moreover, it is unlikely that it will become (to any significant extent) an offset mechanism like the CDM.[126] Therefore, most finance that comes to flow through REDD should be straightforwardly identifiable as state finance.[127] However, the Convention's parties have developed this programme only very slowly. They have not created a centralized body to administer it. REDD as yet has no 'institutional' characteristics. There is no mechanism to generate a flow of REDD finance apart from some voluntary contributions by states like Norway.[128] All this might change when the Paris Agreement goes into force.[129] Yet it should be kept in mind that REDD's 'whole of country' model (to be contrasted with the CDM's piecemeal, project-based approach) is politically sensitive or simply impractical with some developing countries, and is likely to remain so for a long time.[130]

It is ironic that, of all the institutions of climate finance, the one to have expired is the CDM. It is the most 'modern' of the institutions, conceptually incompatible in its pure form with the model of development aid (ad hoc donations of supposedly incremental costs) and the CBDR thinking of pre-Copenhagen times, even though the CDM is confined within the Kyoto Protocol – the treaty that took CBDR thinking to its extreme. The use of emission caps to create climate finance and move it around the world is, when applied to all states simultaneously, the essence of post-Copenhagen thinking.

1.3.4 Adaptation Fund and other adaptation-specific funds

The Adaptation Fund faces several problems. It is under the Kyoto Protocol, whose life will not extend beyond the coming into force of the Paris Agreement. The fund is relatively miniscule and depends for most of its income on the sale of CERs (it is structured as a tax on CER sales), the market for which has greatly diminished as the Protocol has continued to lose relevance. It is therefore an 'inadequate' fund by any measure, and its income is unpredictable.[131] In addition to the Adaptation Fund, there is, under the Convention, the LDC Fund, which covers only the 'urgent and immediate' adaptation needs of developing countries.[132]

Concepts and institutions 41

1.3.5 A new entry: the Green Climate Fund

The international climate change regime created the GCF, a generalist institution for transnational climate finance, in 2010.[133] (It was first announced in the Copenhagen Accord.) Another five years would pass before the new institution began to generate financial flows.[134] The fund is to work through accredited implementing entities which will support projects and programmes using grants, concessional loans, equity, and guarantees.[135] Originally, it was thought that the GCF would channel a 'significant portion' of climate finance.[136] The GCF continues to engender high expectations. The Board of the GCF has repeatedly promised to bring about a 'paradigm shift' in climate finance.[137] Its ultimate objective is 'to become the main channel for public climate finance'.[138] Developed-country governments are more circumspect about the GCF's future. Thus, for example, 'The [GCF] has the potential to become the largest channel for the delivery of international climate finance to developing countries',[139] in which statement we see that the carefully chosen language avoids the term 'public climate finance'. The fund's initial capitalization has been modest.[140] Under the Paris Agreement,[141] the GCF is to 'serve the Agreement' not on its own but together with the GEF. The new fund is not given any special standing or role under the Paris Agreement, nor is the role of the GEF diminished in any way.

The GCF Board has said that it sees its mission as linked with the international effort to avoid the 2°C limit.[142] This is a sign of post-Copenhagen thinking. The Board has also said that it interprets its mandate to 'balance' mitigation and adaptation finance as meaning that the climate finance it controls must be split 50:50 between mitigation and adaptation.[143] It is not clear that these two positions are consistent. In the former case, the finance must be tailored to the outcome sought. In the latter case, use of the finance is determined by a decision on inputs irrespective of outcomes. It is hard to say what the GCF will develop into.

1.4 Conclusion

The most important idea reviewed in this chapter is that wealthy countries are under an obligation to supply new, additional, and predictable finance through institutions established for this purpose, or through bilateral arrangements, to meet the incremental cost of voluntarily cooperating developing countries in launching initiatives that promote the FCCC's article 2 objective. Despite the complexity inherent in each of these elements, overall the idea made good sense in the pre-Copenhagen context, when the contemporary reading of the FCCC's objective suggested gradual, open-ended progress, rather than a timed march to a fixed goal. Following the Cancun COP's adoption of the 2°C limit on warming, the idea that wealthy countries could promote the FCCC's objective by supplying ad hoc amounts of finance to developing countries stopped making sense. In the post-Copenhagen era, input tests – 'Is the money new?', 'Is it additional?' – seem beside the point, because the pressing questions are outcome-oriented: 'Is each country doing its fair share?' And: 'Is the collective action on a trajectory consistent with the warming limit?'

42   *Concepts and institutions*

Notes

1   The IPCC writes that 'The assessment of this topic [of climate finance] is complicated by the absence of agreed definitions, sparse data from disparate sources, and limited peer-reviewed literature' – all signs of the topic's lack of maturity; see Intergovernmental Panel on Climate Change (2014b), *Climate Change 2014: Mitigation of Climate Change: Contribution of Working Group III to the Fifth Assessment Report of the Intergovernmental Panel on Climate Change*, New York: Cambridge University Press, p. 1211 (*5AR WG3*).

2   The history of development aid goes back to 1950; see Stephen Spratt (2009), *Development Finance: Debates, Dogmas and New Directions*, Abingdon: Routledge, p. 171.

3   A term used by Martin Stadelmann, Jessica Brown, and Lena Hörnlein (2012), 'Fast-Start Finance: Scattered Governance, Information and Programmes', in *Carbon Markets or Climate Finance? Low Carbon and Adaptation Investment Choices for the Developing World*, edited by Axel Michaelowa, Abingdon: Routledge, p. 127.

4   On the definition I have just outlined, CDM finance counts as regime or treaty finance, even though the CDM greatly relies on private initiative (including investment). It would be counterintuitive, I think, to embrace a definition of climate finance which is too narrow to embrace the CDM.

5   Organization for Economic Cooperation and Development and Climate Policy Initiative (2015), *Climate Finance in 2013–14 and the USD 100 Billion Goal*, Paris: OECD and CPI, p. 27 ('The measurement and reporting of mobilised private finance is in its infancy').

6   Barbara Buchner *et al.* (2013), *The Global Landscape of Climate Finance 2013*, Climate Policy Initiative, p. 2.

7   Smita Nakhooda, Charlene Watson, and Liane Schalatek (2013), *The Global Climate Finance Architecture*, Washington, DC: Heinrich Böll Stiftung, p. 1.

8   IPCC, *5AR WG3*, p. 1212.

9   Ibid., p. 1211.

10   Chris Buckley (2015), 'China Burns Much More Coal Than Reported, Complicating Climate Talks', *New York Times* (3 November). See also Dabo Guan *et al.* (2012), 'The Gigatonne Gap in China's Carbon Dioxide Inventories', 2 *Nature Climate Change* 672.

11   Liane Schalatek and Neil Bird (2013), *The Principles and Criteria of Public Climate Finance: A Normative Framework*, Washington, DC: Heinrich Böll Stiftung, p. 2.

12   For the OECD's definition of ODA, see Smita Nakhooda *et al.* (2013), *Mobilising International Climate Finance: Lessons from the Fast-Start Finance Period*, Washington, DC: World Resources Institute, p. 45.

13   Farhana Yamin and Joanna Depledge (2004), *The International Climate Change Regime: A Guide to Rules, Institutions and Procedures*, Cambridge: Cambridge University Press, p. 277.

14   See www.oecd.org/dac/stats/the07odagnitarget-ahistory.htm.

15   The FCCC's Standing Committee on Finance mentions several other proposals drawn from various sources: only funds mobilized from new sources, such as a levy on emission trading; only funds delivered through new channels, such as the GCF; only funds in excess of projected ODA calculated using a specified formula; only a specified share of the increase in ODA; only funds in excess of current climate finance; or only climate finance that is not reported as ODA; see Standing Committee on Finance (2014a), *Biennial Assessment and Overview of Climate Finance Flows Report*, p. 56.

16   See Chapter 4. Note that financial additionality has long been practised in the CDM, where the complexity of the concept quickly led to simplification, and further to calls

Concepts and institutions 43

for even more simplification. As I discuss in Section 1.2.2, the CDM's 'additionality' is probably closer in meaning to the concept of incremental cost.

17 Kemal Derviş and Sarah Puritz Milsom (2011), 'Development Aid and Global Public Goods: The Example of Climate Protection', in *Catalyzing Development: A New Vision for Aid*, edited by Homi Kharas, Koji Makino, and Woojin Jung, Washington, DC: Brookings Institution Press, p. 168; and International Institute for Sustainable Development (2015), 'Summary of ADP 2–8 (No. 3) (9 February)', 12 (622) *Earth Negotiations Bulletin* 1, p. 2.

18 Stadelmann *et al.*, 'Fast-Start Finance', p. 128.

19 See also the definition in Charlotte Streck (2001), 'The Global Environment Facility: A Role Model for International Governance?', 1 (2) *Global Environmental Politics* 71, p. 73 ('Incremental costs [are] the extra costs incurred in the process of redesigning an activity vis-à-vis a baseline plane . . . focused on achieving national benefits, in order to address global environmental concerns').

20 Yamin and Depledge, *International Regime*, p. 281.

21 This implication is also found in the definition of incremental cost provided by Schalatek and Bird, *Principles and Criteria*, p. 1 ('agreed full incremental costs [are] the additional costs of transforming business-as-usual fossil-fuel-dependent economic growth strategies into a low-emission climate-resilient development path').

22 See, for example, IPCC, *5AR WG3*, p. 1212 ('The incremental investment is the extra capital required for the initial investment for a mitigation *or adaptation* project in comparison to a reference project'; emphasis added).

23 E.g. energy-efficiency measures can have a nil or even negative cost. But even where there is a positive cost, the country might still have the means to cover it. See Clark C. Gibson *et al.* (2005), *The Samaritan's Dilemma: The Political Economy of Development Aid*, New York: Oxford University Press, p. 37 ('A donor has to be careful not to crowd out . . . necessary local engagement by providing too much support and thereby creating incentives to be passive observers among local people').

24 Luis Gomez-Echeverri (2013), 'The Changing Geopolitics of Climate Change Finance', 13 (5) *Climate Policy* 632, p. 635 ('determining an agreed full incremental cost would require having a reasonably good knowledge and vision of all the mitigation options available, followed by an agreement on one that is most effective by some agreed criteria').

25 Susanne Olbrisch *et al.* (2013), 'Estimates of Incremental Investment for, and Cost of, Mitigation Measures in Developing Countries', in *International Climate Finance*, edited by Erik Haites, Abingdon: Routledge, pp. 32–33 ('A definition of the "full incremental costs" has not yet been agreed, so the financial resources that should be provided to developing countries for mitigation measures cannot be determined precisely').

26 Ibid., p. 33.

27 Erik Haites (2011), 'Climate Change Finance', 11 (3) *Climate Policy* 963, p. 964 ('The full incremental cost could be argued to be the higher capital cost . . . less the present value of the operating cost savings').

28 For the reasons, see ibid., p. 965; see also Olbrisch *et al.*, 'Estimates of Incremental Investment', p. 48; and Yulia Yamineva and Kati Kulovesi (2013), 'The New Framework for Climate Finance under the United Nations Framework Convention on Climate Change: A Breakthrough or an Empty Promise?', in *Climate Change and the Law*, edited by Erkki J. Hollo, Kati Kulovesi, and Michael Mehling, Dordrecht: Springer, p. 212.

29 IPCC, *5AR WG3*, p. 1212. Another example is REDD measures which require little capital investment, so virtually all of the costs are operating costs: Olbrisch *et al.*, 'Estimates of Incremental Investment', p. 43.

30 Yamin and Depledge, *International Regime*, p. 280.

44 Concepts and institutions

31 Cf.: 'The mechanism provides top-up, supplemental financing that makes low-emitting projects competitive against cheaper but higher-emitting alternatives'; CDM Executive Board (2015), *Annual Report*, FCCC/KP/CMP/2015/5, para. 14.

32 In Chapter 5, I refer to a group of large CDM projects that, on any reasonable interpretation of the term, have no additionality.

33 FCCC (2011), *Decision 2/CP.17, Outcome of the Work of the Ad Hoc Working Group on Long-Term Cooperative Action under the Convention*, FCCC/CP/2011/9/Add.1, Annex I ('UNFCCC Biennial Reporting Guidelines for Developed Country Parties'), para. 18.f.

34 IPCC, *5AR WG3*, p. 1214 ('Available data [on climate finance] typically relate to commitments rather than disbursements'). For more on this point, see Chapter 4.

35 Angela Falconer and Martin Stadelmann (2014), *What is Climate Finance? Definitions to Improve Tracking and Scale Up Climate Finance*, Climate Policy Initiative.

36 On the negative impact of unpredictable aid flows, see Spratt, *Development Finance*, pp. 185–186.

37 Alex Bowen (2013), 'Raising Climate Finance to Support Developing Country Action: Some Economic Considerations', in *International Climate Finance*, edited by Erik Haites, Abingdon: Routledge, pp. 97–98.

38 Schalatek and Bird, *Principles and Criteria*, p. 2.

39 Buchner *et al.*, *Climate Finance 2013*, p. 33.

40 Yamin and Depledge, *International Regime*, p. 274 ('the Republic of Korea, Malta and Cyprus, Israel and a number of parties from Central Asia and Central/Eastern Europe are not considered or do not consider themselves to be developing countries').

41 E.g. FCCC (2014), *Decision 5/CP.20, Long-Term Climate Finance*, FCCC/CP/2014/10/Add.2, para. 7 ('[The COP] Calls on developed country Parties to channel a substantial share of public climate funds to adaptation activities').

42 Yamin and Depledge, *International.Regime*, p. 267. See also IPCC, *5AR WG3*, p. 1214.

43 Lin Feng and Jason Buhi (2010–2011), 'The Copenhagen Accord and the Silent Incorporation of the Polluter Pays Principle in International Climate Law: An Analysis of Sino-American Diplomacy at Copenhagen and Beyond', 18 *Buffalo Environmental Law Journal* 1, p. 60.

44 See article 9.1 of the Paris Agreement.

45 FCCC (2011), *Decision 2/CP.17*, Annex I, para. 13.

46 E.g. the United Arab Emirates provided $1.2 billion of climate-related finance in 2013–2014: OECD and CPI, *Climate Finance 2013–14*, p. 23. See also the other examples on the same page.

47 IISD, 'ADP 2–8 (No. 3)', p. 2.

48 A point emphasized by Yamin and Depledge, *International Regime*, p. 273.

49 Aidy Halimanjaya et al. (2013), *Climate Finance Thematic Briefing: Mitigation Finance*, Washington, DC: Heinrich Böll Stiftung, p. 2; cf. Robert L. Hicks et al. (2008), *Greening Aid? Understanding the Environmental Impact of Development Assistance*, New York: Oxford University Press, p. 248.

50 IPCC, *5AR WG3*, p. 1215.

51 E.g. Commonwealth of Australia (2014), *Australia's Fast-Start Climate Finance: July 2010–June 2013*, p. 4.

52 Government of Norway (2014), *Norway's Sixth National Communication under the Framework Convention on Climate Change*, p. 162.

53 Bowen, 'Raising Climate Finance', p. 100 ('The general principle is to tax to finance current spending and borrow to finance public investment. . . . From the perspective of a developed-country government, this suggests that transfers to developing countries should be financed by tax revenue'); and Charlotte Streck and Charlie Parker

Concepts and institutions 45

(2012), 'Financing REDD+', in *Analysing REDD+: Challenges and Choices*, edited by Arild Angelsen *et al.*, Bogor Barat: Center for International Forestry Research, p. 119 ('Market-linked and non-market mechanisms are both forms of public sector finance').

54 Karsten Neuhoff et al. (2009), *Structuring International Financial Support to Support Domestic Climate Change Mitigation in Developing Countries*, Cambridge: Climate Strategies, p. 26.

55 Mattia Romani and Nicholas Stern (2013), 'Sources of Finance for Climate Action: Principles and Options for Implementation Mechanisms in this Decade', in *International Climate Finance*, edited by Erik Haites, Abingdon: Routledge, p. 120 ('grants ... without repayment obligations, which are over and above existing commitments, increase the net resources available to the recipient country [as] do concessional loans, which carry a repayment obligation but have a "grant equivalent" value depending on the nature of their concessionary element'); see also Neuhoff *et al.*, *Structuring International Financial Support*, p. 13 (a concessional loan is the 'direct provision of capital on terms that are advantageous compared to that which would be available from private capital markets'); IPCC, *5AR WG3*, p. 1227; and Standing Committee on Finance, *Biennial Assessment 2014*, pp. 8, 62.

56 E.g. IISD, 'ADP 2–8 (No. 3)', p. 2 ('Saudi Arabia, for the Arab Group, asked that financing be primarily public, including grant-based finance'); and Stadelmann *et al.*, 'Fast-Start Finance', p. 125.

57 Thus the United States counts export credit, whose primary purpose is to facilitate exports, as climate finance: United States (2014), *United States Climate Action Report 2014*, Washington, DC: US Department of State, p. 24.

58 Olbrisch *et al.*, 'Estimates of Incremental Investment', p. 43.

59 Gomez-Echeverri, 'Geopolitics of Climate Finance', p. 641; and United States, *Climate Action Report*, p. 182 ('The U.S. government is looking to use public funds where they are catalytic').

60 Neuhoff *et al.*, *Structuring International Financial Support*, p. 7; and Bowen, 'Raising Climate Finance', pp. 99–100.

61 Gomez-Echeverri, 'Geopolitics of Climate Finance', p. 641; and IPCC, *5AR WG3*, p. 1214.

62 Neuhoff et al., *Structuring International Financial Support*, p. 7.

63 The counterargument is that, until such time as public finance has created a level field (after which private investment will follow naturally, by economic self-interest), it is not appropriate to count private investment as climate finance. With time, government support for mitigation could be phased out completely, but until such time, climate finance is only whatever the government contributes and not the private investment leveraged. As for adaptation finance, where there is no 'level field' to be created, it would probably never be phased out: Spratt, *Development Finance*, p. 203.

64 Derviş and Puritz Milsom, 'Development Aid', p. 155.

65 Spratt, *Development Finance*, p. 2.

66 Derviş and Puritz Milsom, 'Development Aid', p. 155.

67 OECD and CPI, *Climate Finance 2013–14*, p. 22 ('ODA ... continues to be the predominant source of bilateral public climate finance (accounting for 84% of volumes in 2013–14)').

68 Urvashi Narain, Sergio Margulis, and Timothy Essam (2013), 'Estimating Costs of Adaptation to Climate Change', in *International Climate Finance*, edited by Erik Haites, Abingdon: Routledge, p. 74 ('continued development may be one of the best defences against climate change').

69 Neuhoff *et al.*, *Structuring International Financial Support*, p. 26 ('Climate change support is not about aid, with donors and recipients. It is about taking joint responsibility for a global problem').

46 Concepts and institutions

70 Derviş and Puritz Milsom, 'Development Aid', pp. 174–175 ('The financing of activities that benefit the whole world [has] a rationale that is different from that of development aid [i.e. altruistic poverty-reduction]').

71 Romani and Stern, 'Sources of Finance', p. 128 ('adaptation is essentially development in a more hostile climate').

72 See the Introduction to this book.

73 Subject to the consideration that 'keeping the adaptation funds separate from development funds could lead to a serious duplication of effort and the misallocation of scarce resources': Joel B. Smith *et al.* (2013), 'Development and Climate Change Adaptation Funding: Coordination and Integration', in *International Climate Finance*, edited by Erik Haites, Abingdon: Routledge, p. 54.

74 Derviş and Puritz Milsom, 'Development Aid', p. 168. 'Direct access' to climate finance has been defined as the situation where 'project management traditionally played by multilateral, international, and bilateral institutions . . . is taken on by the national funding entity or institution': Gomez-Echeverri, 'Geopolitics of Climate Finance', p. 634.

75 E.g. FCCC (2011), *Decision 3/CP.17, Launching the Green Climate Fund*, FCCC/CP/2011/9/Add.1.

76 Article 9.9 of the Paris Agreement: 'The institutions serving this Agreement . . . shall aim to ensure efficient access to financial resources through simplified approval procedures.'

77 On the GCF's access arrangements, see Schalatek and Nakhooda, *The Green Climate Fund*, p. 3; and Green Climate Fund (2015), *Report of the Green Climate Fund to the Conference of the Parties*, FCCC/CP/2015/3, p. 5.

78 The G77/China group of developing countries prefer the term 'equal allocation' (see IISD, 'ADP 2–8 (No. 3)', p. 2), whereas developed countries use 'balanced allocation'. It is the latter term that prevails in international agreements.

79 Article 9.4.

80 Article 2.1.

81 A typical statement is this: 'Climate finance aims at reducing emissions, and enhancing sinks of GHG and aims at reducing vulnerability of, and maintaining and increasing the resilience of, human and ecological systems'; Standing Committee on Finance, *Biennial Assessment 2014*, p. 19.

82 IPCC, *5AR WG3*, pp. 1149, 1155.

83 Ibid., p. 1148.

84 Ibid., p. 1210.

85 Charlotte Streck (2009), 'Expectations and Reality of the Clean Development Mechanism: A Climate Finance Instrument between Accusation and Aspirations', in *Climate Finance: Regulatory and Funding Strategies for Climate Change and Global Development*, edited by Richard B. Stewart, Benedict Kingsbury, and Bryce Rudyk, New York: New York University Press, p. 71.

86 Axel Michaelowa (2012), 'Manoeuvring Climate Finance around the Pitfalls: Finding the Right Policy Mix', in *Carbon Markets or Climate Finance? Low Carbon and Adaptation Investment Choices for the Developing World*, edited by Axel Michaelowa, Abingdon: Routledge, p. 259.

87 Such a system could be arranged if states wanted it; see William D. Nordhaus (2015a), 'A New Solution: The Climate Club', 62 (10) *The New York Review of Books* 36, p. 37 ('A policy to optimize the global benefits of emissions reductions would require a universal carbon price of $40 per ton [approximately]. Under this policy, countries might set a carbon tax of $40 per ton on all carbon-emitting activities', thus creating an international tax).

88 Article 6.

Concepts and institutions 47

89 Nicholas Stern (2007), *Stern Review Report on the Economics of Climate Change*, UK Treasury, p. 320.
90 Romani and Stern, 'Sources of Finance', p. 126.
91 FCCC, *Decision 2/CP.15 (2009), Copenhagen Accord*, FCCC/CP/2009/11/Add.1, paras 8–9.
92 FCCC (2011), *Decision 3/CP.17*, Annex, para. 38.
93 For a discussion of the term and a weighing up of various options, see Spratt, *Development Finance*, pp. 188–190; Michaelowa, 'Right Policy Mix', p. 256; Stadelmann *et al.*, 'Fast-Start Finance', p. 128; Bowen, 'Raising Climate Finance', pp. 106, 108; Nakhooda *et al.*, *Lessons from the Fast-Start Finance Period*, p. 44; Romani and Stern, 'Sources of Finance', p. 126; and IPCC, *5AR WG3*, p. 1233.
94 Scholars have felt the need to define the FCCC's financial mechanism very broadly, even though such a broad understanding is not justified by the Convention's text. E.g. Yamin and Depledge define 'financial mechanism' as 'the totality of legal, institutional and procedural arrangements that regulate and make possible the flow of financial resources mandated by the Convention': Yamin and Depledge, *International Regime*, p. 283.
95 Ibid., pp. 265–266.
96 FCCC, article 11.5.
97 Neuhoff *et al.*, *Structuring International Financial Support*, p. 26; Derviş and Puritz Milsom, 'Development Aid', p. 166; and FCCC (2014), *Decision 9/CP.20, Fifth Review of the Financial Mechanism*, FCCC/CP/2014/10/Add.2, Annex (summary of fifth review of the financial mechanism), para. 89 ('With the establishment of the GCF, the risk of overlap among the activities financed within and outside the Convention is high'); see also Global Environment Facility (2015), *Report of the Global Environment Facility to the Twenty-First Session of the Conference of the Parties to the United Nations Framework Convention on Climate Change*, FCCC/CP/2015/4, p. 20.
98 United States, *Climate Action Report*, p. 22.
99 Ibid., p. 188.
100 United States (2016), *Second Biennial Report of the United States of America under the United Nations Framework Convention on Climate Change*, Washington, DC: US Department of State, p. 41.
101 Ibid., pp. 41–42.
102 Based on Neuhoff et al., *Structuring International Financial Support*, p. 17.
103 Some example bilateral sources: International Climate Initiative (Germany); International Climate Fund (UK); International Forest Climate Initiative (Norway); International Forest Carbon Initiative (Australia).
104 Neuhoff et al., *Structuring International Financial Support*, p. 10.
105 For the provision of ongoing support, see ibid., p. 18.
106 Ibid., pp. 9, 11; and IPCC, *5AR WG3*, p. 1226.
107 IPCC, *5AR WG3*, p. 1227.
108 Export credit is a form of finance provided by a country to foreign buyers to assist in the financing of the purchase of goods from its national exporters: Nakhooda *et al.*, *Lessons from the Fast-Start Finance Period*, pp. 44–45.
109 Global Environment Facility (2014), *Report of the Global Environment Facility to the Twentieth Session of the Conference of the Parties to the United Nations Framework Convention on Climate Change*, FCCC/CP/2014/2, p. 15.
110 Ibid., p. 15 ('The GEF provides . . . funding to meet the agreed incremental costs of measures to achieve [global environmental benefits], *or the additional costs of measures to achieve adaptation benefits* in the case of the adaptation program'; emphasis added). The GEF does not explain what it means by 'additional costs' or the source of its mandate to supply such costs.

48 *Concepts and institutions*

111 GEF, *2015 Report to COP*, p. 1.
112 Streck, 'The Global Environment Facility', p. 71.
113 See, e.g., Jamie Pittock (2010), 'A Pale Reflection of Political Reality: Integration of Global Climate, Wetland, and Biodiversity Agreements', 1 (3) *Climate Law* 343.
114 Yamin and Depledge, *International Regime*, pp. 285–286.
115 Derviş and Puritz Milsom, 'Development Aid', p. 166; and World Bank (2015), *Common Principles for Climate Change Adaptation Finance Tracking*, p. 1 ('The multilateral development banks consist of the African Development Bank, Asian Development Bank, European Bank for Reconstruction and Development, European Investment Bank, Inter-American Development Bank, and the International Finance Corporation and World Bank from the World Bank Group'). The International Finance Corporation was launched in 1956, with the remit to lend to the private sector in developing countries without government guarantees, and thereby to complement the World Bank's focus on lending to governments: Spratt, *Development Finance*, p. 264.
116 See, e.g. Derviş and Puritz Milsom, 'Development Aid', p. 166.
117 Hicks *et al.*, *Greening Aid*, p. 189.
118 Erik Haites and Carol Mwape (2013), 'Sources of Long-Term Climate Change Finance', in *International Climate Finance*, edited by Erik Haites, Abingdon: Routledge, p. 171.
119 Derviş and Puritz Milsom, 'Development Aid', p. 165.
120 FCCC (2014), *Decision 9/CP.20*, Annex (summary of fifth review of the financial mechanism), para. 85.
121 Ibid., para. 84.
122 In article 6.4.
123 The main argument for this characterization was rehearsed earlier; it is that the CDM does not represent additional effort. However, this is not entirely true, because states agreeing to emission limits can take more ambitious positions knowing that the CDM is standing by as a source of relatively cheap offsets.
124 REDD is, in fact, conceptualized as a mechanism of climate finance, e.g. *Copenhagen Accord*, para. 6 ('We [agree to establish] a mechanism including REDD-plus, to enable the mobilization of financial resources from developed countries').
125 International Sustainability Unit (2015), *Tropical Forests: A Review*, ISU, p. 75.
126 Olbrisch *et al.*, 'Estimates of Incremental Investment', p. 47.
127 Charlotte Streck (2013), 'The Financial Aspects of REDD+: Assessing Costs, Mobilizing and Disbursing Funds', in *Law, Tropical Forests and Carbon: The Case of REDD+*, edited by Rosemary Lyster, Catherine MacKenzie, and Constance McDermott, Cambridge: Cambridge University Press, p. 126.
128 International Sustainability Unit, *Tropical Forests*, pp. 74–75; and ibid., p. 86 ('the overall outlook for REDD continues to be clouded by a significant degree of uncertainty over prospects for assured long-term financing of REDD').
129 See article 5 of the Paris Agreement.
130 Streck, 'Financial Aspects of REDD', p. 127.
131 Derviş and Puritz Milsom, 'Development Aid', p. 165.
132 Yamin and Depledge, *International Regime*, p. 295; and Derviş and Puritz Milsom, 'Development Aid', p. 168.
133 On the GCF's governance system, see GCF, *2015 Report to COP*, p. 41.
134 Ibid., p. 10.
135 Green Climate Fund (2014), *Report of the Green Climate Fund to the Conference of the Parties*, FCCC/CP/2014/8, Executive Summary, para. 5.
136 Copenhagen Accord, para. 8.
137 www.gcfund.org/about/the-fund.html; and GCF, *2015 Report to COP*, p. 10.

Concepts and institutions 49

138 Schalatek and Nakhooda, *The Green Climate Fund*, p. 1. In the same work, p. 3, they accept the GCF Board's claim about a 'paradigm shift'.
139 Commonwealth of Australia (2013), *Australia's Sixth National Communication on Climate Change: A Report under the United Nations Framework Convention on Climate Change*, p. 188.
140 Sanjay Kumar (2015), 'Green Climate Fund Faces Slew of Criticism', 527 *Nature* 419, p. 419.
141 FCCC (2015), *Decision 1/CP.21, Adoption of the Paris Agreement*, FCCC/CP/2015/10/Add.1, para. 58.
142 Green Climate Fund (2015), 'Green Climate Fund Approves First 8 Investments', Press Release, 6 November 2015, p. 2 ('The Green Climate Fund . . . was given the mandate to help keep the planet's atmospheric temperature rise below 2 degrees Celsius').
143 GCF, *2014 Report to COP*, para. 7b.

2 Climate finance in legal scholarship

2.1 Introduction

The previous chapter introduced the conceptual and institutional framework for climate finance, along with some issues that are of particular interest from a legal perspective. In the present chapter I will review the existing literature on climate finance in so far as it is relevant to questions of law.

The literature is divided into two parts. First, I will consider works on *climate law* which have a bearing on climate finance law. As expected, these tend to be written by law scholars. Second, I will review the literature that has a particular focus on climate finance law. Some works in this category are not written by law scholars; however, they attempt to develop legal/normative theses on climate finance. Perhaps the main message in this chapter is that the relevant literature is very poorly developed.

2.2 General scholarship on climate law with implications for climate finance

Climate law is at such an early stage of development that scholars are still trying to work out what it is. The all-round weakness of climate law allows for many competing opinions (scholarly and otherwise) on what climate law consists of. A review of the even more specialized subject matter of *climate finance* law must take this fact into account. We are not setting out to understand a well-developed branch of law, like tort law.

I take 'climate law' to mean the legal obligations that states have taken upon themselves under the climate change regime. What is the content of that law? Scholars who claim to answer this question will sometimes define 'law' broadly, with the result that they end up describing climate change policies, institutions, negotiation processes, etc. – the activities of state fora which have the power to regulate state conduct on climate change – without saying much, or anything at all, about the law itself. Pragmatism and 'the practical'[1] are given preference. Others have written about domestic laws, at times implying that these are responses to international law, and also that international law consists of such responses, whereas in fact the information presented is about domestic law; as for its alleged links with international law, it is a question left unexplored. A common practice

52   *Climate finance in legal scholarship*

in the literature is to assume that elements of general international law, as well as international environmental law, form part of climate law, without explaining what the connection is or how they come to be part of climate law. Scholarly commentary also incorporates ideas about what climate law might become, although it is not always made clear that these are proposals about a possible future and not an account of the present state of the law. There is thus also a tendency, found among law and non-law academics alike, to confuse the law as it is with the law as it ought to be (*lex lata* vs *lex ferenda*).

I will begin with an example that features several of the weaknesses I have just mentioned. Van Asselt, Mehling, and Siebert, in a reflective piece on climate law, write that 'International climate change law and governance' have grown 'more complex over time'.[2] What they mostly have in mind, it turns out, is not law but 'governance', in the sense of meetings of, and measures taken by, parties to the FCCC. They even go beyond the governance activity of states: 'the international legal regime for climate change is part and parcel of a broader system in which rule-making is no longer confined to the state or to intergovernmental negotiations alone'.[3] Climate law is thus broadened to include non-governmental 'rule-making' – and it is left undefinably broad. There follows a suggestion that there may be no such thing as climate law after all: 'what may be the most troubling property of climate law is the gradual erosion of its formal legal nature in recent years'.[4] What seems to have happened in this case is that van Asselt *et al.*, having made the concept of 'climate law' dependent on the informal activity of a range of non-state actors operating outside the FCCC framework, thereafter are unable to locate the law's substance.[5] At another point, they write that 'international climate change law [is] the sum of international legal norms seeking to address the phenomenon of climate change [. . . it is a] body of rules'.[6] Yet their discussion of 'governance' finally overwhelms any discussion of the law, so that the reader never finds out which 'body of rules' supposedly makes up climate law. The title of the paper promises more than it delivers, because what it delivers is not law but a description of how a particular regime is structured.

In 'Light Through the Storm', a review of selected works on 'climate change governance', Mayer expounds his view on the nature of climate change law.[7] He outlines a climate law consisting of two key components: the pre-existing international law principle of 'no harm' (the prevention principle); and a new concept which he calls 'greenhouse gas necessity'. The latter stands for the principle that emission-reduction policies must avoid making people's lives miserable. According to Mayer, from the no-harm principle we can derive the obligation of states to reduce greenhouse gas emissions and desist from further harm to the global environment. It follows that, from a legal point of view, the FCCC must be a particular application of the no-harm principle, for its aim is the same. Mayer's second principle acts as a limitation on the extent of application of the first. The limitation is necessary, he asserts, because there are states in which emissions could not be reduced below a certain point without great human suffering; it is even possible that situations exist where state emissions must be increased to relieve existing suffering. The necessity principle prohibits

Climate finance in legal scholarship   53

(unreasonable, inequitable) individual suffering resulting from state mitigation action. The provenance of Mayer's principle of greenhouse gas necessity is probably human rights law. But he throws no light on this question.

Mayer's conception of climate law can be seen to have implications for a law of climate finance in so far as suffering can be alleviated through the transfer of wealth. Thus, by scaling up the transfer of climate finance to countries with populations on the edge of suffering, emission reductions of greater intensity can be achieved there, without offending against the principle of greenhouse gas necessity – assuming, of course, that there is such a principle.

Mayer's thesis on necessity is unique in the literature.[8] Undoubtedly his point that mitigation action must avoid increased suffering is correct, at some level, as long as it is not an absolute position but a relativistic one (i.e. as long as it takes the form: 'Everyone must bear the brunt of keeping warming below 2° C, but the distribution of any "suffering" must be fair'). By contrast, Mayer's other thesis on the relevance of the no-harm principle to climate law is widely shared among writers in this area. What is this thesis and how does it relate to climate finance, if at all?

The no-harm principle in its original form could be understood as a stand-alone principle, but probably more accurately it is only a limitation clause *within* a principle, namely the principle that states may exploit, as they see fit, the natural environment over which their jurisdiction extends. All three Rio Conventions (including the Convention on Biological Diversity and the Convention to Combat Desertification) restate the principle of environmental sovereignty, in the following terms:

> States have, in accordance with the Charter of the United Nations and the principles of international law, the sovereign right to exploit their own resources pursuant to their own environmental and developmental[9] policies, and the responsibility to ensure that activities within their jurisdiction or control do not cause damage to the environment of other States or of areas beyond the limits of national jurisdiction.

Mayer prefers to read the no-harm element in the above prescription as a separate principle, and not only as a limitation on the sovereignty principle. He writes that 'a specific application of the no-harm principle gives rise to an obligation owed to the international community as a whole to not damage global environmental commons such as high seas, the atmosphere, or the climate system'.[10] It will be seen that Mayer's interpretation expands the scope of the limitation clause in two ways: first, by introducing a prohibition against damage to the 'global environmental commons', which is not mentioned in the original;[11] second, by supplementing state-to-state obligations with an obligation owed by each state to 'the international community as a whole'.

By modifying the principle of environmental sovereignty in these ways, Mayer is supposedly rendering the no-harm principle applicable to the problem of climate change. On this reasoning, a state's greenhouse gas emissions harm

54 *Climate finance in legal scholarship*

the global commons; and thus, unless the state acts to eliminate its emissions, it stands in breach of its obligations to the community of states.

Through modification of the original principle, Mayer is actually constructing a new principle, one that requires states not only to avoid harming other states (given that the environment of another state is a part of that state) but also to avoid harming *physical systems*. He wants to evolve the law away from anthropocentrism and towards an ecocentric responsibility towards physical systems.

One might try to resist Mayer's extension of the customary principle of prevention on legalistic grounds. 'Areas beyond national jurisdiction' in the original formulation means just that: stretches of land or sea (not air, since it is a medium, not the subject of harm) that are not under the jurisdiction of any state, or whose jurisdictional status is disputed. Yet, the most straightforward counter-argument to Mayer's thesis is to observe that, even if he were right, there would be no state breach of obligation from continued greenhouse gas emissions because no state's greenhouse gas emissions over the course of a day or year or decade or even a century cause any damage as such. It is instead the accumulation of more than 200 years' worth of global emissions that is causing the damage. Mayer is developing a principle of *individual* state responsibility to fix a problem of collective responsibility. It cannot work.[12]

There are thus several problems with Mayer's thesis in 'Light Through the Storm'. Mayer confuses, on the one hand, the real obligation of a state to cooperate with other states so as to come to an agreement under the FCCC to manage climate change, with, on the other hand, an invented obligation which all states supposedly have not to harm the community of states or the climate through greenhouse gas emitting activities. Mayer's thesis ignores the fact that no one state can harm the climate – only the international community of states can. The legal obligation relevant to managing climate change is not one owed by one individual state to the community of states, as Mayer claims, but is an obligation upon the community of states itself (and not owed to anyone) to reach an agreement, under the FCCC (or, eventually, the Paris Agreement), on how climate change should be managed through the participation of each and every state. The specific responsibilities of each state will be evident only *after* such a general agreement on the individualization of contributions is concluded. Once that happens, each state will, at last, owe an obligation to the community of states under the agreement. The classical no-harm principle is thus irrelevant to the development of climate law. Therefore, it is also irrelevant to the law of climate finance.

In a work published a year after 'Light Through the Storm', Mayer sets out to reflect on the 'rationale for international climate law'.[13] He argues that the deeper reason for having an international climate law is to preserve long-term global peace and security, which is now under serious threat from global warming. We exist, Mayer writes, in 'complex interdependence'; from which it follows that wealthier states must support weak states to fight climate change. Climate change makes states acutely aware of their complex interdependence, and as this fact dawns on the wealthier states, in particular, so they will ever more ambitiously seek to support capacity-building and sustainable development in developing countries,

Climate finance in legal scholarship   55

'if only to avoid long-term security threats resulting from human destitution and resentment'.[14] This interesting idea is eminently suited to the era of climate change. Complex interdependence explains why every state must act on mitigation; and it is for the same reason that many states must act on mitigation not only within their own sovereign territory but also in that of other states through the transfer of climate finance. However, Mayer does not elaborate the implications of his idea as they relate to climate finance.

Mayer's overall conception of climate law can be seen, in conclusion, to consist of three elements: the principle of no harm; the principle of greenhouse gas necessity; and the principle that, in a world of complex interdependence, state cooperation on climate change is a condition for the maintenance of global peace and security. While the third principle's legal foundations are as unclear as those of the second (complex interdependence may only express an ethical position), Mayer's overall conception does provide for the development of a law on climate finance: transnational finance must flow from richer to poorer states to reduce avoidable emissions, relieve human suffering caused by mitigation action, and maintain peace and security in the face of the unavoidable impacts of climate change. As noted, however, Mayer does not develop a law on climate finance from the elements of this theory, and it is typical of scholarly reflections on climate law not to perceive the centrality of climate finance, for the question of finance is seen, if at all, as one-way development aid rather than the answer of 'complex interdependence' to globally coordinated mitigation.

Having considered two very different discussions on the nature of climate law in the works of van Asselt *et al.* and Mayer, I will now turn to a project of much greater scope and ambition. The *Legal Principles Relating to Climate Change*, the product of a multi-authored collaborative project initiated by the International Law Association, purport to 'stat[e] the most fundamental legal principles that should guide States in their attempts to develop and operate an effective legal regime on climate change'.[15] The circuitous language notwithstanding, the ILA's work is the first systematic attempt to codify international climate change law.

The ILA finds that several 'legal principles' are 'applicable to states' for 'addressing climate change'.[16] Of these, some are (legally) binding while others are 'emerging'.[17] The ILA does not always clearly distinguish between the two. A key notion for the ILA is 'the climate system as a common natural resource' for generations present and future, which the ILA asserts is an emerging concept in international law.[18] It also asserts that states have a legal obligation to 'protect' the climate system as a common natural resource.[19] More concretely, states have a duty to 'prevent harm' to the climate system from 'significant' greenhouse gas emissions from 'development plans, programs or projects'.[20] According to the ILA, the international legal principle of permanent state sovereignty over natural resources, which on the face of the original formulation, quoted above in the discussion of Mayer's work, allows for unlimited exploitation of natural resources, has over time been subordinated to the higher principle of 'common concern of humankind' for the climate system as a common natural resource. The ILA also refers to this as the principle of sustainable and equitable use.[21]

56 *Climate finance in legal scholarship*

It is clear from the start that the ILA makes no effort to downplay its creative approach to international law. The climate system is simply declared to be a natural resource, as if it were a coal deposit or a forest – material and tangible. Granted that we have come to regard the referent of the rather abstract term 'biodiversity' as a natural resource in need of protection – and that we make regular use of other such abstractions – however the climate system is a much more abstract, or statistical, concept than biodiversity and similar terms are. We could, at a stretch, 'mine' biodiversity, but we cannot mine the climate system in even the loosest sense.

I return to the ILA's principle of sustainable and equitable use. Presumably intended as a legal principle, its provenance is not clear. It possibly has a foothold in the traditional no-harm clause which limits state environmental sovereignty, because just as was the case with Mayer, the principle of greatest significance in the ILA's scheme is the prohibition against transboundary harm: 'States have an obligation to ensure that activities within their jurisdiction or control do not cause damage to the environment of other States or of areas beyond the limits of national jurisdiction, *including damage through climate change.*'[22] The classical rule of international law is once again tinkered with and made to apply to the causes of climate change. The ILA interprets the principle as obliging a state (each state) to reduce its emissions of greenhouse gases to avoid further damage to the environment of other states, as well as to 'the atmosphere'. Because the atmosphere is supposedly an object beyond state boundaries, on the ILA's analysis it is protected by the rule against transboundary harm.

Another element of international climate law which according to the ILA constrains the conduct of states is the principle of equity. Within the principle of equity is found the principle of common but differentiated responsibility. CBDR is equity's 'major expression'.[23] For the ILA, CBDR is fundamental to climate law.[24] Equity/CBDR imply that developing countries are entitled to grow their per-capita emissions, because they are 'still low', although the growth must be 'within reason and [occur] in a sustainable manner'.[25] Here, the ILA's scheme overlaps with Mayer's necessity principle in its ethical outlook, its focus on individuals (per-capita emissions), and its tendency to defeat the transboundary harm principle by defending, potentially (given the huge number of people still living in poverty), an absolute growth in greenhouse gas emissions. Neither the ILA nor Mayer seem to be concerned that their account of climate law contains two principles that are in direct opposition to each other, one demanding reduction in emissions, the other necessitating their growth.

Another principle to which the ILA gives prominence is that states are to cooperate in good faith to develop a global solution to climate change.[26] Developed states are to take 'the lead'[27] with more stringent mitigation commitments and through 'assistance' provided to developing states 'to the extent of their need'. The latter element, which the ILA seems to want to extend to mitigation as well as adaptation assistance, implies the existence of a legal obligation on climate finance. It is not clear from the ILA's work whether this finance obligation derives entirely from the good-faith/cooperation principle, or whether it might also have

Climate finance in legal scholarship   57

a basis in the CBDR principle, the no-harm principle, the principle of sustainable and equitable use, the principle of common concern of humankind, or another of the principles and ideas that find their way into the ILA's synthesis, such as the principle of precaution or the notion of historical responsibility. In the result, while the climate law that the ILA constructs out of pre-existing, modified, or newly emergent or invented concepts implies a positive developed-state obligation on climate finance, the ILA does not develop the point or present a legal rationale for it, such as to enable a state to understand how much climate finance to provide and under what conditions.

In general, the ILA claims to offer a complete picture of international climate law, yet its compilation of numerous legal principles and new ideas does not add up to a coherent system of law from which states may deduce any guidance about what they are required to do. Additional considerations that undermine the ILA's proposed synthesis include the following.

First, the ILA does not explain what are 'significant emissions' of individual states or projects, or how such emissions could be shown to cause serious damage to the 'atmosphere' or the 'climate system'.[28] The root of the problem is that the ILA tries to develop a bottom-up law of climate change, when the actual logic of the problem is strictly top down. States have no individual mitigation obligations until they negotiate them under a burden-sharing arrangement linked to a mitigation target. A state individually can neither cause nor prevent climate change harm. This is why states must reach an agreement on who will do what and by when. Each state will then be accountable under that agreement. The customary no-harm rule does not apply, whether prior to the agreement or subsequent to it.

Second, the relationship of mitigation and adaptation is not clear in the ILA's scheme. ('The [ILA] expresses no priority with respect to the adoption of mitigation or adaptation measures, although, where possible, mitigation measures should take priority over adaptation measures.'[29]) It is only after an agreement has been reached on mitigation that it will be possible to calculate the consequent impacts of the implied climate change on particular countries. Actual financial assistance must be provided not on the basis of relative vulnerability (as the ILA suggests[30]), but on estimated likely impacts. And for this, the extent of mitigation that states commit to undertake must first be known.

Third, the ILA must address the methodological point that states have been negotiating the details of an international regime for the control of climate change for more than 25 years, and in this period have put into effect two treaties on climate change, each of which has been ratified almost universally; the states have also adopted hundreds of decisions under these treaties. It cannot plausibly be maintained that general principles of international law that date from before this quarter-century of subject-specific output are more relevant to the problem than that output itself. The ILA's lack of methodological caution accounts for the aimless character of its *Principles*.

Fourth, the ILA sees relevance in the principle of sustainable development being applied to climate change. The sustainable development principle is not a principle

58 Climate finance in legal scholarship

of international law affecting the rights and obligations of states, because although states often affirm its importance, the principle has no substance and therefore cannot be a principle of law.[31] The ILA nevertheless understands sustainable development to mean state *restraint* in emission growth.[32] To solve the problem of climate change, reduction in emissions is needed, not restraint in growth. Growth in emissions, being damaging, cannot at the same time be sustainable, as the ILA claims.[33] The international treaties on climate change seek to manage a reduction in emissions, leaving no useful role for the principle of sustainable development.

In summing up the ILA's contribution to the scholarly literature on climate law, I have explained that it consists of a collection of ideas and principles – some more relevant than others, some more futuristic than others – but is not a coherent system of current law that lays out what the immediate obligations of states are or what legal issues remain to be resolved. While the ILA does not exactly ignore climate finance, it prefers to emphasize its support for the version of the CBDR principle that places most of the responsibility for action on Annex I countries.

At around the time that the ILA was finalizing its *Legal Principles*, another group of scholars, this time not affiliated with any NGO, embarked on a project similar to the ILA's, which issued in the so-called *Oslo Principles on Global Climate Change Obligations*. The Oslo group's objective was 'to identify and articulate a set of Principles that comprise the essential obligations States and enterprises have to avert the critical level of global warming'.[34] As this last element is a reference to the 2°C threshold which states have agreed to avoid, the group's objective implies that the group's search was for *current* legal principles ('well-established law'[35]) relevant to the intention of states not to exceed the warming limit. (The Oslo group uses unusual and imprecise terms, such as 'global obligations' and 'essential obligations', and also sets out to address the responsibility of 'enterprises'. I will limit my discussion below to the group's assertions on the legal responsibility of states.)

One problem with the Oslo group's objective is that it appears somewhat overdetermined. If states have already taken upon themselves under the FCCC regime a legal obligation to avoid 2°C of warming, why is it necessary for the group to identify any other applicable legal principles in international law? The relevance of any such principles as may be found would be worth exploring in the *absence* of the FCCC's and Kyoto Protocol's specific commitments, but once specific commitment are in place, what is the relevance of any less purpose-built obligations? This is the same criticism that I levelled at the ILA's methodology. Neither the ILA nor the Oslo group seem aware of this weakness in their approach. It leads them at times to suggest, absurdly, that the FCCC is irrelevant.[36] As I will explain more fully in Chapter 3, the legally binding 2°C threshold is, at this point in time, still only a 'communal' obligation of states, unable to resolve itself into state-level obligations unless assisted by another legal element, which I have called the modified polluter-pays principle. Other principles of international law (in particular, the principles of polluter-pays and equity) must certainly still be incorporated into climate law in order to construct a complete picture of the current legal obligations of states on climate change. But the *Legal Principles* and

Climate finance in legal scholarship 59

subsequently the *Oslo Principles* simply amass legal elements without regard to structure or precedence.

There are at least 26 principles in the *Oslo Principles*, depending on how one counts them. Foremost among them is the precautionary principle. According to the Oslo group, the precautionary principle, when applied to the problem of climate change, has several implications for states. The implication with the greatest relevance to climate finance is captured in the following statement: 'The measures required by the Precautionary Principle should be adopted without regard to the cost.'[37] From this it may be deduced that transnational climate finance is obligatory, for otherwise poorer countries would not be able to carry out the required measures, which according to the Oslo group must go ahead regardless of cost.

Is it necessary to invoke the precautionary principle for this purpose? The obligation on wealthier countries to provide climate finance to poorer countries is set out in the text of the FCCC; therefore, the Oslo group's version of the precautionary principle is not needed to derive the obligation. The only new element here is the alleged obligation to disregard cost. The provenance of this element is mysterious. It would indeed be remarkable if the law required states to disregard the cost of measures whose cost is potentially astronomical.[38] The Oslo group does not attempt to justify this assertion.

Next in importance in the *Oslo Principles* is the idea (implicit in Oslo Principle 13) that each person alive is entitled to an equal share of the atmosphere.[39] This is a version of the doctrine of 'equitable access to atmospheric space', which the ILA itself criticized as being controversial.[40] The form of this principle – the fact that it is about individuals, not states – suggests that it belongs to international human rights law. The Oslo group does not clarify the doctrine's provenance. The group, we should note, expresses an interest in morals as much as in law: 'Human beings, because of their unique nature and capacities, have an essential duty, as guardians and trustees of the Earth. . . . Avoiding severe global catastrophe is a moral and legal imperative.'[41] Perhaps the equal-share doctrine is a moral position. Even so, it is far from clear that the per-capita initial allocation called for in the *Oslo Principles* is a just position, let alone one that responds to legal imperative. Applied to the problem of climate change and the regime's 2°C limit, the equitable-access principle would mean that a country's emission budget (the 'permissible quantum' of state emissions, in the Oslo group's terms) is equal to the global per-capita emission entitlement compatible with the 2°C limit multiplied by the population of that country. It is, of course, a remarkably simple way to calculate country emission budgets. What the reader of the *Oslo Principles* is not told is whether it represents current international law, a proposal for law reform, a view of 'climate justice', or something else.

With this background, we come to Oslo Principle 18, which is the most relevant to the question of state obligations on climate finance:

> If and to the extent that an above-permissible-quantum country has taken all steps reasonably available but nevertheless has failed to fulfil the obligations in Principle 13 [i.e. to reduce its emissions to its permissible quantum], that

60 Climate finance in legal scholarship

country must provide financial or technical means to below-permissible-quantum countries to achieve the reduction of GHG emissions [which] the responsible above-permissible-quantum country has failed to achieve.[42]

A state climate finance obligation may thus be derived from the Oslo group's equitable-access principle, more easily and with more concrete consequences than from the group's version of the precautionary principle. Essentially the group's thesis on this point is that a state must offset all its emissions above its entitlement by paying another state (or states) to reduce *its* emissions by the relevant amount below *its* entitlement. This is certainly a strategic approach to climate finance, incorporating climate finance fully into the global mitigation effort.

The Oslo group's position is novel and unique in the literature on climate law. However, the alleged obligation of states is only as secure as the underlying principle of individual equitable access to atmospheric space, whose nature and origin are obscure. No such principle exists under classical international law. Within the FCCC process, states have never supported such an access principle, nor have they adopted any positions that would imply it. On the contrary, in instruments such as the Kyoto Protocol, states have accepted that different geographical and social conditions and natural endowments lead to very different dependencies on fossil fuels and other sources of greenhouse gases. Thus, under the Kyoto Protocol, it would be considered absurd to set coal-rich Australia's per-capita emissions at the same level as geothermal-rich Iceland's. With respect to Oslo Principle 18, the group's work reads merely like a proposal that the Oslo group would like to see implemented. It is advocacy more than scholarship; yet even as advocacy it does not make much sense.

Credit should be given to the Oslo group for having formulated what it calls Principle 9: 'Least developed countries . . . have the same obligation [as more developed countries to implement available GHG-reduction measures that entail costs] to the extent that other entities provide the financial and technical means required.'[43] This idea is central to the post-Copenhagen era, being a refutation of the voluntarism that characterized the earlier era. However, the Oslo group hits on the idea almost accidentally, sometimes attempting a top-down reading of the law (which yields the promising results), but at other times settling for bottom-up prescriptions reminiscent of the ILA's.[44]

2.3 Legal or broadly normative scholarship specifically on climate finance

Scholarly works on climate finance from a legal perspective are few. Law scholars who have written on climate finance have not always succeeded in adopting a legal perspective on the subject.[45] There is a tendency to fall back on descriptions of international institutions and processes, or to comment on the size of the financial flows, invariably concluding that they are inadequate. Some such works proceed to consider potential improvements to overcome the difficulties experienced with raising or distributing climate finance. Although informative, these approaches

Climate finance in legal scholarship 61

demand no legal expertise and do not lead to any specifically legal insight. One searches such works in vain for an exposition of the law on climate finance.

On occasion, a legal perspective on climate finance has been attempted by non-lawyers.[46] The interdisciplinary explorations of law scholars are mirrored in those of political scientists (for the most part) who venture into writing on the law. The shortcoming in such cases is a lack of understanding of the sources of law and legal obligation. Commentators fall into the usual traps that await non-lawyers writing on the law. I reiterate that very few works exist in each of these categories.

Climate finance law is a neglected area of scholarship, largely, in my view, because the importance of climate finance had until recently been downplayed by the dominant CBDR model.

A 2009 article by Lin and Streck – both law scholars – whose stated purpose is to consider the legal aspects of climate finance[47] is not, in fact, about international law but about the institutional and regulatory reform needed to better attain certain objectives of the international climate change regime. For example, the authors express their support for a REDD mechanism that is based on national-level accounting.[48] REDD is potentially a major source of climate finance. Lin and Streck suggest that an international body to approve REDD methodologies and projects should be set up for countries that do not yet meet greenhouse gas accounting requirements in full because they are implementing REDD at the subnational level.[49] The authors are right to remind us that there is as yet no REDD governing body comparable to the CDM's Executive Board to administer REDD and standardize its various components, including methodologies. This insight into the design faults of an international mechanism for climate change mitigation and finance does not advance any legal perspective. The work is an example of thinking about climate finance as an administrative process that could be improved. Instead we need new thinking about climate finance as a body of rules that states must comply with.[50]

In a long chapter on climate finance, Yamineva and Kulovesi – another pair of well-regarded law scholars – recognize that rules on monitoring, reporting, and verification of climate finance are necessary for the effectiveness of the climate change regime.[51] However, they do not seem to recognize that the legal rules creating state obligations must be clarified first. They assert that

> The pledge [in the Copenhagen Accord] to mobilize $30 billion of fast-start finance in 2010–2012 can be seen as an attempt to build trust and generate good will in the interim period before a new international architecture for long-term climate finance is operational.[52]

While the trust-building explanation may or may not be true (no evidence in support of it is presented), the *kind* of explanation belongs to political science or psychology. Yamineva and Kulovesi do not consider whether this instance of state conduct might have a plausible legal explanation. A legal explanation could be that the FCCC parties realized in the lead-up to the drafting of the Copenhagen Accord that climate finance obligations needed to have a more prominent role in

62 *Climate finance in legal scholarship*

the climate change regime for the regime's objective to be achieved. Maybe trust-building was a motivation, but was it the only one? Why would Annex I countries suddenly want to add substance to an obligation that had remained an abstraction for more than 15 years? Leaving aside motivations, what about the legal *effect* of the concrete commitments on climate finance in the Copenhagen Accord? Like many scholars of climate law, Yamineva and Kulovesi produce a narrative as if from within the fray of the negotiations, too close to the action to deliver an understanding of legal developments.

States will continue to struggle to meet the regime's ends unless international processes are improved – this is the lesson from the Lin and Streck article and the Yamineva and Kulovesi chapter. Law reform is not a precondition for the needed redesign, because the law – which Lin and Streck do not discuss, as such – is not identified as the cause of current design shortcomings. The approach is interdisciplinary, but only in the weak sense of being non-disciplinary. True interdisciplinarity presupposes developed, mature disciplinary perspectives. A priority of law scholars when a new field of obligation opens up is to develop the legal discipline's characterization of that field. The starting point should be to discover the applicable legal rules for states, explain their foundations, analyse their consistency with related bodies of law, and determine whether there is state adherence to the new legal obligations. If the rules are inadequate (e.g. because they do not align with the treaty regime's objectives or because they conflict with other rules), it is for governments (on the advice of negotiators, economists, and relevant disciplinary experts, including law scholars) to devise proposals on how to reform the law or bring states into compliance with the law. Before coming to that point, it must be possible to perceive a landscape of legal norms.

In his influential book *The Art and Craft of International Environmental Law*, Bodansky only briefly considers the rationale for transnational financial assistance.[53] He notes that, traditionally, development assistance has been voluntary. 'Arguably, however, all countries have an obligation to contribute to the production of global public goods inasmuch as all countries benefit from them.'[54] While this comment is not specifically about climate finance, it suggests that a legal obligation on states to supply climate finance does not yet exist, although 'arguably' it should exist. Bodansky's comment is not entirely accurate because we know for a fact that the FCCC imposes a general climate finance obligation on Annex II parties. Moreover, even if 'all countries' have the obligation that Bodansky claims they do, transnational climate finance is not necessarily relevant to every country, because a country can produce global public goods through efforts that are entirely domestic. The concept of climate finance is otherwise invisible in *Art and Craft*.

Other general works on international environmental law also pay only lip-service to climate finance – or do not mention it at all. In *Principles of International Environmental Law*, Sands and Peel briefly discuss the status of the polluter-pays principle in international law. They write that the 'principle indicates that the costs of pollution should be borne by the person [not the state] responsible for causing the pollution'.[55] They rank its normative force below that of the principles of prevention (no-harm principle) and precaution.[56] They acknowledge that, since

1986, the European Union has applied the polluter-pays principle at the member-state level and not just to entities at the sub-state level.[57] However, Sands and Peel do not discuss the application of the principle to the problem of climate change, apparently because they do not believe that the principle applies generally to states.

In *International Law and the Environment*, Birnie *et al.* use the term 'solidarity assistance' as a general term for transnational finance for environmental purposes, including climate finance. They state that the legal basis for solidarity assistance is the principle of common but differentiated responsibility: CBDR requires an 'equitable balance between developed and developing states [for] it allows for different standards for developing states and it makes their performance dependent on the provision of solidarity assistance by developed states'.[58] The authors are not saying that the CBDR principle *entails* 'solidarity assistance'; they are saying that developing countries should not be pressured to act without appropriate financial support. This view is permeated by voluntarism: neither side is required *ab initio* to either provide solidarity assistance or act on it.[59] Once again, it is not clear how these views come to be upheld in law textbooks when the FCCC clearly creates supply obligations on climate finance. Birnie *et al.* downplay the significance of solidarity assistance as a legal obligation weighing on states: 'economic assistance [is] part of a strategy for engaging developing states in the process of regulating the international environment';[60] and: 'it [is] irrelevant whether developed states have a legal duty to provide assistance'.[61] These two statements are an accurate, if inadvertent, summary of pre-Copenhagen thinking on climate finance.

One work in the literature, subtitled 'A Normative Framework for a Global Compact on Public Climate Finance', stands out for its attempt to use 'existing' principles of international law for the specific purpose of developing a law of climate finance.[62] Schalatek's approach is similar to the ILA's, except that its whole focus is on climate finance. Schalatek believes that a complete law of climate finance already exists in international law; we just need to look closer at the law to see it.[63] Remarkably for a work that sets out to clarify the legal obligations of states, the work's author is not a law scholar and the 'Normative Framework' contains no legal citations. In making her case, Schalatek unfortunately mixes up reality with ideals and inaccurately portrays general principles of law as having the power of specific rules. She treats climate change as an ordinary environmental law problem to which pre-existing principles of environmental law apply automatically. It is a question-begging approach, no different in this respect to the ILA's.

Schalatek correctly observes that 'a comprehensive global climate finance architecture, which collects, allocates and disburses financial resources in an equitable, effective and efficient manner is still elusive'.[64] She argues that the 'core principles' of international environmental law and human rights currently in force adequately express the duties of states on climate finance;[65] they supply the 'normative framework' missing in the climate finance debate.[66] It would be of little interest to go through all of the principles in Schalatek's list, most of which are no different to those collated by the ILA or the Oslo group. I will mention only a few elements of her scheme.

64   *Climate finance in legal scholarship*

Schalatek confuses human rights law (rights of individuals and obligations of a state towards its citizens) with international law between states, believing that from human rights law it is possible to derive obligations that states owe to each other on climate finance.[67] Thus she relies on the observation that climate change can have a negative impact on the fundamental rights of people to reach the conclusion that an insufficient provision of climate finance constitutes a human rights 'violation' by states.[68] States should therefore provide more climate finance. Her arguments are thinly disguised calls for 'climate justice', a hallmark of NGO-type advocacy. Climate-justice activists allege that insufficient state action on climate change not only damages the environment, it undermines the fundamental rights of the poor. On this view, climate finance is of critical importance to safeguard the rights of the poor.

Schalatek's work nevertheless contains discussion of an important principle that eluded the ILA. Schalatek argues that the polluter-pays principle, as expressed in Principle 16 of the Rio Declaration, applies at the level of states in international law, and is the mechanism by which climate finance should be raised.[69] A country's obligation to pay for 'climate action', she writes, should be correlated with a minimum development standard for each of its citizens.[70] Emissions attributed to development above that standard should be charged to the country in question in accordance with the general principle.

Unfortunately, Schalatek's attempt to enlist the polluter-pays principle for climate law quickly loses direction. No legal basis for a 'development standard' is mentioned. While she acknowledges the agreement on the 2°C warming limit, she decides against linking the sufficiency of climate finance to avoidance of that limit.[71] She misunderstands both the polluter-pays principle and the Kyoto Protocol in her claim that the Protocol's Annex B emission limits for Annex I parties represent an application of the polluter-pays principle.[72] (They actually represent state pledges volunteered by states on the basis of inscrutable domestic decisions and bartering at the negotiating table.) She seeks to apply the polluter-pays principle retroactively and hold 'industrialized countries' to their 'historical responsibility' for greenhouse gas emissions[73] – a sure sign that the argument is no longer about the law but about 'moral impetus'.[74] While invoking the polluter-pays principle, Schalatek's outlook is in fact legally conventional, adopting the strong version of the CBDR principle and treating climate finance as a kind of development aid.[75] Her account of climate finance does not amount to a coherent scheme based on existing legal principles.

The polluter-pays principle is taken up again by Schalatek in a later work with Bird. A novel claim here is that the polluter-pays principle can be derived directly from the CBDR principle; thus CBDR itself supposedly obliges states to raise climate finance.[76] However, Schalatek and Bird do not explain how they reached this conclusion. No other work has claimed that the polluter-pays principle is contained within the CBDR principle. Schalatek and Bird refer to climate finance raised through the application of the polluter-pays principle as 'compensatory finance',[77] which suggests that its purpose is primarily adaptation, not mitigation.

2.4 Conclusion

In this chapter I have attempted to show that the scholarly literature to date fails to give a coherent account of climate change law in general and climate finance law in particular. The received works tend to treat climate law as an accumulation of legal principles inherited from general international law and international environmental law. From this amorphous set it is supposedly possible to derive state obligations on climate finance, yet the method of derivation is usually only hinted at in the literature; when attempted, the results have been unconvincing.

Notes

1 Jutta Brunnée and Charlotte Streck (2013), 'The UNFCCC as a Negotiation Forum: Towards Common but More Differentiated Responsibilities', 13 (5) *Climate Policy* 589, p. 603.

2 Harro van Asselt, Michael Mehling, and Clarisse Kehler Siebert (2015), 'The Changing Architecture of International Climate Change Law', in *Research Handbook on Climate Change Mitigation Law*, edited by Geert van Calster, Wim Vandenberghe, and Leonie Reins, Cheltenham: Edward Elgar, p. 1.

3 Ibid., p. 4.

4 Ibid., p. 7.

5 It is 'in the eye of the beholder', they say (ibid., p. 23), and 'in existential flux' (ibid., p. 30).

6 Ibid., p. 5.

7 Benoit Mayer (2014), 'State Responsibility and Climate Change Governance: A Light through the Storm', 13 *Chinese Journal of International Law* 539.

8 Although cf. Lasse Ringius, Asbjørn Torvanger, and Arild Underdal (2002), 'Burden Sharing and Fairness Principles in International Climate Policy', 2 *International Environmental Agreements* 1, pp. 7–8 ('the principle of need [in the climate change context] is that all human beings be granted the "pollution permits" needed to secure basic human needs, including a decent standard of living'). However, these authors also do not explain the provenance of their principle.

9 The CBD, article 3, omits the words 'and developmental'.

10 Mayer, 'State Responsibility', p. 553.

11 Ibid., p. 557 ('an analysis of climate change as harmful to global atmospheric commons, rather than to States or individuals, avoids complex issues of attribution at the stage of establishing the breach of the no-harm principle').

12 His formula, that 'States responsible for having continuously failed to prevent excessive greenhouse gas emissions within their jurisdiction must act without unreasonable delay to reduce these emissions to a level which is excusable because [it is] necessary' (ibid., p. 559), does not get us any further than where we are already (and have been for some time) under the FCCC.

13 Benoit Mayer (2015a), 'Conceiving the Rationale for International Climate Law', 130 (3) *Climatic Change* 371, p. 371.

14 Ibid., p. 380.

15 ILA (2014), *Legal Principles Relating to Climate Change: Report and Draft Declaration for Consideration at the 2014 Washington Conference*, Commentary, para. 1, to Draft Article 1.

16 Ibid., Draft Article 2.

17 Ibid., Commentary, para. 1, to Draft Article 2.

18 Ibid., Commentary, para. 3, to Draft Article 3.

19 Ibid., Draft Article 3, para. 1.

66   *Climate finance in legal scholarship*

20   Ibid., Draft Article 3, para. 5.

21   Ibid., Commentary, para. 6, to Draft Article 3.

22   Ibid., Draft Article 7A, para. 1, emphasis added.

23   Ibid., Draft Article 4, para. 1.

24   Ibid., Commentary, para. 1, to Draft Article 5. The ILA interprets CBDR in the strong sense: ibid., Commentary, para. 12, to Draft Article 5 ('developing countries shall be subject to less stringent mitigation commitments than developed countries and shall benefit from forms of differentiation relating to compliance and assistance').

25   Ibid., Draft Article 4, para. 2(a).

26   Ibid., Draft Article 5, para. 2; and ibid., Draft Article 8, paras 1–2.

27   Ibid., Draft Article 5, para. 3.

28   The ILA develops its thesis all the way through to its absurd conclusion: 'Where there is a reasonably foreseeable threat that a proposed activity may cause serious damage to the environment of other States or areas beyond national jurisdiction, including serious or irreversible damage through climate change to vulnerable States, an environmental impact assessment on the potential impacts of such activity is required' (ibid., Draft Article 7B, para. 5; see also Draft Article 7B, para. 6; and Commentary, para. 19, to Draft Article 7). The idea that environmental impact assessments could solve the problem of climate change is bottom-up thinking taken to its extreme.

29   Ibid., Commentary, para. 8, to Draft Article 7.

30   Ibid., Commentary, para. 5, to Draft Article 6.

31   See Chapter 3.

32   ILA, *Legal Principles Relating to Climate Change*, Commentary, para. 4, to Draft Article 4.

33   Ibid., Commentary, para. 9, to Draft Article 3.

34   Antonio Benjamin *et al.* (2015), *Oslo Principles on Global Climate Change Obligations*, Expert Group on Global Climate Obligations, p. 1.

35   Ibid., p. 1.

36   E.g. Benjamin *et al.*, *Oslo Principles on Global Climate Change Obligations: Commentary*, p. 8 ('States are legally obliged to reduce their GHG emissions, even if they do not conclude (further) international agreements or conventions').

37   Benjamin *et al.*, *Oslo Principles*, p. 3.

38   Traditional formulations of the precautionary principle do not require state compliance with it where the cost of compliance would be 'unreasonable'.

39   See also: 'each human being is entitled to the same GHG emissions'; Benjamin *et al.*, *Oslo Principles: Commentary*, p. 11.

40   ILA, *Legal Principles Relating to Climate Change*, Commentary, para. 4, to Draft Article 4.

41   Benjamin *et al.*, *Oslo Principles*, p. 1; and ibid., p. 1 ('all States and enterprises have an immediate moral and legal duty to prevent the deleterious effects of climate change').

42   Ibid., p. 5.

43   Ibid., p. 4.

44   See, e.g. ibid., pp. 4, 6 (Principles 8 and 21).

45   See, for example, M. J. Mace (2005), 'Funding for Adaptation to Climate Change: UNFCCC and GEF Developments since COP-7', 14 (3) *Review of European Community and International Environmental Law* 225; Laurence Boisson de Chazournes (2007), 'Technical and Financial Assistance', in *The Oxford Handbook of International Environmental Law*, edited by Daniel Bodansky, Jutta Brunnée, and Ellen Hey, Oxford: Oxford University Press; Christiana Figueres and Charlotte Streck (2009), *Enhanced Financial Mechanisms for Post-2012 Mitigation*, Policy Research Working Paper 5008; Friedrich Soltau (2009), *Fairness in International*

Climate finance in legal scholarship 67

Climate Change Law and Policy, Cambridge: Cambridge University Press, pp. 207–227; Jolene Lin and Charlotte Streck (2009), 'Mobilising Finance for Climate Change Mitigation: Private Sector Involvement in International Carbon Finance Mechanisms', 10 (1) *Melbourne Journal of International Law* 70; Haroldo Machado-Filho (2012), 'Financial Mechanisms Under the Climate Regime', in *Promoting Compliance in an Evolving Climate Regime*, edited by Jutta Brunnée, Meinhard Doelle, and Lavanya Rajamani, Cambridge: Cambridge University Press; and Yulia Yamineva and Kati Kulovesi (2013), 'The New Framework for Climate Finance under the United Nations Framework Convention on Climate Change: A Breakthrough or an Empty Promise?', in *Climate Change and the Law*, edited by Erkki J. Hollo, Kati Kulovesi, and Michael Mehling, Dordrecht: Springer.

46 For example, Nele Matz (2002), 'Environmental Financing: Function and Coherence of Financial Mechanisms in International Environmental Agreements', 6 *Max Planck Yearbook of United Nations Law* 473; Liane Schalatek (2010), *A Matter of Principle(s): A Normative Framework for a Global Compact on Public Climate Finance*, Berlin: Heinrich Böll Foundation; Britta Horstmann and Achala Chandani Abeysinghe (2011), 'The Adaptation Fund of the Kyoto Protocol: A Model for Financing Adaptation to Climate Change?', 2 (3) *Climate Law* 415; Smita Nakhooda *et al.* (2013), *Mobilising International Climate Finance: Lessons from the Fast-Start Finance Period*, Washington, DC: World Resources Institute; and Liane Schalatek and Neil Bird (2013), *The Principles and Criteria of Public Climate Finance: A Normative Framework*, Washington, DC: Heinrich Böll Stiftung.

47 Lin and Streck, 'Mobilising Finance'.

48 Ibid., p. 97.

49 Ibid., p. 99.

50 Another paper by Streck, again on climate finance and REDD, suffers from the same shortcomings: Charlotte Streck (2013), 'The Financial Aspects of REDD+: Assessing Costs, Mobilizing and Disbursing Funds', in *Law, Tropical Forests and Carbon: The Case of REDD+*, edited by Rosemary Lyster, Catherine MacKenzie, and Constance McDermott, Cambridge: Cambridge University Press. It contains no discussion whatsoever of first principles or legal requirements; instead, it considers pragmatic options from the point of view of a climate-regime negotiator.

51 Yamineva and Kulovesi, 'Framework for Climate Finance', p. 214.

52 Ibid., p. 210.

53 Daniel Bodansky (2010), *The Art and Craft of International Environmental Law*, Cambridge, MA: Harvard University Press.

54 Ibid., p. 245.

55 Philippe Sands and Jacqueline Peel (2012), *Principles of International Environmental Law*, Cambridge: Cambridge University Press, p. 228.

56 Ibid., p. 229.

57 Ibid., p. 231.

58 Patricia W. Birnie, Alan E. Boyle, and Catherine Redgwell (2009), *International Law and the Environment*, Oxford: Oxford University Press, p. 133.

59 Ibid., p. 134.

60 Ibid., p. 110.

61 Ibid., p. 135.

62 Schalatek, *Normative Framework*, p. 5.

63 Ibid., p. 4.

64 Ibid., p. 5.

65 Ibid., p. 5.

66 Ibid., p. 4.

67 E.g. ibid., pp. 8, 19.

68 Ibid., pp. 18–19.

68 *Climate finance in legal scholarship*

69 Ibid., p. 6.
70 Ibid., p. 6.
71 Ibid., p. 6.
72 Ibid., p. 35.
73 Ibid., p. 18.
74 Ibid., p. 35.
75 What she calls 'compensatory finance': ibid., p. 35.
76 Schalatek and Bird, *Principles and Criteria*, p. 1.
77 Ibid., p. 2.

3 Legal obligations of states relating to climate finance

3.1 Introduction

States, through their participation in the international climate change regime, have accepted legal obligations on climate finance. Some elements of the law are apparent from the treaties themselves, while others require careful exposition. Such an exposition is the aim of this chapter. The chapter offers a restatement of climate law – the first of its kind – including climate finance law. (The challenge of applying the law to the 'facts' of climate finance is taken up in Chapter 4.) The exercise will reveal that climate finance law is an integral part of climate law, so that we cannot make sense of one without an understanding of the other. Throughout, I stay close to 'the law as it is'. I do not attempt to offer a conception of the law as it ought to be.

State obligations can be identified in the relevant treaty texts, in this case the FCCC and Kyoto Protocol. The FCCC recalls certain principles of international law and international environmental law, suggesting their relevance to a nascent climate change law and potentially even to a specific law on climate finance. State obligations can also be found in (1) binding decisions of the state parties, adopted within the treaty frameworks; (2) pronouncements or affirmations of obligations by states and other forms of repeated state practice; (3) general principles of international law; and (4) obligations necessarily entailed by the above. The first of these categories covers the Paris Agreement and the decision adopting it.

In the previous chapter I noted that the method used by the ILA, the Oslo group, and others to analyse climate law resulted in a kind of overdetermination of their answers. It cannot be that the states' legal obligations in response to the problem of climate change are derivable from principles of international law that pre-existed, or were developed in parallel with, the FCCC regime, as the ILA and others imply; for then the climate treaties would be rendered supplementary, when as a matter of fact they are the more specific of the sources and they should be given priority for being deliberately and carefully formulated with an intention to bind states. Another argument against the method used by the ILA *et al.* is that it paradoxically renders invisible the oldest, most highly developed, and least controversial set of legal obligations in the climate change regime: those on state reporting and review.

70 *Legal obligations of states*

The correct approach in mapping out international climate law is to draw on the principles of international law to fill in gaps left by the FCCC regime, to explain the legal rationale of certain aspects of the regime, or to give direction to the interpretation or implementation of the regime's objectives – not to render invisible the detail of the legal scheme created by the regime. Concerning the international law principles recalled and reiterated in the FCCC's preamble, some are of doubtful relevance to the problem of climate change, whereas at least one – the polluter-pays principle – has gained ground since the Copenhagen COP. Thus more is needed than a correct prioritization of sources. Legal clarification seeks consistency in the sources. Principles that defeat the regime's objectives, or are impossible to implement, must be set aside.

One of the most difficult legal questions in this context concerns the relationship between mitigation and adaptation finance. At the *political* level states are always careful to speak of climate finance as relating to a single obligation – 'support' for developing countries – which they discharge by providing mitigation and adaptation finance in 'balanced' proportions. However, as I have observed more than once already, conceptually the two types of finance have completely different rationales. Thus mitigation finance reduces emissions in countries that cannot further reduce their emissions without external assistance. Its rationale is to contain global warming. Adaptation finance responds to damage from climate change actually experienced or otherwise anticipated in specific locations in developing countries – countries that cannot afford to repair or defend themselves against the damage. Some would also say that adaptation finance compensates the poorest developing countries for measures to deal with or avert damage whose causes they have not contributed to. The rationales for mitigation and adaptation finance hardly overlap at all. The ILA, Oslo group, and others do not acknowledge that this rift exists within climate finance law.

3.2 Specific treaty rules on climate finance

The first place in which to look for principles and rules making up a body of law is the relevant legal instruments. To start with, the unqualified legal obligations (the 'shall' statements) in the FCCC could be listed. The exercise, which would be iterated to encompass COP decisions, would result in a list of rules, but not necessarily a body of law. For the latter, it is necessary to be able to state the rationale for the various rules and how they work together. Legal principles (higher-order rules) help make sense of the lower-order treaty provisions. A body of law will have been identified when an interdependence and coherence in the several elements can be made visible – or when it becomes possible to say about that law: 'Now I understand the states' legal obligations and how they serve their collective objective.'

I have divided this section into rules on substance and rules on procedure relating to climate finance. While it may be expected that the substantive and procedural parts of climate finance law develop in parallel with each other, in fact they can have quite independent histories. Procedural law is likely to develop first, as it is

Legal obligations of states 71

less controversial. Thus rules on the accurate and frequent reporting of financial support to developing countries could exist even in the absence of a rule about the amounts to be provided (i.e. in the absence of a particularized substantive law on climate finance). It is also possible, of course, that substantive obligations indicated in broad terms can pre-exist detailed procedural rules.

As a matter of fact, in the FCCC's case, while the treaty outlines substantive obligations on climate finance, it says rather more about the states' corresponding procedural obligations. The pace of development of procedural and substantive law may also differ remarkably within a treaty regime. In the FCCC's case, it is again procedural law that develops most rapidly.

3.2.1 Substantive treaty rules

Substantive treaty provisions on climate finance start off as a few brief provisions in the FCCC. They are only slightly developed in subsequent decisions of the state parties. No major development occurs prior to the Copenhagen Accord. The Accord's changes were incorporated into the body of FCCC decisions at the Cancun COP in 2010.

I begin in the pre-Copenhagen period with the FCCC itself. The FCCC's key article 4.3 was discussed in detail in Chapter 1,[1] and need not be revisited here, except in so far as it refers to 'the need for adequacy and predictability in the flow of funds and the importance of appropriate burden-sharing among developed country Parties'. This is clearly a substantive provision on climate finance. At COP 7, in 2001, it was agreed that 'appropriate modalities for burden sharing among the Parties included in Annex II need to be developed'.[2] No timeframe for the development of such modalities was specified, and none has materialized since.[3]

Article 11.3(d) of the FCCC is a partly substantive provision; it requires the COP to work with the GEF to enable 'determination in a predictable and identifiable manner of the amount of funding necessary and the conditions under which that amount shall be periodically reviewed'. Technology transfer (article 4.5) is related to climate finance and best viewed as a species of it; it is another substantive, 'shall', provision.[4] FCCC article 4.7 conditions the implementation of the commitments of developing countries 'on the effective implementation' of developed-country commitments on climate finance. It, too, falls within the substantive category. At the same time, 'Developing country Parties may, *on a voluntary basis*, propose projects for financing.'[5] This is one of the textual bases for the 'voluntarism' that prevailed in the pre-Copenhagen period.

Lastly, in the FCCC's substantive category, article 11.1 created 'A mechanism for the provision of financial resources on a grant or concessional basis'. The substantive content is that climate finance is to be in the nature of a grant or an instrument with an (unspecified) grant-equivalent component.

There follows the Copenhagen Accord, intended as a bridge between the end of the Kyoto Protocol's first commitment period and the starting date of a new global treaty on climate change (i.e. the interregnum 2013–2020). States signing up to the Accord agreed to hold the increase in global temperature to below 2°C,

72 *Legal obligations of states*

on the basis of equity.[6] It was a major development in substantive climate law. The following paragraph contains most of the Accord's substantive provisions on climate finance:

> Scaled up, new and additional, predictable and adequate funding as well as improved access shall be provided to developing countries, in accordance with the relevant provisions of the Convention, to enable and support enhanced action on mitigation [and] adaptation . . . for enhanced implementation of the Convention. The collective commitment by developed countries is to provide new and additional resources, including forestry and investments through international institutions, approaching USD 30 billion for the period 2010–2012 with balanced allocation between adaptation and mitigation. . . . In the context of meaningful mitigation actions and transparency on implementation, developed countries commit to a goal of mobilizing jointly USD 100 billion dollars a year by 2020 to address the needs of developing countries.[7]

I have discussed this key paragraph in detail in the introduction to this book. It gives a numerical indication of the amount of 'necessary funding' for the 2013–2020 period, while leaving the burden-sharing question unresolved. However, its critical break with the past is its elimination of voluntarism. The funding that 'shall be provided to developing countries [for] enhanced action on mitigation' is funding that, implicitly, shall be acted upon. The Copenhagen Accord does not clarify which developing country will undertake what amount of mitigation, just as it does not clarify which developed country will provide what amount of climate finance. The implied substantive point, however, is that climate finance is the facilitator of universal mitigation action. Voluntarism, as a legal impediment to such action, is struck out.

The Cancun COP decision adopting the elements of the Copenhagen Accord devotes three separate paragraphs to the need for mitigation action by developing countries.[8] It is only a 'will' obligation ('developing country Parties will take nationally appropriate mitigation actions'[9]); it is nevertheless strong enough to spell the end of voluntarism.

Lastly, assuming the Paris Agreement comes into force, what would it add to the substantive law on climate finance?

Article 9.1 of the Agreement alludes to continuity, not change, in state responsibility on the supply of climate finance: 'Developed country Parties shall provide financial resources to assist developing country Parties with respect to both mitigation and adaptation *in continuation of* their existing obligations under the Convention.' Article 8 adopts the FCCC's financial mechanism unchanged. Other elements require of states a 'progression beyond previous efforts' in the mobilization of climate finance (article 9.3), and therefore an actual change – an increase – in the amount of finance supplied. There is thus to be continuity, albeit with additional effort. Under the Paris Agreement, the 'subject' of the obligation to provide climate finance remains the group of developed countries. This collectivity of states has been the informal subject of the finance obligation since

Legal obligations of states 73

the Cancun COP. Cancun made it standard practice, when urging states to contribute – or to contribute more – to climate finance, to avoid reference to the narrow Annex II group preferred by the Convention, and thus quietly to extend the finance obligation to all developed countries.[10]

The COP decision adopting the Paris Agreement contains the outline of a process for increasing the amount of climate finance: 'developed countries intend to continue their existing collective mobilization goal through 2025 in the context of meaningful mitigation actions and transparency on implementation; prior to 2025 the Conference of the Parties [to the Paris Agreement] shall set a new collective quantified goal from a floor of USD 100 billion per year'.[11] Article 13.11 of the Agreement itself provides that 'each Party shall participate in a facilitative, multilateral consideration of progress with respect to efforts under Article 9 [the Agreement's main article on the supply of climate finance], and its respective implementation and achievement of its nationally determined contribution'. The plan for raising climate finance is voluntary pledging in the context of peer pressure.

In sum, developed countries 'intend' to take the lead on supply. The finance goal of $100 billion per year by 2020 is kept at the same level through to at least 2025 (suggesting that 'enhancement' of finance is not expected, and therefore not required, until the second half of the next decade). Lacking a concrete path to the financial ambition of 2020, the parties are urged to develop a 'concrete road map' instead.[12] The $100 billion goal, which was a kind of ceiling in the Copenhagen Accord and has now become a floor, is not supplemented by a new high target. As in the Accord, the continuation and the enhancement of climate finance are conditioned on the meaningfulness and transparency – not further defined – of measures taken by developing countries. Regarding supply, then, there is more continuity than change.

The Paris Agreement does not advance the law on the substantive issue of burden-sharing. The burden of reaching the target of $100 billion by 2020 and keeping it at that level through to at least 2025 still has not been parcelled out among developed states – and there is no indication of any kind of formula for sharing out the agreed financial burden. The COP decision (not the Agreement) does outline a pledge-based mechanism for country contributions to the collective *mitigation* effort: 'the information to be provided by Parties communicating their nationally determined contributions . . . may include . . . how the Party considers that its nationally determined contribution is fair and ambitious, in the light of its national circumstances, and how it contributes towards achieving the objective of the Convention'.[13] Climate finance is not mentioned in this context, even though, in the case of a developed country, a 'fair and ambitious' national contribution cannot be assessed in isolation of the country's contribution to climate finance.

The 2°C warming limit is another substantive legal issue relevant to climate finance. Pre-Copenhagen, the FCCC parties did not acknowledge the link between climate finance and an emission budget. Post-Copenhagen, the newly adopted 2°C limit began to be mentioned in connection with climate finance.[14] In the Paris Agreement's foundational article 2, officially for the first time a connection is made

74   *Legal obligations of states*

between the climate finance to be raised to support mitigation efforts in developing countries and the agreed warming limit: 'This Agreement . . . aims to strengthen the global response . . . by: (a) Holding the increase in the global average temperature to well below 2°C . . . (c) Making finance flows consistent with a pathway towards low greenhouse gas emissions and climate-resilient development.'[15] The 'pathway' in (c) surely incorporates the set of emission trajectories that, in (a), hold the temperature below 2°C.

The coming into force of the Paris Agreement would certainly help to develop the substantive law on climate finance. It elevates to the level of the treaty text obligations that had been established by decision under the FCCC. The Agreement affirms the post-Copenhagen thinking, to the effect that climate finance is critical to the avoidance of 'dangerous' warming. Because the Agreement puts an end to the Annex I/Annex II distinction, pre-existing substantive obligations have been extended, for they now formally apply to the category of 'developed' countries. However, there is little new on the amounts of finance to be supplied or on how states are to share the burden of climate finance. The same pledging system which was created for the 2013–2020 period is continued, augmented only by a 'facilitative, multilateral consideration of progress'. As for the question of how much to prioritize mitigation over adaptation with the climate finance raised, the Agreement simply adopts the old formula: 'to achieve a balance between adaptation and mitigation' (article 9.4).

3.2.2 Procedural treaty rules

Procedural law in the context of climate finance primarily concerns reporting by states of the financial support they have supplied, and includes the 'independent' review of such reports. The process attained a small degree of systematization when the Cancun COP compelled developed countries to report biennially on their provision of financial support to developing countries, beginning in 2013.[16] A procedural rule for holding developing countries accountable for the climate finance they have received has not so far been developed. Overall, reporting on climate finance is an area of neglect in the climate change regime, compared, for example, with state reporting on greenhouse gas emissions, where the law is well developed.

A few provisions not relating to reporting also belong to the category of procedural law. Article 11.3 of the FCCC places an obligation on the COP 'and the entity or entities entrusted with the operation of the financial mechanism' to agree ('shall agree') on arrangements for the 'Determination in a predictable and identifiable manner of the amount of funding necessary and available for the implementation of this Convention and the conditions under which that amount shall be periodically reviewed.' No such arrangements for the determination of 'need' have ever been fully developed. A case in point is that the amounts of climate finance in the Copenhagen Accord were 'spontaneously' generated – they were not determined through any particular process. As for the channels of supply – another procedural matter – article 11.5 of the FCCC allows that 'financial resources related to the implementation of the Convention [may be distributed] through bilateral, regional and other multilateral channels'. In fact, bilateral channels have dominated the supply of climate finance.

The rest of this section will focus on the rules for the reporting of climate finance. The Convention's Annex II parties have been required since the earliest years of the regime to report on their supply of climate finance. Such reports were to be presented, broken down by year, as part of their National Communications.[17] The original focus on the smaller group of Annex II parties changed, for all practical purposes, to encompass Annex I parties as a whole. According to the reporting guidelines on National Communications, as revised in 1999,[18] developed countries were to clarify, among other things, whether the finance they had supplied met the criterion of being 'new and additional'. States were also to report on the channels of distribution used. The 1999 guidelines required the information to be presented in a few simple tables.[19] There was little more to the reporting obligation on finance than what I have described above.

The Copenhagen Accord called for reform:

> Delivery of . . . financing by developed countries will be measured, reported and verified in accordance with existing and any further guidelines adopted by the Conference of the Parties, and will ensure that accounting of such targets and finance is rigorous, robust and transparent.[20]

As a result, in 2010, the Cancun COP revised the guidelines on Annex I National Communications, 'including the development of common reporting formats and methodology for finance'.[21] This led to the advent of Biennial Reports for developed countries (as well as Biennial Update Reports (BURs) for developing countries) to cover the 2013–2020 period. These concise, highly structured, and more frequent reports would become the focus of improvements on reporting on climate finance.

The Biennial Report guidelines[22] require each developed country to have in place, and provide a description of, a 'national approach' for tracking the provision of climate finance.[23] The country is required to distinguish between the mitigation and adaptation finance supplied and to report on each in detail.[24] The contributing states must also lay out 'rigorously, robustly, and transparently' the assumptions and methodologies underlying their national approaches to climate finance. They must use standardized methodologies for reporting climate finance where such methodologies are available.[25] (By 2016, none had been developed.[26]) Lastly, in their Biennial Reports, developed countries are to explain how they determine that the resources supplied 'effectively address' the adaptation and mitigation needs of non-Annex I parties.[27]

In 2011, the COP also put in place some relatively 'soft' reporting arrangements for non-Annex I parties on climate finance. Through their National Communications, non-Annex I parties are encouraged (not obliged) to submit information on finance received from Annex I/Annex II parties, from bilateral or multilateral institutions, and from the GEF. Guidelines were adopted for the preparation of

76 *Legal obligations of states*

developing-country BURs for the 2013–2020 period.[28] Through their BURs, non-Annex I parties are encouraged to submit information on financial constraints and gaps and related technical and capacity-building needs, in addition to information on finance received from the aforementioned sources – as well as, as of 2015, from the GCF. Even though the BURs could in theory help to verify the inflow of climate finance into developing countries,[29] no specific guideline or template in tabular format or otherwise has been developed for reporting climate finance in the BURs. Nor is there any guideline on (or even reference to) reporting on the outcomes achieved with the finance received.[30]

As for 'review' provisions for state reports on climate finance, none existed prior to 2010. Following Cancun, a process to review Annex I reporting on climate finance was incorporated into the review of the Biennial Reports for the 2013–2020 period. The task was added to the reviewing responsibilities of Expert Review Teams. Under this procedure, an ERT completes a report on an Annex I party's Biennial Report, and this 'technical review report'[31] is submitted to the FCCC parties, as the first step in the process of International Assessment and Review.[32] The second step is conducted in the Subsidiary Body for Implementation forum;[33] its purpose is to 'assess' the provision of financial and other support to developing-country parties. It is not clear from the relevant guidelines or the short history of practice to date whether assessment in the SBI is to go beyond basic questions concerning methodological and reporting adequacy.

The BURs of developing countries are not reviewed by ERTs but by 'technical teams of experts' (TTEs), which are constituted and trained to be sympathetic to the issues faced by developing countries.[34] A TTE prepares a 'technical analysis' of a BUR. The TTE's report is then submitted to the FCCC parties for the next step in a process called International Consultation and Analysis.[35] This latter step, also under the SBI, consists of a 'facilitative exchange of views'[36] – a highly attenuated multilateral component that does not specifically provide for any assessment of reporting on the climate finance received by developing countries.

In the lead-up to the Paris COP in 2015, Annex I countries advocated a strengthening of recipient-country reporting on climate finance.[37] (The need for greater transparency on developing-country mitigation actions receiving climate finance was noted already in the Copenhagen Accord[38] and the Cancun Agreements.[39]) The Paris Agreement did not strengthen recipient-country reporting directly (article 13.10 of the treaty merely provides that 'Developing country Parties *should* provide information on financial . . . support needed and received under [Article] 9'), although possibly it will do so through the elaboration of the so-called 'enhanced transparency framework for action and support' (ETF).[40] The framework's purpose 'is to provide clarity on support *provided and received* by relevant individual Parties . . . and, to the extent possible, to provide a full overview of aggregate financial support *provided*',[41] although, it would seem, not *received*. Reporting on outcomes is not even mentioned. Still, it is possible that the ETF, combined with the 'global stocktake',[42] will in time lead to a better accounting of incoming climate finance and the mitigation (and adaptation) outcomes obtained with it.

As for the review of climate finance reporting, the Paris Agreement appears simply to incorporate the processes of International Assessment and Review and International Consultation and Analysis into the new regime, with no noteworthy change,[43] thus perpetuating the differentiated treatment of supplier and recipient states.

3.2.3 Summary of conventional sources

The previous two sections outlined the treaty-based substantive and procedural rules on climate finance. It is far from being an empty space. Much has already been put in place, although much more is still needed before it could be said that a fully rational system of global mitigation action has been achieved.

On the substantive side, we have seen that the obligation to provide climate finance now falls on a group of countries enlarged well beyond its Annex II origins. FCCC parties are obliged to develop a system for the equitable distribution of the burden of providing the climate finance – something they have not done yet. The voluntarism which characterized the participation of developing countries has been rejected and a new obligation is forming, requiring such countries to actively seek climate finance where cost-effective domestic mitigation opportunities exist. The amount of climate finance to be provided by developed countries has not been precisely agreed to; only rough amounts have been promised, by certain dates: up to $100 billion per year by 2020; and at least $100 billion per year from 2025 onward. These amounts are arbitrary figures; yet there is a clear obligation on the FCCC parties to avoid arbitrariness and to link their calculations to 'the objective of the Convention', which, as of 2009, is to keep global warming below 2°C. The Paris Agreement, when in force, will be the first treaty instrument in the history of the climate change regime to link the climate finance obligation with the 2°C limit. Lastly on the substance, the FCCC limits the meaning of 'climate finance' to finance that is, for the most part, public and has a 'grant equivalence'.

On the procedural side, the legal obligations of states mainly relate to the reporting of climate finance. Developed states, as of the Cancun COP, must report biennially on the climate finance they have provided in some detail. Compared with their reporting obligations on greenhouse gas emissions, the rules on reporting climate finance are still elementary. Developing countries have never been obliged to report on the climate finance they have received, and even under the Paris Agreement they are still not obliged to do so. The logic of the Copenhagen Accord, which eliminates voluntarism, by implication requires greater symmetry in reporting, but the FCCC parties have not followed this through. The 'accountable reporting' rule which applies to developed countries and which as of late has been extended to their provision of climate finance requires an 'independent' review of reporting. Thus, it is well accepted that Annex I reports on greenhouse gas emissions must be submitted to review by ERTs. The obligation to submit to independent review has been extended to reporting on climate finance. The whole scheme is lopsided, however, as it is set up to scrutinize supply and not use. There is thus some way to go on improving the regime, yet a body of procedural rules certainly already exists.

78 *Legal obligations of states*

3.3 The relevance, if any, of principles of international law

The remainder of the chapter will consider whether the rules on climate finance derived from the climate treaties and COP decisions can be further developed under the guidance of more general principles of international law. It will be seen that most such principles are not applicable to the law on climate finance, or to climate law in general, and so cannot serve to enrich the body of conventional rules.

3.3.1 Sovereignty over natural resources and prevention of transboundary harm

Principle 21 of the Stockholm Declaration (the no-harm, or prevention principle) is reproduced almost verbatim in the FCCC's preamble.[44] A possible literal application of the no-harm principle to a state's anthropogenic greenhouse gas emissions is that, because those emissions are harmful to other states, they must cease, or else the state will be in violation of international law. It is therefore necessary in a discussion of climate law – even one ultimately focused on climate finance – to begin with a consideration of the relevance of this principle and how it might guide state conduct.

There are two versions of the no-harm principle: the classical, or 'weak', version, which holds that a state may not allow harmful substances to flow out across its borders and harm the environment of neighbouring areas; and the strong version, namely that, in addition to the classical prohibition, a state may not harm or contribute to the harm of any 'global commons' or any 'global physical system'. As discussed in Chapter 2, the ILA adopts the principle under the latter interpretation, claiming that the no-harm principle is highly relevant to the problem of climate change and is prescriptive of state conduct. A similar position is taken by Birnie *et al.*[45] In the latter work, the point is very weakly argued, and not entirely consistently, as its authors also appear to oppose the extension of the classical principle: 'treating the phenomena of global warming and climate change in the same way as transboundary air pollution, which is regional or bilateral in character [is inappropriate]'.[46]

The purpose of the no-harm principle is to protect a state from a certain type of physical interference by another state upon its own territory. The principle of environmental sovereignty, onto which the no-harm principle is grafted, assumes that each state has full control over its natural resources, which it may exploit as it pleases, and also that it has enough control over domestic actors to contain within its jurisdictional bounds any environmental damage that accompanies the exploitation of its domestic resources, so that it does not impact harmfully on neighbouring states. The environmental sovereignty principle does not prohibit domestic environmental damage; on the contrary, it appears to presume that environmental damage will be the rule rather than the exception. Hence the need for a supplementary rule that calls for the containment of damage within state boundaries. It is surprising that this essentially environmentally unfriendly principle has been adopted by environmentally minded scholars and NGOs as a foundation of climate law.

The no-harm principle, by its own wording, aims to prevent injury to other states or to 'areas beyond the limits of national jurisdiction'. Neither the atmosphere nor the climate system are 'areas' beyond the limits of national jurisdiction. Fatally for the strong position, the FCCC does not say that mitigation action by states must be in accordance with the no-harm principle. On the contrary, the FCCC provides that 'all countries, especially developing countries, need access to resources required to achieve sustainable social and economic development and . . . in order for developing countries to progress towards that goal, their energy consumption will need to grow'.[47] Thus the FCCC provides not only for a continuation of greenhouse gas emissions from developing countries, but for an *increase* in them, so, in what is a *reductio ad absurdum*, if it were true that the no-harm principle applies to the causes of climate change, the FCCC is authorizing developing countries to disregard the no-harm principle.

Even if greenhouse gases could be said to cause damage to 'other states', the no-harm principle would still not apply to the problem of climate change if states consent to the damage. While no state explicitly, in writing, consents to such damage, all states are responsible to some extent for the emission of greenhouse gases, both in the past and in the present. Unwilling or unable to terminate their own emissions, they effectively concede that they are in the same position as other states, polluting their neighbours just as their neighbours pollute them back. Even if the principle could be invoked in this context, it would be defeated by the consent – or effective consent – exception.

In conclusion, because the no-harm principle has no meaningful application to the problem of climate change, a fortiori it is not relevant to the law on climate finance.

3.3.2 Principle of precaution

Rio Declaration Principle 15 provides that, 'Where there are threats of serious or irreversible damage, lack of full scientific certainty shall not be used as a reason for postponing cost-effective measures to prevent environmental degradation.' The FCCC incorporates two different statements on precaution;[48] only the second constitutes the precautionary principle expressed in the Rio Declaration:

> The Parties should take precautionary measures to anticipate, prevent or minimize the causes of climate change and mitigate its adverse effects.
>
> Where there are threats of serious or irreversible damage, lack of full scientific certainty should not be used as a reason for postponing such measures, taking into account that policies and measures to deal with climate change should be cost-effective so as to ensure global benefits at the lowest possible cost.

The first of these statements is phrased very generally and appears to be a way of introducing the second. It does not say anything new, as the parties to the FCCC, by adopting the Convention, have already taken the precautionary measures suggested ('should') in the first statement.

80   *Legal obligations of states*

Two versions of the precautionary principle are to be found in the literature. One is weak and closest to the Rio Declaration; it says that a lack of full scientific certainty about cause and effect between a proposed development and its environmental damage should not be used as a reason in environmental policy to ignore the indicated causal link – and that this holds in all cases where the option to proceed cautiously by acknowledging the link does not come at an unreasonable cost.[49] In the stronger version, the precautionary principle 'requires that once environmental damage is threatened, action should be taken to control or abate possible environmental interference even though there may still be scientific uncertainty as to the effects of the activities'.[50] Its main difference from the classical expression of the principle in the Rio Declaration is its positive requirement of *action* in the face of uncertainty. It is a significant departure from the thesis that uncertainty should not serve as a reason to avoid conservative action.

Birnie *et al.* claim that Principle 15 of the Rio Declaration applies 'to problems of global environmental risk, such as climate change . . . in furtherance of the objective of sustainable development'.[51] They offer no explanation of how the principle applies to climate change. They slip from the weak to the strong version of the principle, apparently unaware. On reflection, the strong version (which takes the form: 'Where state conduct threatens environmental harm, the state should take preventative action') is conceptually very close to the strong version of the no-harm principle. The ILA's *Legal Principles* devote a 'draft article' jointly to the precautionary principle and the no-harm principle. It is the only article in the *Principles* to have two halves – a sign that the ILA regards them as being not only conceptually closely related but also of equal importance as substantive law applying to climate change.

Let us consider them in turn. The weak version of the precautionary principle clearly is not relevant to climate law because there is no doubt that (1) we are causing climate change and (2) it is harmful to our way of life.[52] There is no relevant uncertainty, or if there is uncertainty, it is on minor points; no-one is saying that we should keep up the production of greenhouse gas emissions until the minor points are cleared up. As for the strong version, it lacks a legal basis. Leaving that problem aside, it boils down to the view that the environment should be cared for. The first of the two statements in the FCCC, quoted above, might seem like a version of the strong thesis, yet all that that statement says is that states should do the kinds of thing that the treaty itself commits them to do. States are already taking action through the FCCC, and they are considering committing to even stronger action through the Paris Agreement. Thus the precautionary principle, like the no-harm principle, is not applicable to the problem of climate change, or adds nothing to the treaty law we already have.

3.3.3 Sustainable development

Following the pattern established in the previous two sections, the question for this section is whether there is any 'law' on sustainable development that could enrich or have any bearing on the treaty-based law on climate finance.

Legal obligations of states 81

The Rio Declaration incorporates a principle of sustainable development:

> The right to development must be fulfilled so as to equitably meet developmental and environmental needs of present and future generations. In order to achieve sustainable development, environmental protection shall constitute an integral part of the development process and cannot be considered in isolation from it.[53]

The FCCC and the climate change regime as a whole do not recognize a 'right' to development. Is there, nonetheless, a right to *sustainable* development within the regime that would amount to a normative rule?[54] Some elements of the regime would support an argument to that effect. For example, the CDM's objective of creating emission reductions is conditioned on its support for sustainable development; and the Copenhagen Accord assumes that 'the context of sustainable development' is a given.[55] However, if 'sustainable development' were to be defined as all development pathways consistent with avoidance of the 2°C threshold – which is one way to understand 'sustainable development' in article 2 of the Paris Agreement – then sustainable development is an *obligation* of all states, rather than a right of any subgroup of states.

Whether as an alleged right or obligation, what does it stand for?

The Rio Declaration elaborates the above-quoted passage by obliging all states to 'cooperate in the essential task of eradicating poverty as an indispensable requirement for sustainable development' (Principle 5). In the name of sustainable development, it requests states to 'reduce and eliminate unsustainable patterns of production and consumption and promote appropriate demographic policies' (Principle 8). Possibly also under the same concept of sustainable development is the commendation that 'Environmental impact assessment, as a national instrument, shall be undertaken for proposed activities that are likely to have a significant adverse impact on the environment' (Principle 17).

Scholars writing on sustainable development have questioned the concept's lack of precision and normative content.[56] Yet it is apparent from the Rio Declaration's formulations that sustainable development, whatever its meaning or legal status, does not have the power to elaborate or contribute anything specific to the climate change regime. Poverty eradication cannot be said to be the objective of the FCCC; on the contrary, it is often implied that efforts to eradicate poverty will be the cause of increased emissions.[57] Unsustainable production patterns would include the use of fossil fuels (as inputs); however, the climate change regime is already more accurately focused on managing outputs (greenhouse gases) rather than inputs. An EIA can detect and mitigate unwanted impacts at the local level, but it has nothing to say about greenhouse gases from the assessed development, which add to global atmospheric concentrations but have no local impacts.

Nevertheless, support for a 'principle of sustainable development' remains. It can be divided into two tendencies: supporters of a weak version, according to which economic development should be subject to considerations of environmental

82 *Legal obligations of states*

protection, such that lasting environmental damage is avoided or reduced where it is economically feasible to do so.[58] Here 'sustainable development' means 'less damage', not 'no damage'.[59] There are also supporters of a strong version – one that proclaims that no (lasting) environmental damage is to result from any development action. The strong version entails that certain types of development must be phased out completely, and perhaps immediately, so as to prevent further damage. Schalatek supports the strong version, which she applies to climate finance: ' "Do no harm", namely ensuring that a climate intervention does not make matters worse, even if only unintentionally, should be the yardstick against which all climate funding decisions should be judged.'[60] Anton is also in this camp: '[Rio's weak notion] of sustainable development, with its focus on economic growth, has had a destructive impact . . . it has diminished and subordinated international environmental protection to economic growth and social development.'[61]

Both the weak version and the strong version are rife with problems. The former predates the idea of climate change, both chronologically and conceptually. It advocates 'balance' in decision-making, which means acceptance of a certain degree of environmental damage.[62] But it does not tell us how much damage to accept. The FCCC, by contrast, does, at a certain level. It tells us that damage going hand-in-hand with global warming up to 'below' 2°C is acceptable (in the sense of 'allowed' or 'unavoidable').[63] So the FCCC is already more specific than the weak version of the concept of sustainable development. At the level of the development proposal itself, and no matter how large the development may be, it is not possible to make an assessment on the basis of an EIA or any such analysis that includes in the balance a relevant link with climate change. Such a link would have to take into account what the other relevant actors are doing, the impact of the project on what other actors might decide to do, the decisions other actors might take if the project did not proceed, etc.[64] The calculation would have to be projected years into the future. None of this is practically possible.

On this analysis, the weak concept is irrelevant. Under the FCCC, all development within the 2°C limit is 'sustainable development', seeing that the state parties wish to balance economic development and environmental harm in this manner and live with the consequences of 2°C of warming. There is nothing in the weak version that entails that they should be doing anything differently.

The concept of sustainable development first surfaced in the 1970s, when development decisions could be framed as choices between sustainable and unsustainable outcomes. Where a proposed development presented no such choice, in principle it would not be allowed to proceed. It was nevertheless assumed that in most cases such a choice would exist. In this period, prior to 1990, the fact was not fully appreciated that the very basis of human development – an almost total reliance on fossil fuels for energy and food production and a dependence on land-use change to support population and economic growth – were damaging the environment through climate change. In reality, from this new perspective, for any given development the most that could be hoped for was that environmental (i.e. climatic) damage would be minimized, not avoided. Essentially all development was revealed as damaging. When this became clear, the original

Legal obligations of states 83

(weak) version of the concept of sustainable development stopped making sense. But the strong version that has sought to replace it also does not make sense.

The strong version requires of each development decision that it be a 'positive' one. This runs directly into the problem that there is no legal basis for this proposition. Also, it is difficult to see how it would work. As I have noted, almost any growth in, e.g., the energy sector would employ fossil fuels and add to atmospheric concentrations of greenhouse gases. It is only where a development *displaces* a pre-existing harmful development, and does no additional harm itself, that a contribution has been made to sustainable development in the strong sense. Implicit in this is that the principle is not applicable where the choice is between two poor environmental (climatic) outcomes both of which are harmful. An environmentally harmful outcome is, under the strong thesis, by definition unacceptable. The fact that one outcome is better than the other does not initself make the choice of the less harmful one a contribution to sustainable development, unless no better choice exists, including the choice of doing nothing.

Thus, for example, the substitution of a coal-fired power plant with a gas-fired one is not a contribution to sustainable development in the strong sense. Shutting down the coal-fired power plant would be such a contribution, but only if it did not lead to an increase in greenhouse gas emissions elsewhere in the energy sector in the country (or outside the country, if the country imports electricity from its neighbours). Which 'clean energy' development does not itself entail significant environmental damage? Which such development actually suppresses existing 'dirty' production and does not simply serve to meet an increase in demand? One has to search far and wide and still will not easily find an example of sustainable development – short of cessation of development – that fits the strong version of the thesis. Sustainable development in the strong version requires us always to choose the option of positive good, but if there is no practical application to the idea, it cannot help to develop the law we have in place.

It has been naively asserted that sustainable development *is the only way* to fight climate change.[65] On the contrary, we should recall that the IPCC, in its 'below 2°C pathway' scenarios, assumes more nuclear power will be installed, more carbon capture and storage will be created, and more land for solar power or biofuel production will be set aside – in general, that there will be more all-round 'geoengineering' of what is left of the natural environment. Even a modest level of control over climate change thus requires a significant amount of further development that in no ordinary sense of the word could be called 'sustainable'. Even after all the needed geoengineering options have been implemented, the climate change regime's aim to ease warming up to under 2°C and then hold it there entails a high risk of failure. How could this aim be called 'sustainable' in any ordinary sense? Those who sneer at the weak thesis have a point; but the strong thesis they seek to install in its place is utopian and has no basis in law.

When the natural environment is already damaged through climate change, and the real choice is between maintaining it in its present damaged state or damaging it more, no development can be 'sustainable'. The focus must shift to the containment of the damage done, although without any assurance of success. Under

84 *Legal obligations of states*

the FCCC, all change up to the threshold of 'dangerous' is, legally, acceptable. The climate change regime has ceased to be a system of environmental protection – which it might well have been had states been ambitious enough back in 1992. Those who see the notion of sustainable development as being relevant to climate law mistake the current FCCC regime for a system of environmental protection; in truth, it is a system of controlled environmental damage. Sustainable development, even if it were a legal principle, has nothing to say to a regime that, quite realistically, accepts severe damage as a given.

3.3.4 Equity and the principle of common but differentiated responsibility

The Rio Declaration introduces the principle of common but differentiated responsibility with the statement: 'States shall cooperate in a spirit of global partnership to conserve, protect and restore the health and integrity of the Earth's ecosystem.'

It continues:

> In view of the different contributions to global environmental degradation, States have common but differentiated responsibilities. The developed countries acknowledge the responsibility that they bear in the international pursuit of sustainable development *in view of the pressures their societies place on the global environment* and of the technologies and financial resources they command.[66]

The italicized phrase implies that other countries exercise little or no 'pressure' on the global environment in comparison with developed countries. One quarter of a century after the Rio Declaration, this is no longer true (if it ever was). In most developed countries, strict environmental laws have taken hold, and environmental damage is both much less than it used to be and much less than it is in some developing countries.

The CBDR principle is alluded to in the FCCC's preamble:

> the global nature of climate change calls for the widest possible cooperation by all countries and their participation in an effective and appropriate international response, in accordance with their common but differentiated responsibilities and respective capabilities and their social and economic conditions.

It will be noted that this provision is not about the CBDR principle itself (for the differentiation of responsibility is simply assumed in the quoted passage), but about what I call the principle of good-faith cooperation. The cooperation principle is present also in the opening sentence of the Rio Declaration's Principle 7 (above). In both cases, the concept of differentiated state responsibility serves to explain how the cooperation principle should be implemented. Yet, in the climate change regime, it is the CBDR principle that receives most of the attention of scholars, whereas the cooperation principle is hardly ever mentioned.

The FCCC returns to state differentiation in article 3.1, which seems to lay down two principles side by side – equity and CBDR:

> The Parties should protect the climate system for the benefit of present and future generations ... on the basis of equity and in accordance with their common but differentiated responsibilities and respective capabilities. Accordingly, the developed country Parties should take the lead in combating climate change and the adverse effects thereof.[67]

In both FCCC passages quoted, the drafters have added the words 'and respective capabilities' to the Declaration's wording. This could mean that state responsibility is to be determined with reference to state 'capability'. In the Declaration, the phrase 'the technologies and financial resources they command' is a measure of capability. So this is probably what the FCCC also means. (The Paris Agreement adds the words 'in the light of national circumstances' to the end of the FCCC's already unwieldy phrase.)

The CBDR principle is thus certainly invoked in the FCCC, although there is a lack of clarity about what it stands for. There is a possibility that it means no more than that the climate change regime should be implemented equitably among all states.

Of the two principles, equity (or equitable utilization) is a well-established general principle of international law,[68] whereas CBDR is not.[69] Perhaps because CBDR stood for nothing in particular at the start of the climate change regime, it could be given a definition that suited the politics of the early years – when allusion to a 'historical responsibility' of rich countries was a more forceful argument than it is today.[70]

CBDR quickly acquired a very precise form in the climate change regime: it created a 'sharp distinction between Annex I and non-Annex I states',[71] placing a 'firewall' between developed and developing countries.[72] This polarized manifestation received its purest expression in the Kyoto Protocol, which divided the world into 'two poles: developed countries, which had to accept cuts in emissions, and the rest, with no binding commitments'.[73] Some scholars concede that 'only one particular interpretation of the CBDR principle ... has so far dominated the climate negotiations'.[74]

Even though that particular interpretation represents only one possible manifestation of the CBDR idea, the polarized manifestation became the regime's defining principle. It was eventually held up as 'central to the realization of climate justice'.[75] The Kyoto Protocol's 'exclusive focus on emissions reduction commitments for Annex I Parties ... was consonant with the CBDR principle', affirm Brunnée and Streck.[76] CBDR, thus defined, was said to be 'essential to the legitimacy and hence viability of a long-term, global regime'.[77] Some scholars also accepted the CBDR principle's central, guiding, role in relation to climate *finance*,[78] even though the principle did not have any clear implications for climate finance.

86   *Legal obligations of states*

Polarization began to unravel at the Bali COP, and came to an end a few years later, in Cancun.[79] The Durban Platform, note Brunnée and Streck, 'lacks any explicit reference to the differentiation of responsibilities between Parties, the differences in historic emissions of developed and developing countries, and the leadership role of developed countries'.[80] Given that the FCCC's version of CBDR was an artificial creation, and had no independent legal basis or accepted meaning pre-1992, it should have faded away completely, as it seemed to have done in Durban. Instead, purportedly, it has been retained under a new definition. The essence of the new definition is captured by Ulfstein and Voigt: 'States are supposed to be treated equally [for which] their differences and national circumstances must be taken into account.'[81] This is so close to being a restatement of the equity principle that it leaves little room for a separate principle of CBDR. Scholars have failed to see this. Starting from a complete differentiation between two groups of states, but retreating now to a position of equal treatment of all states subject to capacity, the CBDR principle has merged back into the principle of equity in article 3.1 of the FCCC. It no longer has anything significant to say on its own.

Yet there are still those who insist that the original principle lives on, albeit under a more subtle definition.[82] They fail to appreciate that the basic post-Copenhagen position is that each state has a legal responsibility to act on mitigation, subject to its ability, objectively and reasonably assessed, to bear the cost of doing so. Pre-Copenhagen, under the influence of the original CBDR principle, there were two groups, one with legal responsibility and one without. The shift from two groups to one was not one of degree; it was a change of state. (The original CBDR's 'differentiated' meant principled differentiation of states into two categories; it did not mean 'different' mitigation obligations along a spectrum.) This is why I have described the Copenhagen Accord as bringing about a fundamental change in legal arrangements among states. Whereas the CBDR's polarization placed full responsibility for action on the Annex I group, thus marginalizing climate finance, under the new arrangement, in every instance where financial support is offered, a non-Annex I country with mitigation opportunities has a legal obligation to act on mitigation. Its capacity limits are only a practical matter and can be altered by climate finance. There is no longer any legal substance to differentiation. Equity is the principle left.

The link between equity and CBDR depends on how the latter is implemented. If CBDR divides states into two groups, then the link is weak, and after a while states will complain (as they have) that the division is inequitable. If, on the other hand, CBDR is made relative to the national circumstances of each state, as seems to be the case under the Paris Agreement, then CBDR and equity become indistinguishable as principles. When this happens, it may be that another principle is needed, one that can distribute the mitigation burden in accordance with the principle of equity. The process that removed the polarization and reduced CBDR to a restatement of equity left a vacuum where there used to be a guiding principle for action. Can international law offer another principle to replace CBDR in the climate change regime, or must the regime be content with the law it has developed through treaties and decisions?

3.3.5 The polluter-pays principle and burden-sharing among states

The Rio Declaration, Principle 16, emphasizes the importance of the polluter-pays principle as a policy instrument for 'national authorities':

> National authorities should endeavour to promote the internalization of environmental costs and the use of economic instruments, taking into account the approach that the polluter should, in principle, bear the cost of pollution, with due regard to the public interest and without distorting international trade and investment.

In contrast with many of the Declaration's principles, this one appears not to seek to bind states in their interactions with each other. Instead, it urges governments to adjust the prices of goods and services within their jurisdiction so that prices reflect the cost of their environmental impact.

We know how the polluter-pays principle works for state authorities,[83] for it is extensively used by them to regulate local environmental problems, such as particulate matter, noise pollution, or traffic congestion. A local authority may calculate what amount of particulates, noise, or traffic is tolerable for, say, a stretch of road or bridge; it may then introduce a toll that reduces pollution indicators to the tolerable range.

At this level, the polluter-pays principle is not only a regulatory device with many practical applications and a good track record;[84] in many jurisdictions it is recognized as a principle of law[85] because it tackles head-on the inequity which results from failing to price environmental externalities.[86] Such failure has led to situations where those who pollute more than others (or who consume products which pollute more than others) benefit, because the damage (the cost of government clean-up, reduced environmental quality, etc.) usually falls equally on all citizens.

What about the regulation of greenhouse gases, which present a global, not a local, environmental problem? There are two ways to approach this question. First, the polluter-pays principle can have an application with greenhouse gases at the domestic level,[87] in particular where the state (or region, in the case of the European Union) has adopted a cap on emissions. The state cap represents a concession that the state must bear the cost of reducing national emissions from a BAU level to the level represented by the cap. The greater the difference, the greater the cost to the state. One way or another, the cost of maintaining the cap will be passed down to the state's citizens.

The latter case is significantly different from the archetypal one outlined two paragraphs above, because the inequity addressed through the pricing of greenhouse gas emissions within the domestic jurisdiction is not an inequity that exists within that jurisdiction alone but one that exists within the international community of states as a whole.

Second, the principle may be applied at the level of a state's relationship with other states, where 'the economic agent playing a decisive role in the pollution'[88]

88 *Legal obligations of states*

is the state itself. A state has this role because it may adopt policies and pass laws that reduce domestic emissions – or it may decline to do so.

Applied at this level, as international law, the principle requires a state to bear a cost for some part of its contribution to the global greenhouse effect. The principle is not concerned about how a state, in its domestic arrangements, meets the cost it has chosen to bear (or has been assigned) internationally. The state may very well choose to price domestic emissions in order to spread around the cost of the international obligation among its citizens and create broad-based mitigation incentives, but it may also use other methods to rein in emissions (e.g. incentives to increase energy efficiency; fuel-switching; etc.) that do not exact a payment for pollution.[89]

It is important to distinguish the two answers to the question I posed earlier. In this section, I am concerned with the second one, since this is the one most relevant to international law.

The polluter-pays principle is a principle of equity. It applies to states in their international relations with each other (as much as to individuals or firms in domestic law).[90] Nothing in the language of Principle 16 of the Rio Declaration prevents the principle from attaching to a state in its dealings with other states.[91] 'The Principle has been considered since 1990 as a general principle of international environmental law.'[92] At this level, the polluter-pays principle stands for the proposition that a state must cover the environmental cost of its globally consequential pollution and not simply let other states suffer it. Thus, it has a similar effect to the no-harm principle. However, it is free of that principle's limitations. Because all states contribute to the greenhouse effect, and because states have decided that some enhancement of that effect will have to be tolerated, the polluter-pays principle only applies to a certain portion of the greenhouse gas pollution that a state releases into the world's environment.[93]

The polluter-pays principle normally operates in a context where the setting of a price, or bearing of a cost, is not an arbitrary exercise.[94] It is not simply an ad-hoc attack on BAU practices – it is an attempt to reduce BAU pollution to a new, predefined, level. The climate change regime has, as of 2010, created such a target that enables a rational application of the principle. The cost to be borne by states must be such as to maintain an emission budget compatible with avoidance of 2°C of warming. All state targets would necessarily be below BAU for each of the states, thus imposing a cost on country economies. Under this arrangement, states would receive emission allowances adding up to a 'safe' global budget.[95] They would be allowed to trade their emission allowances and would be fined for excess emissions. The fine for emissions above the target (i.e. the fine for climatic 'pollution') would be steep enough to ensure that a state would rather pay to create domestic mitigation or purchase emission allowances from other states than pay the fine. Thus the polluter-pays principle at the international level would work by discouraging pollution, not by allowing pollution subject to a fee. Revision rules would ensure that short-term state targets remain on track to meet the long-term stabilization goal.[96] A version of this system was trialled by the Kyoto Protocol.[97] Because the countries which the Kyoto Protocol made subject to the principle (the

Annex I parties) were all wealthy, there was no compunction in theory about fining them, if necessary, and no provision was made to support them financially to meet their targets should the need arise.

The polluter-pays principle has its limitations. As a general principle, it has no capacity to prescribe individualized cost obligations for states. The principle supports the proposition that states with the highest emissions per capita must make the largest reductions, other things being equal; but other things are not equal. The distribution of mitigation burdens is a complex matter of international policy and equity that remains unresolved.[98]

A country's mitigation burden is a factor[99] of its emissions per capita, its mitigation opportunities, and its wealth (GDP per capita or another indicator of wealth). Each of these three factors necessarily represents a relative assessment against global data. The highest responsibility falls on a wealthy country whose emissions are high and whose low-cost mitigation opportunities are plentiful. A country with low per-capita emissions and few low-cost mitigation opportunities which is also a poor country will have a relatively insignificant or non-existent mitigation burden despite its (legal) mitigation obligation. Most countries lie in-between these extremes. Wealthy countries with relatively low (per capita) and falling emissions for which additional domestic mitigation is comparatively expensive occupy the same part of the spectrum of mitigation burdens as poor countries with low but growing emissions and plentiful, reasonably priced, mitigation opportunities. To discharge their responsibilities, these countries must cooperate. Climate finance increases a developing country's ability to mitigate, ideally making it equal to its burden, calculated as the product of its per-capita emission trend, mitigation opportunities, and wealth. Along the spectrum also lie countries that, while 'developing', do not require climate finance to discharge their responsibility, or require only a small amount of climate finance relative to their size as emitters.[100] The pre-Copenhagen approach did not have all countries locked into this one equation as the post-Copenhagen model does.

It is clear, therefore, that a general equity principle must be engaged with to moderate the application of the polluter-pays principle, which is a species of the general principle of equity.[101] Equity must adjust the costs to a state of a unit of domestic emission reduction; or, in what amounts to the same thing,[102] it must place a burden on wealthier states to achieve emission reductions by subsidizing poorer states to carry them out, subject to the spectrum analysis above. Climate finance enables the equitable application of the polluter-pays principle.[103] Conceivably, however, a wealthy country could be expending such a substantial effort domestically (i.e. emission reductions per capita beyond BAU are high) that it is not required to supply climate finance. But this would only make sense if it were the most cost-effective use of its additional expenditure. The modified polluter-pays model does not accommodate wasteful domestic spending where it is possible to achieve more mitigation with the same expenditure used as climate finance. In practice, domestic spending is likely to have benefits additional to emission reduction, and these would have to be taken into account in deciding cost-effectiveness.[104]

90 *Legal obligations of states*

The role played by the polluter-pays principle in the climate change regime is to provide a legal rationale and justification for the transition to the post-Copenhagen model, whereby all states must mitigate, subject to capacity. It settles on the regime as an additional layer of legal principle, not already contained within it. The principle is important for making the legal case that all states must contribute to the collective cost of keeping global warming under control. It implies that negotiation of a legally binding burden-sharing agreement is unavoidable in the long term.[105] Knowledge of this legal obligation is not insignificant, because it maintains pressure on states to come to an agreement on how to share the collective cost of mitigation, in the knowledge that, until they do so, they will be in non-compliance with a legal principle. These elements of legal obligation are not visible except through the lens of the polluter-pays principle.

States have been in a self-congratulatory mood since the Paris COP. They are now focused on fleshing out the details of their agreement. Yet the Paris outcome offers no more than an elementary step towards the creation of substantive mitigation obligations or towards an agreement to share the burden of the emission budget globally among states. It is only an agreement to work towards an agreement. The Agreement's NDC scheme is bottom-up (and not budget-driven). Even if the NDCs' mitigation commitments were legally binding instead of just voluntary, they could still not guarantee the climate finance needed to avoid a 2°C rise in warming. 'Practical', bottom-up, options[106] are not consistent with international law, which implies a top-down agreement that achieves the 2°C limit. The Paris Agreement shies away from obliging states to reach agreement on how to share the burden. It postpones the inevitable.

3.4 Synthesis of treaty-based and other sources of law

Having considered all the sources relevant to the development of international climate change law, we are now in a position to summarize that law, with a particular focus on climate finance. As expected, as yet only a few legal rules exist in international law to induce state action on climate change.

I begin with the general substantive rules:

> *The containment rule.* Global warming must be kept below 2°C. The amount of state mitigation action implied by this limit requires so great an effort that some states would have to bear an excessive cost per mitigation unit, whereas others could not afford even a modest cost. Therefore, international climate finance is necessary to smooth out cost differences among states.

> *The equity rule.* The collective mitigation obligation that all states share under the climate change regime (i.e. the containment rule) must be shared among states equitably through a burden-sharing agreement. From the equivalence rule (see below), it follows that the burden of *climate finance* must also be equitably distributed. The equity rule places a positive obligation on all countries to contribute to mitigation where enabling conditions are in place.

The good-faith negotiation rule. Until an agreement is reached on the equitable allocation of mitigation burdens, states are to engage in voluntary mitigation efforts or support other states to do so through climate finance. In parallel, states must engage in uninterrupted negotiations in good faith towards the production of an equitable burden-sharing agreement. This is a substantive, not procedural, rule because it requires good faith, not the mere occurrence of negotiations.

The equivalence rule. Mitigation obligations are to be met through domestic reduction actions or through financial transfers that support mitigation programmes and projects in other countries. Thus mitigation obligations can be converted into climate finance obligations, and vice versa.

The prioritization rule. The balancing of mitigation and adaptation funding must be subordinated to the containment rule. Sufficient mitigation funding must be made available by states to avoid breaching the 2°C limit. Climate finance must therefore prioritize mitigation funding. Adaptation finance should also be raised, but it cannot have the same priority.

There are also two general procedural rules:

The accountable reporting rule.[107] States contributing climate finance must report their financial support transparently and allow for its independent expert verification. Receiving states must do the same in relation to the use of finance and the mitigation outcomes achieved by it. Receiving states should not be exempt from independent expert verification but may need to have the costs associated with verification covered through climate finance.

The re-assessment and re-negotiation rule. States must accept and respond to scientific feedback (e.g. from the IPCC) on their progress with containing the emission budget. Where the progress is found to be insufficient, states must return to the negotiating table to reconsider the total burden and its state-level distribution.

Under my analysis, the content of conventional law, with its elaboration in state-party decision-making, must be given priority when outlining the applicable law. The more difficult task has been to identify a general legal principle that sets the overall direction for the climate change regime. I considered each of the principles that are regularly put forth in fulfilment of that role – the no-harm principle, the principle of precaution, the concept of sustainable development, and the CBDR principle – and found them all wanting. The only general principle relevant to the elaboration of conventional climate law in the direction which it has set itself since Copenhagen is the polluter-pays principle.

The adoption of the polluter-pays principle has substantive-law implications for developing countries: they must now engage in mitigation as a matter of legal obligation and not only by voluntary choice (assuming that they have cost-effective emission-reduction opportunities available to them and that finance is

92   *Legal obligations of states*

made available to them to cover incremental costs). The impact of the principle's application is softened (modified) by the principle of equity. The modified polluter-pays principle relies for its authority on the acceptance of the polluter-pays principle as a principle of international law applying to the problem of climate change.

From the moment when the climate change regime set the warming limit at 2°C and extended mitigation obligations to all countries, it effectively adopted the polluter-pays principle. Many pieces began to fall into place at that point, including the rationale for climate finance as providing flexibility and equity in the application of the polluter-pays principle to the problem of climate change. By contrast, the CBDR model that prevailed until then cannot explain the *dis*continuum effected by the Copenhagen transition, from a time when only a few states had mitigation obligations to a time when all of them did. It has been said that 'the notion of CBDR is the anchor provision of the global climate regime'.[108] But that legal position has now been completely rejected.

The new climate law emphasizes cooperation and reciprocity. The transfer of finance must be pursuant to a plan that stands a chance of solving the underlying problem. It is a collaborative endeavour, responsibility for which is not only on the country with the obligation to provide finance. It necessarily follows from an obligation of supply-and-receipt that there is an obligation of *appropriate* use of climate finance, because the former obligation arises from the requirement of quantified (budgeted) mitigation action, which means that the obligation is not met unless the relevant action is taken. Thus recipient states have accepted an important obligation to carry out real, additional, and verifiable mitigation (and adaptation) actions with the received finance.

The new law makes no unrealistic assumption about equal individual (personal) 'ownership' of the atmosphere.[109] Avoidance of 2°C or more of warming is not calculated with reference to any assumed equal ownership. It is at most equivalent to saying that people in developing countries, generally, have higher per-capita emission 'rights', although they still have to bear a cost – if only a nominal one – for their individual emissions. Still, the role that equity plays in the current legal scheme should not be exaggerated. The reason why wealthy states are so willing to embrace it, is, after all, self-interest. Each state has an interest in keeping the climate system from spiralling out of control. The wealthier states know that, for this, they must bear a cost.

The CBDR principle never allowed climate finance to become a conceptually central notion. Under CBDR, climate finance existed only as an optional mitigation mechanism that a minority of states contributed to and that recipient states subscribed to voluntarily. The only essential role accorded by the pre-Copenhagen FCCC regime to climate finance was for purposes unrelated to mitigation, namely to support costs of LDC adaptation and to fund periodic reporting by developing countries. With CBDR displaced by the polluter-pays principle, climate finance gained a legal foothold in international law.

Since 2010, the majority of countries make, or plan to make, emission reductions. They therefore incur, or plan to incur, a certain cost for their pollution.

Legal obligations of states 93

Some developing countries (including China) may be able to absorb most of the cost themselves, whereas others will rely to a significant degree on financial assistance provided to them by other states for the purpose of mitigation. Developing countries will still be able to increase their levels of greenhouse gas pollution in support of their economic development. But in contrast with the CBDR approach, the growth is no longer, legally, unlimited. Even if indirectly, it is limited by the 2°C target. Under a non-legal analysis, the two situations look the same. From a legal point of view, they are different.

The elimination of a CBDR-type of differentiation also affects procedural rules. Developing countries have until recently not had to engage in 'accountable reporting'. They have not had to report their emissions annually or use the strictest accounting methods. The mitigation effects of projects in developing countries funded with climate finance, typically the CDM, have been calculated against projected BAU emissions for the developing country concerned, which are easy to manipulate (see Chapter 5). The modified polluter-pays model implies a legal obligation on all states to engage in accountable reporting. When accountable reporting is fully implemented for all states, developing countries will be more careful about how they utilize mitigation finance, because at that point their national emission accounts will have become the measure of their mitigation efforts, not the reductions claimed from project-based accounting.

I have argued that the polluter-pays principle, tempered by equity, has become central to international climate law. It supplies a legal standard against which state conduct may be judged. It is a standard in which the notion of climate finance is central. The principle is the logical cornerstone of the climate change regime. However, the politics of the regime insist on continuity, concealing foundational change. The legal scheme outlined in this chapter therefore is neither fully accepted nor fully realized.

Notes

1 See Sections 1.2.1–1.2.4.
2 FCCC (2001), *Decision 7/CP.7, Funding under the Convention*, FCCC/CP/2001/13/Add.1, para. 1(d).
3 Cf. Farhana Yamin and Joanna Depledge (2004), *The International Climate Change Regime: A Guide to Rules, Institutions and Procedures*, Cambridge: Cambridge University Press, p. 270: 'issues relating to financial burden-sharing have taken place largely in the GEF . . . during replenishment negotiations, rather than in the COP. . . . This approach to burden-sharing cannot be described as a binding rule but it guides expectations.'
4 'The developed country Parties and other developed Parties included in Annex II shall take all practicable steps to promote, facilitate and finance, as appropriate, the transfer of, or access to, environmentally sound technologies and know-how to other Parties, particularly developing country Parties, to enable them to implement the provisions of the Convention.'
5 FCCC, article 11.1, emphasis added.
6 FCCC, *Decision 2/CP.15 (2009), Copenhagen Accord*, FCCC/CP/2009/11/Add.1, para. 2.
7 Ibid., para. 8.

94 *Legal obligations of states*

8 FCCC (2010), Decision 1/CP.16, *The Cancun Agreements: Outcome of the Work of the Ad Hoc Working Group on Long-Term Cooperative Action under the Convention*, FCCC/CP/2010/7/Add.1, paras 2(d), 48, and 52.

9 Ibid., para. 48.

10 Ibid., para. 18; and ibid., para. 52 ('in accordance with Article 4, paragraph 3, of the Convention, developed country Parties shall provide enhanced financial . . . support'). Note also that article 9.1 of the Paris Agreement refers to the 'continuation of [the] existing obligations' of developed countries (not Annex II parties) on climate finance.

11 FCCC (2015), *Decision 1/CP.21, Adoption of the Paris Agreement*, FCCC/CP/2015/10/Add.1, para. 53.

12 Ibid., para. 114.

13 Ibid., para. 27. The wording is the same as in FCCC (2014), *Decision 1/CP.20, Lima Call for Climate Action*, FCCC/CP/2014/10/Add.1, para. 14.

14 E.g. Standing Committee on Finance (2014a), *Biennial Assessment and Overview of Climate Finance Flows Report*, p. 67 ('An important question posed at the outset of the [Biennial Assessment] was whether it was possible to assess whether climate finance is helping to achieve the overarching goal of the Convention of keeping climate change within 2 degrees'); Green Climate Fund (2015), 'Green Climate Fund Approves First 8 Investments', Press Release, 6 November 2015, p. 2 ('The Green Climate Fund . . . was given the mandate to help keep the planet's atmospheric temperature rise below 2 degrees Celsius'); and International Institute for Sustainable Development (2015), 'Summary of ADP 2–8 (No. 3) (9 February)', 12 (622) *Earth Negotiations Bulletin* 1, p. 1 ('The African Group called for a clear link between a quantitative financial goal and temperature goal').

15 Cf. FCCC (2015), *Decision 1/CP.21*, para. 52 ('in the implementation of the Agreement, financial resources provided to developing countries should enhance . . . their climate change actions with respect to both mitigation and adaptation to contribute to the achievement of the purpose of the Agreement as defined in Article 2').

16 FCCC (2010), *Decision 1/CP.16*, para. 40.a.

17 FCCC (2001), *Decision 7/CP.7*, para. 1(e–f). The system of National Communications is an attempt to operationalize the reporting obligations of state parties to the FCCC.

18 FCCC (1999), Decision 4/CP.5, *Guidelines for the Preparation of National Communications by Parties Included in Annex I to the Convention, Part II: UNFCCC Reporting Guidelines on National Communications*, FCCC/CP/1999/6/Add.1, paras 51 and 53.

19 FCCC (1999), *Guidelines for the Preparation of National Communications by Parties Included in Annex I to the Convention, Part II: UNFCCC Reporting Guidelines on National Communications*, FCCC/CP/1999/7 (annex to Decision 4/CP.5), pp. 93–95.

20 *Copenhagen Accord*, para. 4.

21 See FCCC (2010), *Decision 1/CP.16*, paras 40(a), 41.

22 FCCC (2011), *Decision 2/CP.17, Outcome of the Work of the Ad Hoc Working Group on Long-Term Cooperative Action under the Convention*, FCCC/CP/2011/9/Add.1, Annex I: UNFCCC Biennial Reporting Guidelines for Developed Country Parties, paras 13–19; see also FCCC (2012), *Decision 19/CP.18, Common Tabular Format for 'UNFCCC Biennial Reporting Guidelines for Developed Country Parties'*, FCCC/CP/2012/8/Add.3, table templates 7, 7(a), and 7(b), which seek to streamline climate finance reporting.

23 FCCC (2011), *Decision 2/CP.17*, Annex I: UNFCCC Biennial Reporting Guidelines for Developed Country Parties, para. 14.

24 Including on the source of funding; the financial instrument used (e.g. a grant or concessional loan); the economic sector to which the finance was directed; and the method of determination of newness and additionality of the supplied finance: ibid, para 18.

Legal obligations of states 95

25 Ibid., para. 15.
26 Cf. FCCC (2014), *Decision 11/CP.20, Methodologies for the Reporting of Financial Information by Parties Included in Annex I to the Convention*, FCCC/CP/2014/10/Add.2, para. 1 ('a decision on the methodologies for the reporting of financial information, as referred to in decision 2/CP.17, paragraph 19 [is still pending]'); and ibid., para. 3 ('the secretariat [is] to prepare a technical paper [drawing on] information submitted by Parties on appropriate methodologies and systems used to measure and track climate finance'). See also Organization for Economic Cooperation and Development and Climate Policy Initiative (2015), *Climate Finance in 2013–14 and the USD 100 Billion Goal*, Paris: OECD and CPI, p. 33 ('The existing reporting guidelines and Common Tabular Formats developed in 2012 provide no internationally agreed definitions or methodology for basic financial reporting'). Hence FCCC (2015), *Decision 1/CP.21*, para. 57, 'Requests the Subsidiary Body for Scientific and Technological Advice to develop modalities for the accounting of financial resources provided and mobilized through public interventions in accordance with Article 9, paragraph 7, of the Agreement.'
27 FCCC (2011), *Decision 2/CP.17*, Annex I: UNFCCC Biennial Reporting Guidelines for Developed Country Parties, para. 16.
28 Ibid., Annex III.
29 A point made by the Standing Committee on Finance, *Biennial Assessment 2014*, p. 6 ('To form a comprehensive picture of climate finance, information on both finance provided by developed countries and finance received by developing countries is needed'); see also Joel B. Smith *et al.* (2013), 'Development and Climate Change Adaptation Funding: Coordination and Integration', in *International Climate Finance*, edited by Erik Haites, Abingdon: Routledge, p. 66.
30 Recipient states no doubt must account for their actions to the direct suppliers of climate finance, whether these are individual states (in bilateral finance) or institutions (in multilateral finance). Yet this cannot serve as a substitute for international reporting as it is invisible at the international level. (Cf. Expert Review Team (2014), *Report of the Technical Review of the First Biennial Report of Finland*, FCCC/TRR.1/FIN, para. 41: 'Indicators . . . used to measure the achievement of the objectives of financial support . . . are project or fund-specific, [but] there are no specific climate indicators being developed for the specific purpose of the UNFCCC.')
31 In the TRR, section II.C (Progress towards achievement of target) precedes and is independent of section II.D (Provision of finance to developing countries), indicating that the Biennial Reporting process does not perceive a relationship between the two. Moreover, there is no target to be reported/reviewed under section II.D, on finance. In order to grasp the changes occasioned by the Paris Agreement, we must be alert to such subtle differences between current practices and the slightly better-integrated practices envisaged by the Paris Agreement.
32 IAR was established pursuant to FCCC (2010), *Decision 1/CP.16*, para. 44. For the technical review procedure and guidelines, see FCCC (2011), *Decision 2/CP.17*, Annex I, and FCCC (2013), *Decision 23/CP.19, Work Programme on the Revision of the Guidelines for the Review of Biennial Reports and National Communications, Including National Inventory Reviews, for Developed Country Parties*, FCCC/CP/2013/10/Add.2, Annex, paras 61–71. See also FCCC (2014), *Decision 13/CP.20, Guidelines for the Technical Review of Information Reported under the Convention Related to Greenhouse Gas Inventories, Biennial Reports and National Communications by Parties Included in Annex I to the Convention*, FCCC/CP/2014/10/Add.3.
33 FCCC (2011), *Decision 2/CP.17*, Annex II, para. 9.
34 In contrast with ERTs, in which developed and developing countries are equally represented, the majority of TTE members are from developing countries, and their training courses are different from those taken by ERT members in their focus on

96 *Legal obligations of states*

challenges faced by developing countries: FCCC (2013), *Decision 20/CP.19, Composition, Modalities and Procedures of the Team of Technical Experts under International Consultation and Analysis*, FCCC/CP/2013/10/Add.2, Annex, para. 5.

35 ICA was established through FCCC (2010), *Decision 1/CP.16*, para. 63.

36 FCCC (2011), *Decision 2/CP.17*, Annex IV, para. 6.

37 For the US position on this, see International Institute for Sustainable Development (2015), 'Summary of ADP 2–8 (No. 3) (9 February)', 12 (622) *Earth Negotiations Bulletin* 1, p. 2.

38 *Copenhagen Accord*, para. 5.

39 FCCC (2010), *Decision 1/CP.16*, para. 53.

40 Paris Agreement, article 13.1. While article 13.1 purports to create an 'enhanced transparency framework for action and support', the article, further along, separates support from action: the action is tied in with the NDC process (article 13.7), whereas the support is disconnected from the core provisions of the agreement (article 13.9). Cf. *Copenhagen Accord*, para. 5.

41 Paris Agreement, article 13.6.

42 See Paris Agreement, articles 14.1 and 14.3.

43 Paris Agreement, articles 13.11, 13.12, 13.14, and Decision 1/CP.21, para. 98.

44 The preamble's wording is: 'States have . . . the sovereign right to exploit their own resources pursuant to their own environmental and developmental policies, and the responsibility to ensure that activities within their jurisdiction or control do not cause damage to the environment of other States or of areas beyond the limits of national jurisdiction.'

45 Patricia W. Birnie, Alan E. Boyle, and Catherine Redgwell (2009), *International Law and the Environment*, Oxford: Oxford University Press, pp. 130, 143, 145.

46 Ibid., p. 130.

47 FCCC, preamble.

48 FCCC, article 3.3.

49 E.g. Birnie et al., *International Law and the Environment*, p. 161.

50 David Freestone (1994), 'The Road from Rio: International Environmental Law after the Earth Summit', 6 (2) *Journal of Environmental Law* 193, p. 211. For the strong version, see also Birnie *et al.*, *International Law and the Environment*, p. 157; ibid., p. 163 ('No longer is it necessary to prove that serious or irreversible harm is certain or likely before requiring that appropriate preventive measures be taken. Evidence that such harm is possible will be enough to trigger an obligation or to empower states to act'); and Michael Weisslitz (2002), 'Rethinking the Equitable Principle of Common but Differentiated Responsibility: Differential Versus Absolute Norms of Compliance and Contribution in the Global Climate Change Context', 13 (2) *Colorado Journal of International Environmental Law and Policy* 473, p. 497.

51 Birnie et al., *International Law and the Environment*, p. 157.

52 Ibid., p. 156 ('if the evidence is sufficiently conclusive to leave little or no room for uncertainty in the calculation of risk, then there is no justification for the precautionary principle to be applied at all').

53 Principles 3 and 4.

54 FCCC, article 3.4 ('The Parties have a right to . . . *promote* sustainable development').

55 *Copenhagen Accord*, para. 1.

56 W. M. Adams and D. H. L. Thomas (1993), 'Mainstream Sustainable Development: The Challenge of Putting Theory into Practice', 5 (6) *Journal of International Development* 591, p. 601 ('In practice the implementation of "sustainable development" is deeply problematic'); Vaughan Lowe (1999), 'Sustainable Development and Unsustainable Arguments', in *International Law and Sustainable Development*, edited by Alan Boyle and David Freestone, Oxford: Oxford University Press, p. 30; Marc Pallemaerts (2003a), 'International Law and Sustainable Development: Any

Progress in Johannesburg?', 12 (1) *Review of European Community and International Environmental Law* 1; Birnie *et al.*, *International Law and the Environment*, pp. 126–127; and Sam Headon (2009), 'Whose Sustainable Development? Sustainable Development under the Kyoto Protocol, the "Coldplay Effect", and the CDM Gold Standard', 20 (2) *Colorado Journal of International Environmental Law and Policy* 127, p. 156.

57 E.g. *Copenhagen Accord*, para. 2.

58 E.g. Birnie *et al.*, *International Law and the Environment*, p. 125 ('given the breadth of international endorsement for the concept [of sustainable development] few states would quarrel with the proposition that development should in principle be sustainable and that all natural resources should be managed in this way').

59 Robert B. Gibson (2005), *Sustainability Assessment: Criteria and Processes*, London: Earthscan, pp. 122–125; David Freestone (2010), 'The World Bank and Sustainable Development', in *Research Handbook on International Environmental Law*, edited by Malgosia Fitzmaurice, David M. Ong, and Panos Merkouris, Cheltenham: Edward Elgar, pp. 153–154 ('[The World Bank] has made considerable progress in mainstreaming sustainable development considerations into its work . . . but . . . huge additional financial resources . . . will be needed to ensure that all major energy investments in developing countries are *low carbon*'; emphasis added); and Mukul Sanwal (2012), 'Rio+20, Climate Change and Development: The Evolution of Sustainable Development (1972–2012)', 4 (2) *Climate and Development* 157, p. 157.

60 Liane Schalatek (2010), *A Matter of Principle(s): A Normative Framework for a Global Compact on Public Climate Finance*, Berlin: Heinrich Böll Foundation, p. 5.

61 Donald K. Anton (2013), 'The "Thirty-Percent Solution" and the Future of International Environmental Law', 10 *Santa Clara Journal of International Law* 209, p. 217.

62 Birnie et al., *International Law and the Environment*, p. 146.

63 Nathan Rive *et al.* (2007), 'To What Extent Can a Long-Term Temperature Target Guide Near-Term Climate Change Commitments?', 82 (3–4) *Climatic Change* 373, p. 377 ('The aim of climate action is not to prevent all change—only change that may be defined as "dangerous" ').

64 Lowe, 'Sustainable Development', p. 29.

65 E.g. Madeleine Heyward (2007), 'Equity and International Climate Change Negotiations: A Matter of Perspective', 7 *Climate Policy* 518, p. 529 ('sustainable development and combating climate change are mutually reinforcing processes'); and Martin Parry (2009), 'Climate Change is a Development Issue, and Only Sustainable Development can Confront the Challenge', 1 (1) *Climate and Development* 5, p. 5.

66 Rio Declaration, principle 7, emphasis added.

67 Cf. article 4.2 of the FCCC: 'The developed country Parties and other Parties included in Annex I . . . shall adopt national policies and take corresponding measures on the mitigation of climate change [that] demonstrate that developed countries are taking the lead in modifying longer-term trends in anthropogenic emissions consistent with the objective of the Convention.'

68 Birnie et al., *International Law and the Environment*, p. 123.

69 Dinah Shelton (2007), 'Equity', in *The Oxford Handbook of International Environmental Law*, edited by Daniel Bodansky, Jutta Brunnée, and Ellen Hey, Oxford: Oxford University Press, p. 657.

70 Weisslitz, 'CBDR', p. 476; Simon Caney (2005), 'Cosmopolitan Justice, Responsibility, and Global Climate Change', 18 *Leiden Journal of International Law* 747, p. 774; and Shelton, 'Equity', p. 656.

71 Geir Ulfstein and Christina Voigt (2014), 'Rethinking the Legal Form and Principles of a New Climate Agreement', in *Toward a New Climate Agreement: Conflict,*

98 *Legal obligations of states*

    Resolution and Governance, edited by Todd L. Cherry, Jon Hovi, and David M. McEvoy, Abingdon: Routledge, p. 195.

72 Ibid., p. 191.

73 Lin Feng and Jason Buhi (2010–2011), 'The Copenhagen Accord and the Silent Incorporation of the Polluter Pays Principle in International Climate Law: An Analysis of Sino-American Diplomacy at Copenhagen and Beyond', 18 *Buffalo Environmental Law Journal* 1, p. 17.

74 Ulfstein and Voigt, 'Legal Form', p. 192.

75 Edward Cameron, Tara Shine, and Wendi Bevins (2013), *Climate Justice: Equity and Justice Informing a New Climate Agreement*, working paper, WRI and Mary Robinson Foundation, p. 2.

76 Jutta Brunnée and Charlotte Streck (2013), 'The UNFCCC as a Negotiation Forum: Towards Common but More Differentiated Responsibilities', 13 (5) *Climate Policy* 589, p. 593.

77 Ibid., pp. 601–602.

78 E.g. Karsten Neuhoff *et al.* (2009), *Structuring International Financial Support to Support Domestic Climate Change Mitigation in Developing Countries*, Cambridge: Climate Strategies, p. 5; and Yulia Yamineva and Kati Kulovesi (2013), 'The New Framework for Climate Finance under the United Nations Framework Convention on Climate Change: A Breakthrough or an Empty Promise?', in *Climate Change and the Law*, edited by Erkki J. Hollo, Kati Kulovesi, and Michael Mehling, Dordrecht: Springer, p. 195.

79 FCCC (2010), *Decision 1/CP.16*, para. 48 ('developing country Parties will take nationally appropriate mitigation actions . . . supported and enabled by technology, financing and capacity-building, aimed at achieving a deviation in emissions relative to business as usual emissions in 2020').

80 Brunnée and Streck, 'Differentiated Responsibilities', p. 596. Ulfstein and Voigt make the same observation in 'Legal Form', p. 192.

81 Ulfstein and Voigt, 'Legal Form', p. 190.

82 Brunnée and Streck, 'Differentiated Responsibilities', p. 596 ('The process of softening the edges of the principle of CBDR'); ibid., p. 597 ('the trend towards a more nuanced differentiation'); and Ulfstein and Voigt, 'Legal Form', p. 195.

83 For general formulations of the polluter-pays principle, see Organization for Economic Cooperation and Development (1992), *The Polluter-Pays Principle: OECD Analyses and Recommendations*, Doc. OCDE/GD(92)81, pp. 5, 8–9; Jonathan Remy Nash (2000), 'Too Much Market? Conflict between Tradable Pollution Allowances and the "Polluter Pays" Principle', 24 *Harvard Environmental Law Review* 465, p. 478; Simon Caney (2005), 'Cosmopolitan Justice', pp. 753–754; and Boris N. Mamlyuk (2009), 'Analyzing the Polluter Pays Principle through Law and Economics', 18 (1) *Southeastern Environmental Law Journal* 39, pp. 44–45, 47.

84 Wherever the polluter-pays principle is implemented, it is virtually guaranteed to be effective. For examples, see Intergovernmental Panel on Climate Change (2014b), *Climate Change 2014: Mitigation of Climate Change: Contribution of Working Group III to the Fifth Assessment Report of the Intergovernmental Panel on Climate Change*, New York: Cambridge University Press, pp. 1163–1164.

85 OECD, *Polluter-Pays Principle*, p. 9 (the polluter-pays principle was embodied in the Single European Act in 1987 and in the Treaty of Maastricht in 1992); Nash, 'Polluter-Pays Principle', pp. 471–472 (on the influence of the polluter-pays principle on US domestic environmental law); Barbara Luppi, Francesco Parisi, and Shruti Rajagopalan (2012), 'The Rise and Fall of the Polluter-Pays Principle in Developing Countries', 32 *International Review of Law and Economics* 135, p. 136; Philippe Sands and Jacqueline Peel (2012), *Principles of International Environmental Law*, Cambridge: Cambridge University Press, p. 231.

Legal obligations of states 99

86 Mamlyuk, 'Polluter Pays Principle', p. 42 ('In the legal sense, the polluter pays principle embodies the general equitable notion that polluting entities should bear the costs of their pollution').

87 Mattia Romani and Nicholas Stern (2013), 'Sources of Finance for Climate Action: Principles and Options for Implementation Mechanisms in this Decade', in *International Climate Finance*, edited by Erik Haites, Abingdon: Routledge, p. 119; Joseph E. Aldy (2015), 'Pricing Climate Risk Mitigation', 5 *Nature Climate Change* 396; William D. Nordhaus (2015b), 'The Pope and the Market', 62 (15) *The New York Review of Books* 26; Gernot Wagner (2015), 'Push Renewables to Spur Carbon Pricing', 525 *Nature* 27.

88 OECD, *Polluter-Pays Principle*, p. 8.

89 Nevertheless, there are strong arguments for pricing greenhouse gas emissions domestically in all countries; see Alex Bowen (2013), 'Raising Climate Finance to Support Developing Country Action: Some Economic Considerations', in *International Climate Finance*, edited by Erik Haites, Abingdon: Routledge, p. 99.

90 It has long been obvious to economists that an approach in which states are charged for greenhouse gas pollution offers the best solution to the problem of climate change: see Nicholas Stern (2007), *Stern Review Report on the Economics of Climate Change*, UK Treasury, p. 469; Christoph Böhringer and Carsten Helm (2008), 'On the Fair Division of Greenhouse Gas Abatement Cost', 30 (2) *Resource and Energy Economics* 260, pp. 271–272; Ross Garnaut (2011), *The Garnaut Review 2011: Australia in the Global Response to Climate Change*, Port Melbourne, Victoria: Cambridge University Press, p. 38; Jeff Tollefson (2015a), 'Fossil-Fuel Divestment Campaign Hits Resistance', 521 *Nature* 16.

91 Contrary to the interpretation given by Sands and Peel, *Principles of International Environmental Law*, pp. 228–229, which is completely without support.

92 OECD, *Polluter-Pays Principle*, p. 9; see also Nash, 'Polluter-Pays Principle', pp. 466, 469 (with extensive citations given in the footnote to this text), 471; and Weisslitz, 'CBDR', p. 499.

93 The polluter-pays principle does not always have to be implemented in such a way as to price pollution in accordance with the cost of repair. *Avoidance* of harm is also an implementation method. In the case of climate change, some damage is accepted as inevitable (the consequences of global warming up to 2°C), while higher degrees of damage are sought to be avoided through imposing costs on each state. In this context, it is not about internalizing the cost of the damage but about internalizing the cost of limiting the damage to an agreed level.

94 Oran R. Young (2014), 'Does Fairness Matter in International Environmental Governance? Creating an Effective and Equitable Climate Regime', in *Toward a New Climate Agreement: Conflict, Resolution and Governance*, edited by Todd L. Cherry, Jon Hovi, and David M. McEvoy, Abingdon: Routledge, p. 25.

95 Stern, *Stern Review*, p. 471.

96 Ibid., p. 316.

97 The Kyoto Protocol did not refer to a global budget, and thus was fundamentally different from the model described here, despite superficial similarities.

98 On the problem of negotiating burden-sharing among states, see Lasse Ringius, Asbjørn Torvanger, and Arild Underdal (2002), 'Burden Sharing and Fairness Principles in International Climate Policy', 2 *International Environmental Agreements* 1.

99 Stern, *Stern Review*, p. 468 ('There is no single formula that captures all dimensions of equity, but calculations based on income, per capita emissions and historic responsibility [are relevant]').

100 Feng and Buhi, 'Copenhagen Accord', p. 46 ('Later in the day [16 December 2009], these major emerging countries announced [China, India, Brazil, and South Africa] their intention to collectively reduce carbon emissions by 2.1 gigatons by 2020 but,

100 *Legal obligations of states*

in a major show of force, insisted that they do it voluntarily and without outside verification'); and ibid., pp. 59–60 ('While He Yafei [Vice Foreign Minister of China] pledged that his country did not expect money from the US or other "rich countries", he insisted that "financial resources for the efforts of developing countries [are] a legal obligation"'). This was the first expression of position that some non-Annex I parties would engage in mitigation *without* financial assistance. See also ibid., p. 50 ('[On 18 December 2009] Premier Wen [of China] stressed that China is voluntarily reducing its emissions growth rate and has "not attached any condition to the target or linked it to the target of any other country"').

101 Caney, 'Cosmopolitan Justice', p. 763.
102 Heyward, 'Equity and International Climate Change Negotiations', p. 526.
103 Böhringer and Helm, 'Fair Division', p. 273.
104 Sonja Klinsky and Hadi Dowlatabadi (2009), 'Conceptualizations of Justice in Climate Policy', 9 (1) *Climate Policy* 88, p. 93.
105 Stern, *Stern Review*, p. 473 ('Frameworks for international collective action that recognise a global long-term quantity constraint on emissions must distribute responsibility for meeting the overall limit to nation states [on the basis of equity]').
106 E.g. Brunnée and Streck, 'Differentiated Responsibilities', p. 591.
107 For an elaboration of this concept, see Alexander Zahar (2015a), *International Climate Change Law and State Compliance*, Abingdon: Routledge, ch. 2.
108 Brunnée and Streck, 'Differentiated Responsibilities', p. 590.
109 Heyward, 'Equity and International Climate Change Negotiations', p. 521 ('[Argument that] no one owns the atmosphere and ... its "distribution" should thus be equal. ... Egalitarian principles are not generally applied to the sharing of environmental resources').

4 State performance of obligations on climate finance

4.1 Introduction

The temporal focus of this chapter, running from the conclusion of the Copenhagen COP to the time of writing, encompasses a period of rapid growth in the supply of climate finance. The 2009 COP moved climate finance to the very top of the states' agenda. It has remained there since.

The focus period is constituted of the three years of Fast-Start Finance (2010–2012) and the first three years (2013–2015) of 'mid-term finance' (2013–2020). (There is no official name for the latter period.) I will also briefly discuss what is called 'long-term finance', i.e. the period from 2021 onward. I will focus on state supply and reporting of climate finance and the extent to which it can be regarded as compliant with the law set out in Chapter 3. For background purposes, I will also provide some information on pre-2010 finance.

We saw in Chapter 3 that the international law on climate finance is in a transitional phase, exiting a period of broadly formulated state obligations, in which climate finance was conceptually cut off from the regime's mitigation responsibility, and entering a period of specific obligations aimed at keeping warming below 2°C, with climate finance and mitigation law integrated into one and the same objective, namely the equitable allocation of mitigation burdens to all countries. A law in transition, by definition, does not provide clearly formulated or even clearly recognized obligations against which a state's performance may be judged. Therefore, no assessment of state compliance with current climate finance obligations could reach precise conclusions on the commission or avoidance of legal 'breaches' of international law. The most that could be hoped for at the threshold of a new era is an understanding of the extent and consistency, including self-consistency, of state action on climate finance.

We have also seen that the emerging law responds to a realization that an urgent increase in mitigation 'ambition' is required. As a consequence of the adoption of the 2°C warming limit and the ascendancy of the modified polluter-pays principle to the position of a dominant legal norm in the climate change regime, the isolation of *adaptation* finance has only become more pronounced. This makes the assessment of state performance on adaptation all the more difficult. Logically, in post-Copenhagen thinking, finance must first be raised to reduce pollution sufficiently to meet the global target of staying below 2°C. After that –

102   *State performance of obligations*

or ideally on top of that – more finance must be raised to support adaptation actions, or at least those actions considered urgent and necessary for human welfare and which the states affected cannot reasonably afford to implement from their own resources. However, the latter obligations could almost be part of a different international treaty – one on humanitarian assistance, development aid, or disaster relief – because they cannot be reconciled with the dominant logic of the emerging climate law. Despite the Paris Agreement's continuation of the rhetoric of 'balance' in the two forms of climate finance, adaptation is now bound to remain the poor cousin of mitigation, because priority at this extremely critical stage must legally be given to the removal of the causes of the problem of climate change, not the treatment of the impacts on humans, which will only keep getting worse for as long as the causes are not brought under control.

It might seem harsh to express the law in this way. Yet there is also a harshness in those who insist that no less than half of climate finance should go to adaptation. Whereas mitigation finance benefits all living beings, adaptation finance essentially benefits only humans.

Still, it would not be correct structurally, or indeed morally, to push the adaptation issue over to a different international treaty: the need for adaptation has been created, no less, by the climate change regime itself, which, after a quarter-century's worth of lack of real effort and ambition, has come to accept warming of up to 2°C and all that it entails as tolerable. The pressing need for adaptation action being largely the result of decisions made (or shied away from) since 1992 under the auspices of the FCCC, this same regime must now find ways to attenuate its own impacts, while still prioritizing mitigation.

It should nevertheless be kept in mind that, when it comes to adaptation finance, its legal rationale rests on a different basis than mitigation finance. We should not blur the law to downplay the mitigation/adaptation tension.

4.2 'Need' for climate finance

It will be recalled from Chapter 1 that the rule on incremental cost means that Annex I countries are required to supply only the incremental costs of mitigation projects, with developing countries bearing the projects' baseline costs. For mitigation, therefore, 'need' could be interpreted as 'total need for incremental cost'. For adaptation, whose benefits are only local, the concept of incremental cost does not apply.

A scholarly opinion often heard is that finance efforts under the FCCC have been 'insufficient to meet the growing funding needs by developing countries for adaptation and mitigation'.[1] This is meant as a factual assessment, but more likely it is a priori, for a standard for the assessment of sufficiency is usually missing from such accounts. With adaptation finance, funding agencies themselves tend to be extremely vague about what it is.[2] Even limiting ourselves to mitigation finance, the rule on incremental cost cannot fully answer the question of the objective need for climate finance in the present or future. The total incremental cost at a given point in time cannot be calculated except with reference to

State performance of obligations 103

mitigation projects known to be seeking Annex I support at that point in time – an extremely limited notion of mitigation finance 'need'.

4.2.1 Assessments of need for mitigation finance

In the past decade, international organizations have periodically produced estimates of the need for mitigation finance. They have not always clearly distinguished mitigation finance from other forms of finance (especially adaptation finance). An FCCC study from 2007 is in this category; it estimated additional 'investment' needed in 2030 at $380 billion, of which $177 billion would be for developing countries.[3] 'Investment' is a term commonly used in this context, possibly to suggest capital costs (as opposed to operating costs), or else to suggest the involvement of private sources of finance which are seeking a return on their 'investment'. Such studies make a host of assumptions, of course. The earlier ones used atmospheric concentrations (usually 450 ppm or 550 ppm) of CO_2 in their modelling. A 2006 World Bank study estimated that new investment needed in *the power sector* in developing countries would need to start at $160 billion per annum, and rise to $190 billion per annum, over the period 2010–2030, for a more-likely-than-not stabilization at 450 ppm CO_2.[4]

It will be seen straight away that issues of comparability arise between studies. Different assumptions and sectoral preferences lead to (what appear to be) significantly different estimates of mitigation finance need. The findings of the two aforementioned studies, both a decade old, are out of date, not least because climate finance did not increase by anything close to the amount suggested by them as necessary. Moreover, the inclusion in their estimates of private investment that is not necessarily specifically 'leveraged' with public funds creates doubt about whether the amounts discussed are climate finance in the sense of the FCCC, or something more ill-defined.

Other studies on mitigation finance need include an IEA 2009 report on energy-related CO_2 emissions.[5] The IEA calculated the average incremental investment need for 2021–2030 in developing countries at $377 billion per annum. The study does not distinguish public from private finance, nor does the stated per-annum amount of needed finance reflect the consequential reduced investment in fossil-fuel supply or transmission-and-distribution infrastructure, which would be significant.[6] The IEA uses the 2°C limit in its calculations. Reviewing various studies, Haites writes that estimates of incremental capital cost needed for mitigation in developing countries range from $175 billion to $565 billion in 2030; whereas estimates of incremental operating cost (which is more complex to calculate, leading to fewer such studies[7]) are substantially lower: $140–$175 billion per year in 2030.[8] Studies used by the IPCC for developing-country mitigation costs in 2030 range from approximately $50 billion to $625 billion.[9] Buchner *et al.* report estimates of annualized additional 'investment' needed for mitigation ranging from $490 billion per year in 2010–2020 to $910 billion per year in 2010–2050; these amounts are constituted of both public and private investment.[10]

104 *State performance of obligations*

The various studies, using different models and definitions, do not give a clear answer overall to the question of need. This does not mean that a clear overall answer is not attainable. But for that, states must agree on a methodology for the calculation of climate finance need under the FCCC, which in turn requires states to be clear about how much domestic mitigation they can achieve without external assistance, given the strictures of the 2°C limit. States must openly concede that climate finance is a key factor in the equation which, together with (internationally unsupported) domestic mitigation, determines the extent of global mitigation. Instead, states still treat climate finance as a separate item of expenditure to which an ad hoc value may be assigned. Olbrisch *et al.* claim that the Copenhagen goal of mobilizing $100 billion per year by 2020 'falls within the low end' of mitigation need estimates.[11] The truth is that the estimates are all over the place – it is impossible to tell whether $100 billion is at the low or high end. Because states are nowhere close to agreeing on a methodology to calculate climate finance need, the most accurate characterization of the $100 billion is that it is arbitrary.

The FCCC has attempted without much success to gather information on mitigation need through a Nationally Appropriate Mitigation Action recording system.[12] Under the Paris Agreement's NDC process it is possible that the quality of such information will improve. Each developing country should, in principle, be able to account for its domestic mitigation opportunities, their cost (reported, say, in bands, from cheapest to most expensive), and the mitigation opportunities which, due to their overall cost, are beyond the capacity of the country itself to act on from within its own resources. This kind of information must be enabled to reach a level of reasonable reliability and comparability. It must be possible to distinguish information on genuine mitigation need from a mere pitch for more development aid. To raise quality, the international regime could expand its mechanism of independent expert review to scrutinize these elements of NDCs. As matters stand, the Paris Agreement neither provides for, nor excludes, such an expansion.

Three Intended Nationally Determined Contributions exemplify how little is still known about mitigation need. Papua New Guinea submits in its INDC that

> Little domestic finance is available but Government assistance will be provided where possible. . . . The transition to renewable energy in the electricity sector thus would need to be mostly financed from external sources. The first step would be to quantify the funding needed.[13]

Clearly, this country has not even begun to look at mitigation need in a systematic way. South Africa, by contrast, claims in its INDC to have already analysed 'the incremental costs of mitigation actions' and to have found that 'significant finance and investment will be required'.[14] It gives some examples of incremental costs for projects: expand renewable energy over ten years: $3 billion per year; decarbonize electricity by 2050: $349 billion through to 2050; switch to 20 per cent hybrid electric vehicles: $488 billion by 2030; etc. However, 'Further work is needed to prepare detailed business plans' for these costs.[15] India also claims to have estimated its mitigation needs, at least approximately: 'a preliminary estimate [of international climate finance needs] suggests that at least $2.5 trillion (at 2014–15 prices) will be required for meeting India's climate change actions between now and 2030' – i.e. more than $150 billion per year for every year between 2016 and 2030.[16]

These countries evidently still labour under the mentality that climate finance for a country can be worked out in isolation from what the rest of the world plans to do on mitigation. They are not alone in this way of thinking. The climate regime may have transitioned into the post-Copenhagen period, but the practice of states lags way behind the theory.

4.2.2 Assessments of need for adaptation finance

The fundamental problem with the concept of 'adaptation finance need' is that many forms of pressure for human adaptation – in response to severe weather events or cycles of drought, for example – exist anyway, with or without the influence of climate change.[17] Thus finance for adaptation to changing environmental conditions has been a significant part of traditional development work. How do the FCCC parties distinguish adaptation needs caused by climate change from other adaptation needs (baseline needs) for which they have no legal responsibility under the Convention?

Despite the clear methodological difficulties,[18] 'need' estimates for adaptation finance have been produced. An FCCC report from 2007 calculated that an additional per-annum amount of $28 billion to $67 billion would be needed by 2030 for adaptation in developing countries; in 2010, a World Bank study estimated the costs for the same period as lying between $80 billion and $90 billion per year.[19] The latter range is of the same order of magnitude as the total current annual ODA[20] – a huge 'need' emerging only about a decade down the road! A further study, by UNEP, has the developing-country cost of adapting to climate change ranging, in 2030, from $140 billion to $300 billion for the year, and from $280 billion to $500 billion for 2050.[21]

As Smith *et al.* explain, adaptation-need studies proceed by estimating the capital cost required for infrastructure measures, such as sea walls and water reservoirs, in a future year or period (usually excluding operating and capacity-building costs).[22] Because the concept of incremental cost does not apply to adaptation finance,[23] these studies lack a method for separating costs to be met by the developing country itself from costs to be met with regime finance. Instead, the total estimated cost is labelled 'adaptation finance need', even though it cannot be justified that the full cost of developing-country adaptation to climate change – assuming that such an amount could be distinguished from a 'baseline' adaptation cost – is to be met by developed countries. After all, developing countries themselves also contribute significantly to the causes of climate change.

The FCCC has not developed a system for the estimation of need for adaptation finance except for inviting developing countries to list wanted adaptation projects as part of the National Adaptation Programme of Action process.[24] One method

106 *State performance of obligations*

used for the estimation of adaptation need has been to take the estimated cost of a sample of projects from the NAPA list and extrapolate from that the 'need' of all developing countries.[25] Yet, about one-third of NAPA projects are for vulnerability reduction, meaning that these are essentially development projects that also happen to reduce vulnerability to climate change.[26]

At the individual fund level, the situation is no clearer. It is often claimed that this or that climate fund for adaptation is in dire need of replenishment. Regarding the LDC Fund, which is exclusively for adaptation, the FCCC COP said that 'additional contributions are needed if the Fund is to meet the full costs of addressing the urgent and immediate adaptation needs of the LDCs'.[27] Here, by 'urgent and immediate adaptation needs of the LDCs', the COP meant nothing more than that there existed five new projects which the fund had approved but for which no money was left in the fund. It is a purely ad-hoc, bottom-up approach. A similar approach is used by the GEF when it claims to estimate the LDC Fund's needs for 2014–2018 at $700–$900 million.[28]

As with mitigation, the Paris Agreement is silent on how estimates of need for adaptation finance will be improved.[29] India, in its INDC, claims that it would need around $206 billion between 2015 and 2030 for adaptation projects in agriculture, forestry, water resources, ecosystems, etc.; additional (unspecified) 'investments' would be needed to strengthen the country's 'resilience' and disaster management.[30] India's position appears to be that all of this need should be sourced to international regime finance.

4.3 Supply of climate finance

The previous section showed that there is no agreement on how to define or calculate the 'need' for mitigation or adaptation finance. Because need is indeterminable at the present time, the question of whether supply meets need cannot be resolved.[31] Thus we are left to consider supply cut off from need. Nevertheless, even cut off from need, the question of supply is important because potentially it is evidence of the seriousness with which states approach their emission-reduction obligations.

4.3.1 Introduction and methodological issues

As with the question of need for climate finance, the main issue for a discussion on supply is methodological. Any attempt to estimate how much climate finance has been supplied by developed to developing countries over a given period faces several challenges. I begin with a summary of definitional issues.[32]

The FCCC's Standing Committee on Finance has noted that there is 'no agreed definition of climate finance flows from developed to developing countries'.[33] Finance data, whether obtained from states or multilateral funds, often represent the total 'investment' or cost rather than the portion attributable to the creation of emission reductions (i.e. the incremental cost). For finance to count as climate

State performance of obligations 107

finance under the FCCC, it must be 'new and additional'; however, there is no common understanding of how the baseline for this criterion should be defined.[34] Thus reported data may be assumed to refer to a mix of new budget allocations and diverted ODA funds.[35] An additional problem is that data on 'supply' usually relate to commitments rather than disbursements.[36] Actual supply may differ substantially from commitments. Some countries define climate finance to include private finance, whether 'leveraged' by the state or not.[37] This increases the amount of 'climate finance' that a state may take credit for; however, it complicates the assessment of the state's effort and ambition. In relation specifically to adaptation finance, states themselves concede that no clear criteria exist for when to count a development-assistance project as a climate-adaptation project;[38] therefore, any overview of supply of adaptation finance will necessarily be ad hoc (or based on 'expert judgment').[39] While efforts are being made to tighten definitions, they are usually of limited scope – limited, for example, to definitions used by MDBs.[40] Also, they do not have retrospective effect, so they reduce comparability over time.

Second, tracking climate finance, under any definition, is difficult. For a complete picture of climate finance, information on both finance supplied by developed countries and finance received by developing countries would be needed.[41] However, as I explained in Chapter 3, FCCC procedural rules do not require developing countries to report to the FCCC on climate finance received. Undoubtedly, many could not, due to lack of capacity.[42] This methodological issue will not be fixed soon, therefore. As for the rules applying to the reporting of supply by developed countries, these have been, and remain, weak.[43] Not until 2014, when ERTs began to check climate finance information contained in developed-country Biennial Reports, was there some form of independent quality control of reported information on finance. Apart from such regulatory blind spots, the supply of climate finance is often hard to measure because of the complexities in how the finance is channelled; it tends to pass through several intermediary channels before reaching its destination.[44] Some of the reported flows constitute gross flows rather than net contributions, or they may include domestic finance from developing countries.[45] Even where genuine climate finance can be tracked to its destination, it may only be a precondition for the implementation of a project – the exact nature of the project may still have to be decided or implemented.[46]

As a result of the aforementioned problems, climate finance supplied in any year, or period of years, cannot be determined accurately,[47] and estimates of climate finance supplied span a wide range.[48] While some effort is now being made to overcome definitional and reporting shortcomings, progress is slow (e.g. the Paris Agreement does not require developing countries to account for climate finance received). It is not always easy to tell whether supply has increased from one reporting period to the next,[49] although over longer stretches of time it has undoubtedly increased (see below). The methodological caveats outlined here should be kept in mind throughout the remainder of the chapter, as they affect much of the information discussed herein.

108 *State performance of obligations*

4.3.2 Early climate finance, 1992–2009

In the first decade or more of the regime, climate finance was not distinguished from general aid (ODA) as a separate line of assistance. Estimates of climate finance for the time look at whether the aid committed for traditional ODA reasons also incidentally targeted the objectives of the FCCC. On one such estimate, between 1998 and 2000 the member states of the OECD's Development Assistance Committee spent $2.7 billion (7.2 per cent of total ODA) on climate-related activities.[50] In addition, during that period, around $320 million was given to the GEF, which at the time assigned about one-third of its funds to climate-related projects.[51] These figures give an indication of how long it took for climate finance to move up the agenda of the FCCC parties: in the 12-year period from the signing of the FCCC until 2003, GEF grants to climate-related activities totalled $1.6 billion.[52]

A major study of 'climate aid' in the period 1988–2008 by Hicks *et al.* approximately covers the early climate finance period. The authors find that funding for climate aid projects 'jump[ed] from $2.33 billion total in the 1980s to $8.4 billion in the 1990s',[53] led by the MDBs and the GEF, and in bilateral contributions by Japan and the United States.[54] (The authors of the study are not suggesting that 'climate finance' pre-existed the FCCC, only that funding for energy efficiency, renewable power generation, and other projects now considered 'climate related' pre-existed the FCCC.) Intuitively, the jump in the 1990s might be attributed to the advent of the FCCC; however, a general trend to support 'environmental aid' projects already existed prior to 1992.[55] One can only speculate about the state response to the FCCC in its early years – the increases noted above might have already been in train.

Concerning the later years of the 'early period', Olbrisch *et al.* report that funding for projects in developing countries with mitigation as a principal or significant objective averaged about $5.8 billion per year in the period 2006–2008.[56] Their figure is comparable with the IPCC's 'medium confidence' estimate of $10 billion per year, on average, for the 2005–2010 period, based on Annex II party reports.[57] Only a small proportion of these amounts passed through the FCCC's financial mechanism: Annex II party contributions to the GEF, the Special Climate Change Fund, and the LDC Fund averaged just under $0.6 billion per year in the course of 2005–2010.[58]

An important source of climate finance during the early period was the CDM.[59] The Mechanism's operations peaked around 2009, following which they evened out through to 2012, finally commencing a rapid decline to the present.[60]

4.3.3 Fast-Start Finance period, 2010–2012

The major question for this period is whether developed states met the Copenhagen Accord's Fast-Start Finance (FSF) promise of $30 billion. Attempts by scholars and NGO experts to detect increased flows of climate finance began about half-way through the period.[61] Difficulties were immediately encountered in trying to

State performance of obligations 109

separate out FSF from existing flows in the various overlapping funding channels.[62] In the absence of an agreed definition, different states came to understand FSF differently.[63] The Accord provides that FSF will be 'new and additional',[64] but because the criterion is not further defined, the early studies had to make their own assessment.[65] Comparing pre-Copenhagen funding pledges with FSF data, Stadelmann *et al.* conclude that around half of the finance claimed as FSF had been promised or planned before Copenhagen.[66]

The first FSF study to be published after the close of the period found that 37 countries claimed to have made FSF contributions; the total was $35 billion.[67] Of this amount, 47 per cent took the form of concessional and non-concessional loans, guarantees, and insurance, whereas 45 per cent was in the form of grants and related instruments.[68] The study points out that non-concessional public finance (reported as Other Official Flows, or OOF, as opposed to ODA) played a substantial role in developed countries' efforts to meet the FSF commitment. (The main purpose of OOF is to support 'investor' countries' own economic and business interests.[69]) The study also found that finance claimed as FSF was directed to diverse recipients, including NGOs and private companies; only around 33 per cent targeted developing-country governments.[70]

Despite the methodological issues I outlined earlier, the states' own assessment of the FSF period has tended to be positive,[71] most likely because of a general agreement supported by the various independent studies that there was a significant overall increase in climate finance during 2010–2012, notwithstanding the lack of agreed definitions for key concepts.[72]

4.3.4 Mid-term finance, 2013–2020

The period of mid-term finance is covered by the promise given in Copenhagen to scale up climate finance to $100 billion per year by the end of the decade. At this point in time it is too early to tell whether, or in which sense, the promise will be met. As discussed in earlier chapters, the $100 billion goal is 'old school' – it follows the logic of the CBDR era when climate finance was in the margins of the mitigation effort and was not linked to a temperature limit. The amount seemed large when it was first announced, but now that the 2°C threshold has become established as law, 'large' is not enough: climate finance must be related to, i.e. complement, (self-funded) mitigation, with the aim of remaining within the global emission budget. The $100 billion figure sounds even less impressive when we consider that it is definitionally much more 'flexible' than the FSF figure (which was meant to be raised from public sources only). In another sense it is also completely inflexible: the finance goal for 2020 has effectively closed discussion on the levels of climate finance for the 2013–2020 period, just as the mitigation pledges attached to the Copenhagen Accord (the 'quantified economy-wide emission reduction targets'[73]) closed discussion on the mitigation effort through to 2020. The very purpose of the Accord, indeed, was to focus attention on the post-2020 era and leave states pretty much alone in the 2013–2020 period.

110 *State performance of obligations*

The $100 billion goal was a ceiling on ambition as well as a door slammed shut on further negotiation. While the ADP maintained a track on increasing ambition prior to 2020,[74] nothing came of it; only the track for the post-2020 period delivered a concrete result in the form of the Paris Agreement.

The method of scaling up from the $10 billion per annum of new finance in the FSF period to the $100 billion of new finance in 2020 was left undefined. The COP merely 'encouraged' developed-country parties 'to further increase their efforts to provide resources of at least to the average annual level of the fast-start finance period for 2013–2015'.[75] That is, another $30 billion of climate finance became the expectation for the triennium starting in 2013; we note that the COP did not say 'new and additional'. There is currently no consensus on whether progress towards the $100 billion goal is being made or not.[76]

Data are emerging for the early years of mid-term finance, although they are necessarily choppy. In April 2014, $4.43 billion was pledged to the GEF for its sixth operating period (July 2014 to June 2018).[77] During the biennium 2014–2015, the GEF allocated $400.6 million to 52 mitigation projects in developing countries, leveraging an additional $3.5 billion in co-financing from unspecified sources.[78] These figures do not suggest any rapid scaling up of GEF finance.[79] Initial resource mobilization for the GCF netted pledges totalling $10.2 billion;[80] a modest figure, in context, subject to several qualifications.[81] We must await a second fund-pledging round for some clarity on the Fund's per-annum spending power. There is even some evidence that, when all sources are considered under a very broad definition of climate finance, the available amount fell between 2012 and 2013.[82] The authors of this study explain that the overall decrease could be due to the falling cost of some renewable-energy technologies; these savings 'mean that in some cases more renewable energy is actually being deployed for less investment'.[83] Nevertheless, the study's authors characterize the apparent drop as 'alarming'.[84] The study also finds that, despite the FCCC parties' aim to diversify the sources of climate finance they control in order to scale up to $100 billion quickly, almost all developed-to-developing-country climate finance in 2013 came from public sources.[85] Evidence from another study suggests an increase in climate finance a year later, i.e. from 2013 to 2014, although the scope of the two studies is different.[86]

4.3.5 Long-term finance under the Paris Agreement

The Paris Agreement's coverage of climate finance was discussed in Chapter 3. While the Agreement makes a link for the first time in the regime's history between climate finance and the 2°C threshold, in other respects it perpetuates 'old school' thinking, with the $100 billion target kept in place until 2025. Only the INDCs elaborate on the post-2020 period,[87] but since they are likely to change as they evolve into NDCs, very little basis presently exists upon which to speculate about long-term finance.

The key question for 2020 and beyond, of course, is whether states will be able to raise their mitigation ambition through the bottom-up NDC process prescribed by the Paris Agreement, relying on their shared awareness of an ever-decreasing global emission budget to pull them upwards faster. Once an ambitious collective mitigation position is reflected in the commitments of individual states, climate finance will necessarily begin to flow in sufficient quantities, given the fact that mitigation, climate finance, and the emission budget are linked in a single equation.

4.4 Impact and effectiveness of climate finance

What do we know about the real-world impact of climate finance? Specifically, do we know whether it results in the mitigation or adaptation benefits it claims to fund? These simple questions are very difficult to answer, because, when it comes to climate finance, the international regime is still in pre-Copenhagen mode, focused on raising inputs rather than controlling outputs.

As explained in Chapter 3, state reporting on climate finance is weakly developed, even taking into account the improvements brought about by the Biennial Reports, a process which took off only in 2014. The Paris Agreement does not require states receiving climate finance to report the amounts received, let alone what is achieved with them.

I am not suggesting that such information does not exist, only that it is not available from within the regime itself. The FCCC parties have implemented systems that ensure high-quality information on greenhouse gas emissions emitted in developed countries. These are, of course, output-focused reports. Information on developing-country emissions, by contrast, is unreliable, outdated, or in some cases does not exist at all. It would be futile to try to understand the impact of climate finance from the national emission inventories of the minority of developing countries that periodically submit them. The only option presently is to try to investigate the results obtained with particular bundles of climate finance supplied. Yet, the regime does not systematically collect such information either.

The CDM Executive Board has repeatedly proclaimed its interest in the measurable 'benefits' delivered by the CDM. If we consider the CDM to be a form of climate finance, it presents an exception to the situation I have just outlined. That is, in the case of the CDM only, we can easily relate finance to emission reductions, because both the finance and the reductions are verified and reported under the Kyoto Protocol's regime.[88]

Works do exist claiming to assess the 'effectiveness' of climate finance in general. Such a term implies an examination of impacts, whereas the authors of these works invariably mean something quite different, e.g. the 'transparency' or 'sufficiency' of climate finance.[89] Moreover, states themselves will make pseudo-claims about effectiveness; e.g. 'Australia's $599 million fast-start finance commitment ... which is delivering effective adaptation and mitigation outcomes'.[90] Australia does not actually show that it follows up on the outcomes. With regard to the adaptation outcomes, in particular, any attempt to assess impact would quickly founder on definitional issues, since no adaptation indicators have been agreed to,[91] or are likely to be agreed to.[92]

112 *State performance of obligations*

At the fund level of the FCCC's financial mechanism, a recent effort by the GEF has sought to construct a narrative on outcomes achieved with regime finance; e.g. 'The 52 projects are *expected to avoid or sequester* over 256 Mt CO_2 eq. in total over their lifetime, reaching 34 per cent of the overall GEF-6 GHG emission reduction target of 750 Mt CO_2 eq.'[93] However, the GEF cannot escape the fact that it does not follow up on the performance of funded projects, thus limiting itself to impact 'expectations'.[94] The FCCC concedes that realized emission reductions could be substantially different from those expected.[95] The GEF's narrative on adaptation funding also does not go beyond a declaration on expectations.[96]

The 2014 assessment of climate finance carried out by the Standing Committee on Finance noted: 'Climate finance providers are starting to assess the impact of mitigation finance on emissions. . . Adoption of such approaches is nascent. . . . Methodologies for assessing impact on resilience and effective adaptation are much less developed'.[97] The Committee concluded:

> we lack the information to make a precise assessment [of 'whether climate finance is helping to achieve the overarching goal of the Convention of keeping climate change within 2 degrees'] in part because of a limited understanding of finance for climate change responses.[98]

Most scholars and other experts agree.[99]

4.5 Conclusions on state 'compliance' with climate finance obligations

Legal commentary has criticized the 'adequacy' of climate finance. It has thereby at least implied that states are not meeting their obligations. But such a legal assessment is very complex, and could come only at the end of a process that requires much preliminary work in clarifying law and facts, as I have attempted to do in Chapters 3 and 4.

The conclusion of this chapter is not that climate finance is inadequate. Adequacy must be judged against the objective of the climate change regime, i.e. the 2°C limit. State parties have accepted, however implicitly, that the modified polluter-pays principle structures their obligations, but they have not yet agreed on how to discharge their obligations. States must begin to commit to domestic mitigation action as well as to funding for assisted external (developing country) mitigation action, which together must add up to sufficient mitigation to stay on the safe side of 2°C, before the sufficiency of climate finance can be assessed.

Short of the ideal, some more modest assessment criteria might be used, such as 'sufficiency' of action on FSF or on reaching the 2020 finance target – cut off though these are from the FCCC's objective. Yet even these more modest criteria are difficult to assess. Thus although the FSF period was of short duration, had a precise target, and was subjected to intense scrutiny, it is still not possible to tell whether its $30 billion promise was met or what outcomes were obtained with the finance delivered during that period.

State performance of obligations 113

Notes

1 Yulia Yamineva and Kati Kulovesi (2013), 'The New Framework for Climate Finance under the United Nations Framework Convention on Climate Change: A Breakthrough or an Empty Promise?', in *Climate Change and the Law*, edited by Erkki J. Hollo, Kati Kulovesi, and Michael Mehling, Dordrecht: Springer, p. 206. See also Richard B. Stewart, Benedict Kingsbury, and Bryce Rudyk (2009), 'Climate Finance for Limiting Emissions and Promoting Green Development', in *Climate Finance: Regulatory and Funding Strategies for Climate Change and Global Development*, edited by Richard B. Stewart, Benedict Kingsbury, and Bryce Rudyk, New York: New York University Press, p. 17 ('these multilateral funds [GEF, CIF, etc.], even taking into account projected bilateral ODA, are nowhere near large enough for what is needed'); Mattia Romani and Nicholas Stern (2013), 'Sources of Finance for Climate Action: Principles and Options for Implementation Mechanisms in this Decade', in *International Climate Finance*, edited by Erik Haites, Abingdon: Routledge, p. 118; and Standing Committee on Finance (2014a), *Biennial Assessment and Overview of Climate Finance Flows Report*, p. 67 ('global finance for climate action is presently inadequate').
2 World Bank (2015), *Common Principles for Climate Change Adaptation Finance Tracking*, Washington, DC: World Bank, p. 1 ('adaptation [is] a crosscutting development issue').
3 Susanne Olbrisch *et al.* (2013), 'Estimates of Incremental Investment for, and Cost of, Mitigation Measures in Developing Countries', in *International Climate Finance*, edited by Erik Haites, Abingdon: Routledge, p. 35.
4 Ibid., p. 37.
5 Ibid., p. 36; and Barbara Buchner *et al.* (2014), *The Global Landscape of Climate Finance 2014*, Climate Policy Initiative, p. v.
6 Intergovernmental Panel on Climate Change (2014b), *Climate Change 2014: Mitigation of Climate Change: Contribution of Working Group III to the Fifth Assessment Report of the Intergovernmental Panel on Climate Change*, New York: Cambridge University Press, p. 1233 (*5AR WG3*).
7 See Section 1.2.2 for an explanation.
8 Erik Haites (2011), 'Climate Change Finance', 11 (3) *Climate Policy* 963, p. 966.
9 Ibid., p. 966.
10 Barbara Buchner *et al.* (2013), *The Global Landscape of Climate Finance 2013*, Climate Policy Initiative, p. 33.
11 Olbrisch *et al.*, 'Estimates of Incremental Investment', p. 47.
12 FCCC, *Decision 2/CP.15 (2009), Copenhagen Accord*, FCCC/CP/2009/11/Add.1, para. 5 ('Nationally appropriate mitigation actions seeking international support will be recorded in a registry along with relevant technology, finance and capacity building support').
13 Papua New Guinea (2015), *Intended Nationally Determined Contribution Under the United Nations Framework Convention on Climate Change*, p. 6.
14 South Africa (2015), *South Africa's Intended Nationally Determined Contribution*, p. 9.
15 Ibid., p. 9.
16 India (2015), *India's Intended Nationally Determined Contribution: Working Towards Climate Justice*, p. 31.
17 Haites, 'Climate Change Finance', p. 966.
18 E.g. ibid., p. 966 ('The adaptation measures specified provide some degree of resilience to the uncertain future climate. What is the appropriate level of climate resilience?'); Buchner *et al.*, *Climate Finance 2013*, p. 33 ('difficulties in defining adaptation'); and Joel B. Smith *et al.* (2013), 'Development and Climate Change

114 *State performance of obligations*

Adaptation Funding: Coordination and Integration', in *International Climate Finance*, edited by Erik Haites, Abingdon: Routledge, p. 57 ('the sensitivity of adaptation costs to the choice of development (baseline) has not been explored').

19 Smith *et al.*, 'Climate Change Adaptation Funding', p. 56.
20 Urvashi Narain, Sergio Margulis, and Timothy Essam (2013), 'Estimating Costs of Adaptation to Climate Change', in *International Climate Finance*, edited by Erik Haites, Abingdon: Routledge, p. 79.
21 UN Environment Programme (2016), *The Adaptation Finance Gap Report 2016*.
22 Smith *et al.*, 'Climate Change Adaptation Funding', p. 56.
23 See Section 1.2.2.
24 The GEF has financed the preparation of 51 National Adaptation Programmes of Action: Global Environment Facility (18 August 2015), *Report of the Global Environment Facility to the Twenty-First Session of the Conference of the Parties to the United Nations Framework Convention on Climate Change*, FCCC/CP/2015/4, p. 3.
25 Smith *et al.*, 'Climate Change Adaptation Funding', p. 55; and GEF, *2015 Report to COP*, p. 3.
26 Smith *et al.*, 'Climate Change Adaptation Funding', p. 63.
27 FCCC (2014), *Decision 9/CP.20, Fifth Review of the Financial Mechanism*, FCCC/CP/2014/10/Add.2, Annex (summary of fifth review of the financial mechanism), para. 45.
28 GEF, *2015 Report to COP*, p. 3.
29 The COP decision adopting the Paris Agreement calls on the Adaptation Committee 'To consider methodologies for assessing adaptation needs with a view to assisting developing country Parties, without placing an undue burden on them'; FCCC (2015), *Decision 1/CP.21, Adoption of the Paris Agreement*, FCCC/CP/2015/10/Add.1, para. 42(b).
30 India INDC, p. 31.
31 FCCC (2014), *Decision 9/CP.20*, Annex (summary of fifth review of the financial mechanism), para. 43.
32 For more information on definitional issues, see Chapter 1.
33 Standing Committee on Finance, *Biennial Assessment 2014*, p. 42; see also Smita Nakhooda, Charlene Watson, and Liane Schalatek (2013), *The Global Climate Finance Architecture*, Washington, DC: Heinrich Böll Stiftung, p. 1 ('no clear definition of what constitutes climate finance').
34 Nakhooda et al., *Climate Finance Architecture*, p. 1.
35 Charlotte Streck (2011), 'Ensuring New Finance and Real Emission Reduction: A Critical Review of the Additionality Concept', 5 (2) *Carbon and Climate Law Review* 158, p. 166.
36 Martin Stadelmann, Jessica Brown, and Lena Hörnlein (2012), 'Fast-Start Finance: Scattered Governance, Information and Programmes', in *Carbon Markets or Climate Finance? Low Carbon and Adaptation Investment Choices for the Developing World*, edited by Axel Michaelowa, Abingdon: Routledge, p. 132; and Charlotte Streck (2013), 'The Financial Aspects of REDD+: Assessing Costs, Mobilizing and Disbursing Funds', in *Law, Tropical Forests and Carbon: The Case of REDD+*, edited by Rosemary Lyster, Catherine MacKenzie, and Constance McDermott, Cambridge: Cambridge University Press, p. 114.
37 Standing Committee on Finance, *Biennial Assessment 2014*, p. 6.
38 Government of Norway (2014), *Norway's Sixth National Communication under the Framework Convention on Climate Change*, p. 162.
39 Standing Committee on Finance, *Biennial Assessment 2014*, p. 38.
40 Ibid., p. 24. A joint approach by MDBs to climate adaptation finance reporting has been in effect only since 2011.

State performance of obligations   115

41 Ibid., p. 6.
42 Ibid., p. 32.
43 Nakhooda *et al.*, *Climate Finance Architecture*, p. 2 ('limited transparency and consistency in reporting . . . absent of a common reporting format, or independent verification').
44 Stadelmann *et al.*, 'Fast-Start Finance', p. 126.
45 Romani and Stern, 'Sources of Finance', p. 126.
46 Standing Committee on Finance (2014a), *Biennial Assessment 2014*, p. 24.
47 Buchner *et al.*, *Climate Finance 2013*, p. 35 ('unreliable data and large information gaps'); Olbrisch *et al.*, 'Estimates of Incremental Investment', pp. 43–44; Government of Norway, *Sixth National Communication*, p. 176; and Organization for Economic Cooperation and Development and Climate Policy Initiative (2015), *Climate Finance in 2013–14 and the USD 100 Billion Goal*, Paris: OECD and CPI, p. 15.
48 Standing Committee on Finance, *Biennial Assessment 2014*, p. 8.
49 FCCC Subsidiary Body for Implementation (2014), *Compilation and Synthesis of Sixth National Communications and First Biennial Reports from Parties Included in Annex I to the Convention: Executive Summary*, FCCC/SBI/2014/INF.20, p. 13.
50 Farhana Yamin and Joanna Depledge (2004), *The International Climate Change Regime: A Guide to Rules, Institutions and Procedures*, Cambridge: Cambridge University Press, p. 271.
51 Axel Michaelowa and Katharina Michaelowa (2007), 'Climate or Development: Is ODA Diverted from Its Original Purpose?', 84 *Climatic Change* 5, p. 7.
52 Yamin and Depledge, *International Regime*, p. 271.
53 Robert L. Hicks et al. (2008), *Greening Aid? Understanding the Environmental Impact of Development Assistance*, New York: Oxford University Press, pp. 48–49.
54 Ibid., p. 49.
55 See ibid., p. 188, Table 7.1a.
56 Olbrisch *et al.*, 'Estimates of Incremental Investment', p. 45.
57 IPCC, *5AR WG3*, p. 1210; cf. Standing Committee on Finance, *Biennial Assessment 2014*, p. 44.
58 IPCC, *5AR WG3*, p. 1216.
59 CDM Executive Board (2012b), *Benefits of the Clean Development Mechanism 2012*, p. 8.
60 Daisuke Hayashi and Stefan Wehner (2012), 'Mobilizing Mitigation Policies in the South through a Financing Mix', in *Carbon Markets or Climate Finance? Low Carbon and Adaptation Investment Choices for the Developing World*, edited by Axel Michaelowa, Abingdon: Routledge, p. 168.
61 E.g. Stadelmann *et al.*, 'Fast-Start Finance', p. 118.
62 Ibid., p. 119.
63 Smita Nakhooda *et al.* (2013), *Mobilising International Climate Finance: Lessons from the Fast-Start Finance Period*, Washington, DC: World Resources Institute, p. i; and Standing Committee on Finance, *Biennial Assessment 2014*, p. 56.
64 Copenhagen Accord, para. 8.
65 Stadelmann *et al.*, 'Fast-Start Finance', p. 121; see also Olbrisch *et al.*, 'Estimates of Incremental Investment', p. 47; and Smith *et al.*, 'Climate Change Adaptation Funding', p. 61.
66 Stadelmann *et al.*, 'Fast-Start Finance', p. 128.
67 Nakhooda *et al.*, *Lessons from the Fast-Start Finance Period*, p. i; cf. Standing Committee on Finance, *Biennial Assessment 2014*, p. 6 ('The amount of fast-start finance committed and reported by developed countries for the period 2010–2012 exceeded $33 billion').
68 Nakhooda et al., *Lessons from the Fast-Start Finance Period*, p. ii.
69 Ibid., p. 21.

116 *State performance of obligations*

70   Ibid., p. iii.
71   FCCC (2012), *Decision 1/CP.18, Agreed Outcome Pursuant to the Bali Action Plan*, FCCC/CP/2012/8/Add.1, preamble to Part V; and United States (2014), *United States Climate Action Report 2014*, pp. 54–55 ('The United States provided $7.5 billion during fiscal years 2010, 2011, and 2012 . . . meeting . . . America's fair share of the collective pledge').
72   IPCC, *5AR WG3*, pp. 1210–1215; United States (2014), *Climate Action Report*, p. 174 ('The $4.7 billion in appropriated assistance [being part of the US FSF] represents a fourfold increase in annual climate assistance since 2009'); Government of Norway, *Sixth National Communication*, p. 161 ('by any definition [Norway's FSF contribution] can therefore be classified as "new and additional" [because of its strong growth]'); and Commonwealth of Australia (2013), *Australia's Sixth National Communication on Climate Change: A Report under the United Nations Framework Convention on Climate Change*, p. 12.
73   Copenhagen Accord, para. 4.
74   FCCC (2011), *Decision 1/CP.17, Establishment of an Ad Hoc Working Group on the Durban Platform for Enhanced Action*, paras 7–8.
75   FCCC (2012), *Decision 1/CP.18*, para. 68.
76   Group of 18 States and the European Commission Providing Bilateral Climate Finance (2015), *Joint Statement on Tracking Progress Towards the $100 Billion Goal*, p. 2; and OECD and CPI, *Climate Finance 2013–14*, p. 14.
77   FCCC (2014), *Decision 9/CP.20*, Annex (summary of fifth review of the financial mechanism), para. 34.
78   GEF, *2015 Report to COP*, p. 2.
79   During GEF's fifth period, i.e. July 2010 to June 2014, about $1.2 billion was programmed for mitigation projects: FCCC (2014), *Decision 9/CP.20*, Annex (summary of fifth review of the financial mechanism), para. 34; see also GEF, *2015 Report to COP*, p. 3; cf. FCCC (2014), *Decision 8/CP.20, Report of the Global Environment Facility to the Conference of the Parties and Guidance to the Global Environment Facility*, FCCC/CP/2014/10/Add.2, para. 2; and Standing Committee on Finance, *Biennial Assessment 2014*, p. 45.
80   FCCC (2014), *Decision 7/CP.20, Report of the Green Climate Fund to the Conference of the Parties and Guidance to the Green Climate Fund*, FCCC/CP/2014/10/Add.2, para. 3.
81   Sanjay Kumar (2015), 'Green Climate Fund Faces Slew of Criticism', 527 *Nature* 419, pp. 419–420; cf. Green Climate Fund (21 September 2015), *Report of the Green Climate Fund to the Conference of the Parties*, FCCC/CP/2015/3, p. 5.
82   Buchner et al., *Climate Finance 2014*, p. iv.
83   Ibid., p. v; cf. ibid., p. vii ('Of all mitigation finance, 78% went toward renewable energy').
84   Ibid., p. 19.
85   Ibid., p. 19; cf. FCCC Subsidiary Body for Implementation (2014), *Compilation and Synthesis of Sixth National Communications and First Biennial Reports from Parties Included in Annex I to the Convention: Executive Summary*, p. 13.
86   OECD and CPI, *Climate Finance 2013–14*, p. 24 ('Total climate finance outflows from the six major MDBs attributed to developed countries reached $18 billion in 2014, from $12.9 billion in 2013').
87   See, e.g. Republic of Brazil (2015), *Intended Nationally Determined Contribution Towards Achieving the Objective of the United Nations Framework Convention on Climate Change*, pp. 3–4; and Mexico (2015), *Intended Nationally Determined Contribution*, p. 2.
88   However, when it comes to sustainable development benefits, the CDM is unexceptional. Its main report on the subject obtains its information almost exclusively

State performance of obligations   117

from the Project Design Documents produced by CDM project developers pre-implementation: CDM Executive Board (2012b), *Benefits of the CDM 2012*, p. 14. For more on this point, see Alexander Zahar (2015a), *International Climate Change Law and State Compliance*, Abingdon: Routledge, §6.3.2.

89   See, e.g. Smita Nakhooda (2013), *The Effectiveness of Climate Finance: A Review of the Global Environment Facility*, ODI working paper; and Smita Nakhooda and Marigold Norman (2014), *Climate Finance: Is it Making a Difference? A Review of the Effectiveness of Multilateral Climate Funds*, ODI, p. 43.

90   Commonwealth of Australia, *Sixth National Communication*, p. 187.

91   FCCC (2014), *Decision 9/CP.20*, Annex (Summary of Fifth Review of the Financial Mechanism), para. 65.

92   Stadelmann *et al.*, 'Fast-Start Finance', p. 133. For a more optimistic view, see Sam Barrett (2013), 'Local Level Climate Justice? Adaptation Finance and Vulnerability Reduction', 23 (6) *Global Environmental Change* 1819, p. 1826.

93   GEF, *2015 Report to COP*, p. 19, emphasis added.

94   Cf. 'The total amount of direct and indirect mitigation impact *expected* from these projects [615 mitigation projects as at June 2013] is 2.6 and 8.2 billion tonnes of CO_2 eq. emissions, respectively': FCCC (2014), *Decision 9/CP.20*, Annex (Summary of Fifth Review of the Financial Mechanism), paras 72–73, emphasis added; and Global Environment Facility (2 September 2014), *Report of the Global Environment Facility to the Twentieth Session of the Conference of the Parties to the United Nations Framework Convention on Climate Change*, FCCC/CP/2014/2, pp. 3–4 (where 'impact' is discussed in terms of the funded projects' 'likelihood of achieving' project objectives).

95   FCCC (2014), *Decision 9/CP.20*, Annex (Summary of Fifth Review of the Financial Mechanism), paras 72–73.

96   E.g. GEF, *2015 Report to COP*, pp. 30, 32; and FCCC (2014), *Decision 9/CP.20*, Annex (Summary of Fifth Review of the Financial Mechanism), paras 74–75.

97   Standing Committee on Finance, *Biennial Assessment 2014*, p. 8.

98   Ibid., p. 67.

99   Hicks *et al.*, *Greening Aid*, pp. 254–255; Axel Michaelowa (2012), 'Manoeuvring Climate Finance Around the Pitfalls: Finding the Right Policy Mix', in *Carbon Markets or Climate Finance? Low Carbon and Adaptation Investment Choices for the Developing World*, edited by Axel Michaelowa, Abingdon: Routledge, p. 264; Stadelmann *et al.*, 'Fast-Start Finance', pp. 125, 137; and Buchner *et al.*, *Climate Finance 2014*, pp. viii, 19.

5 The philosophy of the control of nature

5.1 2°C as geoengineering

'Geoengineering' is a dystopic term associated with a world in terminal decline, yet what is the FCCC with its 2°C target if not a form of geoengineering? To appreciate this point, it will be necessary to review the main ideas in this book so far:

1   In the context of the climate change regime and its objective (article 2 of the FCCC), mitigation and climate finance are two expressions of the same idea. 'Additional' mitigation, as required by the treaty, always (by definition) means additional finance. When the additional effort is carried out domestically, it is called mitigation; when it is exported it is called climate finance, and this finance is used for mitigation elsewhere. Climate change thus is (potentially) controlled through climate finance. However, instead of integrated regulation of mitigation and climate finance, the two areas have traditionally been uncoordinated.

2   The climate change regime's CDBR principle dominated the pre-Copenhagen order, confining the obligation for mitigation action to a minority of states, and treating climate finance as a form of development aid. This 'CBDR mitigation model' supported voluntarism, i.e. the doctrine that differences in state capacity call for a distinction between compulsory and voluntary state mitigation. The CBDR principle's binary reading was rejected at the Copenhagen COP in 2009. The principle survives, yet has been so diluted in the Paris Agreement in 2015 as to have lost any normative meaning to distinguish it from a general principle of equity.

3   In the place of CBDR, the 'modified polluter-pays principle' has become the dominant principle of the climate change regime – although legal analysis is necessary to bring out this fact. The principle requires all states to pay for their greenhouse gas pollution, subject to an equity adjustment. The polluter-pays principle supplements the treaty-based climate change regime. It is the only general principle of international law which forms a core part of climate change law.

4   A state's obligation to mitigate is limited by state capacity. Where capacity can be extended through climate finance, the capacity limitation is lifted and

120 *The philosophy of the control of nature*

no country harbouring unexploited cost-effective mitigation opportunities may reasonably decline to participate in mitigation actions. This is the legal hallmark of the post-Copenhagen era. It is rich with implications.

5 The 2°C limit on global warming is now indisputably agreed to by states. States have impliedly accepted responsibility to stay within a global emission budget consistent with the limit. Given that a significant amount of the additional mitigation this implies must be found in developing countries, the warming limit also implies a climate finance budget for use in developing countries. The size of that budget can be calculated once it is known how much additional (unsupported) domestic mitigation developed and developing countries are willing to undertake. This is a precondition for the individualization of the FCCC's general mitigation burden.

6 The Paris Agreement is a step closer to compulsory mitigation action for all states – and thus a rejection of voluntarism. However, while it makes certain *processes* compulsory for all, it does not make compulsory the additional mitigation action needed to avoid 2°C. The Agreement's bottom-up NDC system, whose substantive effect will (supposedly) increase over time through peer pressure (a top-down element), *might* succeed in managing the emission budget. But it also might not. The Paris Agreement is unable to reduce the uncertainty on this point because in substance it is still voluntarist. It refrains from full implementation of the post-Copenhagen mitigation model.

7 Up until the Paris Agreement, there was no acceptance that climate finance must be linked to the 2°C temperature limit and used to manage the emission budget. The Paris Agreement succeeds in making the link, for the first time. In other respects, the Agreement is 'old school' on climate finance. The amounts of climate finance promised in the Copenhagen Accord were arbitrary; in the COP decision adopting the Paris Agreement they are no less arbitrary. The Paris COP's decision hesitated to give the quantity of climate finance a clear rationale by linking it to the carbon budget, even though the Paris Agreement itself makes that link.

8 The amounts of climate finance supplied to date are not clearly reported on by states, are difficult to estimate from the available information, cannot be said to be either a 'sufficient' or an 'insufficient' response to the problem of climate change, and their outcomes are obscure. The Paris Agreement takes some steps to improve reporting on climate finance; however, it does not make reporting compulsory for developing countries, nor does it require reporting on outcomes.

9 Calls for 'balancing' mitigation and adaptation finance continue. This is another case of 'old school' thinking. Given an amount of climate finance raised, the post-Copenhagen logic requires that it be spent on mitigation, because the regime's overarching objective is to keep warming below 2°C. This creates a problem for the incorporation of adaptation finance into the regime – a problem that the Paris Agreement ignores. Adaptation finance is still best thought of as a form of development aid. However, the climate change regime justifiably retains control of adaptation finance, since the alternatives

to doing so are worse. States must first of all accept that the two kinds of finance have different rationales and therefore cannot be 'balanced'; the management of climate finance will be helped by a more honest narrative on adaptation finance.

10 In brief: states are not currently in compliance with the post-Copenhagen climate law they have themselves created. They are now focused on fleshing out the Paris Agreement, but this will not be enough to fix the compliance problem, as the Agreement is only a pale reflection of the post-Copenhagen logic. Elaboration of the regime must go beyond mere elaboration of the Paris Agreement.

Beneath this structure lies another element. While the post-Copenhagen regime, in design if not in implementation, is a fully rational, paradigmatic shift from the earlier CBDR-dominated design, it is built on the assumption that nature can be engineered to suit our needs. This narrative assumption presumes that we have or will have the knowledge and technology necessary to keep global warming from reaching 2°C, even though, as yet, we have not agreed on the precise arrangements. Once those are agreed to, we can begin work on managing the temperature rise, easing it up to 1.9°C, or even up to only 1.5°C if we find reason to be more cautious. Talk of a 'budget', of sharing its burden among states, of periodically revising it in response to changes in atmospheric CO_2 concentrations or global warming rates or experienced impacts, of using finance strategically, etc., all imply a mechanism which, although not mechanical like a solar-management mirror suspended in the sky, notionally is a lever through which we can modulate our interference with nature and thereby nature's responses.

This element of the new regime is its vulnerable underbelly. I call it the ethic of control. No account of the current regime, not even a legal one, should fail to acknowledge it.

The climate change regime, with its global 2°C target, is one of the clearest examples of the ethic of control. The ethic has been described before,[1] although only in relation to regional features, e.g. river courses, and never in relation to an all-enveloping physical system such as the climate. My study of climate finance shows how far it reaches. With the ethic of control extended to climate change, the ethic itself has become all-encompassing. The FCCC, as reinvented post-Copenhagen, is the ethic of control writ large.[2] Anthropogenic climate change will be tolerated, we now say, within limits. Those limits will be defined and managed by us. It is a geoengineering ideology, distinct from the geoengineering instruments which leave most of us horrified. Yet an ideology, too, when seen clearly for what it is, can elicit feelings of rejection for being too risky.

5.2 Climate finance and the precarious control of nature

The current law on climate finance – the very idea of climate finance as a mitigation-control mechanism – is thus not above criticism. The most caustic criticism that could be levelled against it turns out to be a philosophical one.

122 *The philosophy of the control of nature*

It attacks the presumption that, through climate finance, nature – the global climate system – can be controlled. On this view, the modified polluter-pays principle is nothing more than a control mechanism through which the philosophy of nature-control is to be implemented. Climate finance is a core element of the post-Copenhagen plan to control the earth's surface temperature; as long as we are prepared to spend enough money on the task, we will succeed. Given that the law on climate finance is central to climate law itself, this criticism impacts climate law as a whole. But why be cowed by this criticism? Why have doubts about the ethic of control? All of us want a predictable natural environment to live in. Our prowess in so many fields surely justifies our belief that we can control the climate, among many other things. The ethic of control could, if necessary, be made to seem more pragmatic, and thus less implausible, by joining it to a principle of continuous review. Control through a feedback loop that responds to information verified by scientists each year, say, as opposed to each five (as under the IPCC assessment process now), is less presumptuous and more risk-averse, if appropriate policy responses can be implemented with the same frequency. The ethic of control, at its most pragmatic, would be realized, given a highly responsive international regime. Or so one might argue.

5.2.1 *Chance and self-delusion*

There are nevertheless good reasons to doubt even the most pragmatic manifestations of the ethic of control. The issues I will raise below originate from within the climate change regime itself. Some of the impacts of climate change (melting icecaps, rising sea levels, destructive storms) are so vast in scale, complex, and self-reinforcing that they question the extent of human control no matter how pragmatically it is exercised. Closer to home, the current international regime is in fact highly *unresponsive* to feedback. The FCCC's pledge period up to 2020 and the Kyoto Protocol's second commitment period, for example, are each eight years long. There is to be no change in ambition during these periods. The Paris Agreement promises only two global stocktakes per decade; NDCs are to be revised only every five years; the $100 billion pledge on climate finance need not be increased until after 2025; etc. The arrangements through to 2020, but even the Paris Agreement itself, are more about not inconveniencing states too much than about creating a pragmatic attempt at control.

Significant uncertainty about the sensitivity of the climate system to anthropogenic interference suggests that the ethic of control is delusional. If the FCCC's 2°C limit is to be realized through an emission budget, states must accept that there is uncertainty in the causal relationship between the management of the budget and global warming.[3] Thus the IPCC speaks in terms of 'a likely probability' that scenarios 'generally' in the range of 430–480 ppm CO_2 eq will maintain temperature increases below 2°C 'this century'.[4] A best-estimate budget of 1,780 Gt CO_2 beginning in 2011 would give a 66 per cent chance or better that the 2°C limit could be maintained.[5] When estimates of other greenhouse gases are included, the CO_2 budget is lowered to about 1,000 Gt CO_2 for a 'likely chance' of staying

The philosophy of the control of nature 123

below 2°C.[6] This level of uncertainty means that the FCCC (and Paris Agreement) would be gambling on, rather than controlling, events.[7] The extent of control could be improved somewhat by switching to a system of continuous review, as I noted above; however, there is no sign of such a radical change in state mentality in the offing.

Scenarios that have a greater than 66 per cent chance of keeping the temperature increase to below 2°C by the end of the century have global emissions at 42 Gt CO_2 eq in 2030. It is the median figure; the range is 31–44 Gt CO_2 eq.[8] Because of the poor condition of international reporting on greenhouse gas emissions (only Annex I parties produce regular, independently checked, inventories), our knowledge of global emission totals is another factor affected by significant uncertainty. The global emission estimate for Kyoto Protocol-controlled gases for 2014 is 52.7 Gt CO_2 eq, with an uncertainty range of 47.9–57.5 Gt CO_2 eq.[9] If the FCCC were to create an interim emission budget for 2030, it would need to rapidly reduce the uncertainty in global emission reporting. Yet, there is no plan to do so prior to 2020. The National Communications and BURs of developing countries are elementary in this respect. At present it is not known whether universal improvements to emission reporting will be prioritized under the Paris Agreement. Even if they were, it would take until 2030 before all major emitters are reporting their emissions accurately. The NDC process is itself highly unpredictable. Overall, it seems unlikely that the FCCC parties will set an appropriate budget for 2030. (The current BAU policy trajectory for 2030 is 58–62 Gt CO_2 eq.[10]) But even if the states were to do so, it is unlikely that they would have in place the means to manage it, given the present poor state of developing-country reporting.

Groups pressuring states to commit to more ambitious mitigation action prefer not to stress the fact that the greater the ambition of states' adopted targets, the less likely it is that they will be met. It is true that greater ambition is needed to keep the temperature from rising above 2°C; it is also true that greater ambition means more wishful thinking and thus less control over the outcome. Certain assumptions about negative-emission technology are illustrative in this respect. All IPCC scenarios consistent with the current pathway of emissions to 2020 assume that 'net zero' total greenhouse gas emissions will be achieved sometime before 2075.[11] These scenarios further assume that CO_2 removal technologies, in particular carbon capture and storage, will be implemented before that date.[12] Far more ambitiously, they assume that carbon capture and storage will be coupled to widespread bioenergy production – with all the impacts on arable land and food prices that this entails.[13] However, to date, capturing CO_2 from power plants has proved more difficult and expensive than many had at first imagined.[14] The reliance on negative-emission technology being widespread already by 2050 involves 'magical thinking'.[15] It joins a long line of 'simplified assumptions . . . far from messy reality'.[16] It does not inspire confidence in the ethic of control of nature.

Recent self-congratulatory COPs – especially the Paris one, at the conclusion of which participants showered themselves in praise not fully deserved – have obscured the scale of the climate challenge.[17] Paradoxically, the Copenhagen turn

124 *The philosophy of the control of nature*

to dealing rationally with the challenge, which was a necessary if belated advance on what had gone before, now has to begin to grapple with the realization that the control ethic underlying the advance is itself irrational due to the uncertainties involved, the slow pace of reform, and the conviction among a growing number of experts that 'stopping warming at 2°C is no longer feasible'.[18]

5.2.2 Inherent vice: fossil-fuel subsidies

It is common practice in government to try to solve a problem with one hand while making it worse with the other. In this way, several political constituencies may be satisfied at once, especially where the complexity or obscurity of the subject matter does not enable the supposed beneficiaries to see that the government's approach overall does not benefit their interests, or may even harm them.

Government policy on climate change is notoriously incoherent. In Chapter 4 I looked rather narrowly at the supply of climate finance to assess state compliance with the relevant obligations of states. But what if, from a wider perspective, that supply is neutralized by support given to conflicting activities? 'More climate finance' must surely also mean 'less anti-climate finance'. Has the increase in climate finance since 1992 been paralleled with a reduction in state-supported fossil-fuel subsidies, for example? Information on such subsidies would allow us to sharpen our reflections on the ethic of control.

In May 2010, the World Bank made a $3 billion loan to South Africa's Eskom company, to be used to build the world's largest coal-fired power plant.[19] (An additional $750 million was loaned to Eskom for renewable-energy projects.) The Eskom project illustrates 'the underlying tension between the development and climate agendas'.[20] The same MDBs that channel the developed states' climate finance also support conventional fossil-fuel technologies that speed up climate change.[21] The Hicks *et al.* study from 2008 found that while MDBs had 'greened' their support substantially over the period 1980–2000, they continued to give about four times as much to 'dirty' projects as to projects with environmental benefits.[22] In the United States, the Obama Administration introduced the Clean Power Plan to make power companies cut carbon emissions; meanwhile, in the Powder River Basin, which spans parts of Wyoming and Montana and is the source of more than 40 per cent of the coal burned in the United States, production subsidies amount to nearly $3 billion dollars a year.[23] Simply making coal companies operating in the Basin pay fair market value for their government leases would reduce emissions. Instead, the United States has 'a coal policy that's totally incoherent, aim[ing] at getting U. S. power plants to use less coal [while] still subsidizing coal companies to produce more of it'.[24] In China, the government flaunts its domestic climate policies with one hand while profiting from the expansion of emission-intensive infrastructure in its client states with the other. Since 2010, Chinese state-owned enterprises

> have finished, begun building or formally announced plans to build at least 92 coal-fired power plants in 27 countries. [Their combined capacity is] more

The philosophy of the control of nature 125

than enough to completely offset the planned closing of coal-fired plants in the United States through 2020.[25]

In the United Kingdom, old coal plants are being taken offline without new ones being built to replace them; at the same time, the UK government is granting £436 million in subsidies over 15 years to diesel generators to build back-up energy for the national grid: 'The subsidies on offer are so appealing that even solar-power developers, which have recently had their own subsidies cut, are building diesel generation on their sites as a way of maximising their returns.'[26] In this case, the solar-energy developer branched into fossil-fuel production because it represented a profitable opportunity. Is there a self-contradiction at some level? Would one be justified to posit that mitigation action and the finance that powers it bring about ideological change in society, or is that wishful thinking? For all we know, climate change, as a global problem, makes individuals or firms feel *less* responsible about the impact of their conduct than they do in relation to their impact on local issues, such as waste recycling. There is evidence of ideological change at the governmental level – e.g. the signing of the Paris Agreement – but the facts on fossil-fuel subsidies[27] also tell us that governments are well able to pursue internally incoherent policies which finally account for the lack of ambition at the international level. When fossil-energy subsidies in developing countries amount to hundreds of billions of dollars a year,[28] the incentive to increase climate finance under the FCCC is easily exhausted.[29]

5.2.3 Negative social and environmental impacts of climate finance

The FCCC narrative tends to emphasize the 'synergies' of climate finance and underplay its internal contradictions. For example: 'several REDD projects may have strong adaptation components . . . renewable energy projects may promote climate change adaptation'.[30] This positive outlook supports the philosophy of control. It seeks to reassure us that climate finance will help us solve the climate change problem while also protecting other environmental and social values. To assuage doubt, the regime adopts legal safeguards or commits to 'added benefits' that explicitly or implicitly condition the provision and use of climate finance.[31] These act as implementation constraints on states' obligations on climate finance. Some constraints exist only at the policy level, while others have the quality of legal obligation. Human rights are said to act as their own implementation constraint on climate finance: 'Mitigation and adaptation policies and their funding can . . . be evaluated in terms of their likely human rights impact and have to be rejected or altered if the fulfillment of these rights is threatened.'[32] Another example is the Kyoto Protocol's requirement that projects funded through the CDM are to deliver sustainable development benefits for the host country. Such benefits go beyond the core business of the CDM, which is to deliver emission reductions at lowest cost. Nevertheless, Protocol parties would probably not have agreed to set up the CDM if it were not for the promise of added social benefits for host countries.

126 *The philosophy of the control of nature*

In a separate section, below, I discuss what we can learn from the CDM experience about the degree of control over outcomes attained through climate finance. In the present section I begin with a more general consideration. It may be assumed that mitigation projects made possible with climate finance should not have maladaptive effects, and also that adaptation projects should not be emission-intensive. In other words, we may assume that climate finance seeks to have coherent (non-self-defeating) outcomes; it should produce mitigation and adaptation benefits at the same time, or at least have no adverse side-effects on one when benefiting the other. If an incompatibility existed and were significant, one funding stream would undermine the other to some extent. Does the FCCC regime regulate climate finance so as to avoid this problem?

For decades, most ODA funding for development projects damaged the environment, natural as well as social.[33] The situation began to improve around 2000, when MDBs, among other distributors of transnational finance, expanded the conditions they impose on project outcomes.[34] Yet 'multiple conflicts, between the objectives of climate and development policy', continue.[35] Mitigation projects with counteradaptive human or ecological impacts include the construction of large hydropower plants in densely populated areas, causing resettlement, social unrest, and loss of productive assets for the poor;[36] wind-energy growth – the fastest-growing source of power worldwide – is damaging bird species already struggling for survival;[37] biofuel development risks sustainability in biodiversity, local environmental quality, and socio-economic rights;[38] forest-carbon management and other forms of CO_2 removal create environmental as well as social dis-benefits;[39] and transnational funding for methane-capture projects at landfills is taking work away from millions of waste pickers.[40] Adaptation projects with emission-intensive or other negative socio-environmental impacts include the building of seawalls causing destruction of coastal ecosystems; agriculture and irrigation projects supporting natural habitat conversion; fossil-fuel-dependent economic development in general;[41] and a diversion of finance from traditional aid objectives, including poverty alleviation, which is not always the main objective of adaptation finance.[42]

REDD is the only context in which the FCCC regime formally attempts to regulate the outcomes of climate finance. Possibly this is because the risks of REDD – a mechanism which is as yet essentially unimplemented[43] – are huge.[44]

In summary, climate finance could cause all manner of environmental damage. Such damage could undermine the objectives of other environmental regimes, and thus create resistance from other quarters to increasing the flow of climate finance. Even mitigation and adaptation outcomes which the regime itself is supposed to control can exist in contradiction to each other – with the outcomes of one undermining those of the other. These issues, or potential issues, are not monitored within the climate change regime;[45] they further add to the precariousness of the regime's assumed control of nature.

5.2.4 CDM finance and its compromises

The CDM has accumulated more than a decade's worth of international experience with a market-based mechanism for climate finance. The CDM Executive Board

The philosophy of the control of nature 127

has repeatedly praised the CDM as a model of climate finance that should be emulated on a larger scale.[46] The Board estimated the revenue generated from the sale of CERs by the end of 2011 at above \$9.5 billion,[47] and total 'investment' in CDM projects as of June 2012 at \$215.4 billion.[48] The Paris Agreement provides for the design of a mechanism with features comparable to the CDM's.[49]

While the CDM has undoubtedly created many benefits, and while its marginalization since around 2012 is due to circumstances beyond its control,[50] the CDM is also a lesson in how climate finance can go sour, in two ways: it may not deliver the emission reductions it claims to deliver; and it may lead to destructive consequences whose occurrence the CDM does not recognize or take responsibility for. The Kyoto Protocol parties did not adopt any safeguards for the CDM, on the model of the (later) REDD safeguards adopted under the FCCC[51] (which are largely non-operationalized,[52] as well as, of course, unimplemented, due to the glacial implementation of REDD[53]).

Under the CDM, in theory, BAU projects are screened out and not registered. A project proponent must convince the Executive Board that the proposed project is 'additional'. It has been said that the CDM's rules for baseline determination and additionality testing are 'surprisingly stringent'.[54] However, project proponents have a strong incentive to try to avoid these rules; the more successful they are in this respect, the more money they can make off international climate finance – at the expense of the emission reductions claimed by their projects, which are thereby diminished or rendered non-existent. The Executive Board may have 'performed remarkably well with regard to specifying rules for additionality testing . . . but less with regard to actually preventing non-additional projects'.[55]

Perhaps the most devastating critic of the CDM's claims to emission reductions and sustainable development has been Philip Fearnside. From a research base in Manaus, Fearnside has focused his work on Brazil's programme of hydroelectric dam construction. He describes the programme as aiming to convert essentially all of the Amazon River's tributaries into 'continuous chains of reservoirs' for the production of electricity.[56] Many of these dams are registered CDM projects. Dam projects at this scale are a phenomenon not confined to Brazil.[57] In fact, the leading CDM hydropower country is China, followed by India, with Brazil in third place.[58] The global amount of emission reductions being claimed by these large CDM-registered dams at one point was 104 Mt CO_2 eq per year – which, as Fearnside points out, is about the same as Brazil's annual emissions from fossil fuels.[59] Because CERs are bought by polluters to cancel out their own, actual, emissions, the CDM's role as a mitigation-control mechanism falters where the emission reductions that a CER purports to stand for are non-additional – i.e. can be shown to be 'reductions' that would have happened anyway because the project which produced the CER would have gone ahead even without the CDM's financial support.

Fearnside lays out the methodological compromises that have led to undercounting hydropower emissions in the CDM. I will preface them with a couple of introductory concepts. A dam produces methane emissions in two ways: they

128 *The philosophy of the control of nature*

bubble up through the reservoir surface; or they escape after the water has passed through the turbines and is released into the river course below. The 'power density' of a dam is the ratio of installed power capacity and the dam's reservoir area. A CDM regulation allows zero emissions to be claimed for the dam if the power density is over 10 W/m². This is a fiction; an increase in the power-to-surface ratio may reduce emissions in some circumstances, but it does not eliminate them. In the case of a dam of high power density, the water passing through the turbines is normally drawn from the reservoir's deepest layer, which is virtually devoid of oxygen, and where decomposition of organic matter generates methane instead of CO_2.[60] (The global warming potential (GWP) of methane, which until 2012 was set, under the CDM, as 21 times that of CO_2 over a 100-year period, was revised upward by the IPCC in 2013, to 28 times higher.[61] Most CDM dams began construction prior to 2012, when the Executive Board was using, as it turns out, a wrong GWP metric for methane. While this is not the Board's fault, it further illustrates how uncertainty over physical processes undermines the ethic of control.) As the methane transits from its containment under high pressure at the bottom of the reservoir into the open air below the turbines, it is released from the churned water into the atmosphere.[62] Fearnside writes that Brazil played a key role in the CDM Executive Board's decision to allow dams with power densities over 10 W/m² to claim zero emissions.[63]

Fearnside fills in the larger picture of climate finance as it operates in the real world – one that the FCCC through its individual funds and mechanisms is not able, or does not want, to see. Using data on the Santo Antônio CDM dam in the Brazilian Amazon, Fearnside calculates the difference between the project's baseline emissions, as claimed, and its actual emissions with the produced methane included.[64] Santo Antônio's electricity is almost entirely consumed at a vast distance from the dam, about 2,400 km away, in the city of Sao Paulo. A transmission line, one of the longest in the world, has been purpose-built to link the dam with the city. The average loss in power transmission for Brazil is 20 per cent; however, the CDM project only considers transmission loss up to a point a mere 5 km from the dam, where the electricity supposedly enters the national grid. Up to that point, transmission loss is only 3.2 per cent. This greatly affects the number of CERs the project can claim.[65] Fearnside posits a gas-fired thermal plant built on the outskirts of Sao Paulo which delivers the same amount of electricity to the city.[66] It is just such a plant that the Santo Antônio dam theoretically eliminates to receive CERs.[67] For a fair comparison with the baseline scenario, the posited gas-fired plant's emissions would have to be reduced by at least 20 per cent for the transmission loss and by another significant amount for the dam's own greenhouse gas emissions. In the latter category, in addition to the deep-water methane discussed above, are releases of CO_2. In Amazonian dams this happens during the construction period and subsequent settlement of a dam's surrounding areas and associated development of agriculture, when deforestation activity is carried out near the dam.[68] None of this is factored into CDM baseline scenarios.[69]

Would the CDM dams in the Amazon have been built anyway? Here again Fearnside's research is invaluable. The dams he studied were all under construction

The philosophy of the control of nature   129

or had been already built before they applied for CDM registration.[70] This fact, as Fearnside observes, offers 'an unambiguous demonstration of non-additionality that all people can understand'.[71] The CDM's 'investment test' for additionality allows a project to claim additionality by showing that a calculated internal rate of return for the project is lower than a 'benchmark' (minimum acceptable) internal rate of return identified by the project developer. This difference is taken to mean that the project is unprofitable and would not go ahead without climate finance. Santo Antônio's investors set the benchmark at 17.31 per cent – and it was accepted by the CDM Executive Board. Fearnside writes: 'Some measure of common sense is required. . . . Few companies or investors can expect to make a return on investment of 17% per year, after taxes, over and above inflation and sustained over a period of 10 years' – i.e. the CDM's crediting period.[72] Yet, even though supposedly coming in below the 'benchmark', vast amounts were invested in Santo Antônio dam years before it was registered as a CDM project.[73]

The market for CERs crashed shortly after 2008. Many CDM projects, large and small, should have begun to fail too. Instead, they survived. Dam projects I visited in Vietnam in 2014 which had begun operations after 2008 had this to say about their registration: CDM status lent them a certain standing with banks and investors; however, none of those projects had undertaken the complex process of applying for credits, given the state of the CER market. They had chosen to forego the income. In other words, all of them were non-additional from the start. Two rice-husk bioenergy CDM projects I visited in the Philippines in 2014 were in the same position. The majority of randomly selected projects in my sample were non-additional.

All told, while the CDM's Amazonian dams claim emission-free electricity, in fact they produce large amounts of greenhouse gases, especially during the first ten years of their operation, which coincide with the CDM's crediting period.[74] Moreover, they would have been built anyway. CDM finance spent on them creates emission reductions on paper only. Yet the certificates issued are used to reduce legal responsibility for very real emissions produced elsewhere.

A climate finance mechanism such as the CDM has to be workable and attractive to investors under the most complex of project conditions. There is an incentive for all involved to ignore information that casts doubt on the mechanism's supposed beneficial impacts. There is even evidence that states will actively resist rules of climate finance that are perceived to reduce potential profits, as is most clearly seen in the Brazilian government's influence 'in creating and broadening the loopholes'[75] in the CDM's regulation of hydroelectric dam projects. Looking at the CDM's experience with dams, one wonders how many large projects funded from other sources of climate finance – e.g. finance passing through the MBDs or channelled from state to state as bilateral finance – are in fact dirty, non-additional projects, which consume 'climate finance' that in substance is nothing more than conventional development finance.[76] As I noted in Chapter 4, we do not have meaningful information at the regime (FCCC) level to help us understand the outcomes of climate finance. Even in the case of the data-rich CDM, regime-level information is not enough, as demonstrated by Fearnside's meticulous

130   *The philosophy of the control of nature*

follow-up investigations. 'Control' becomes precarious in such a situation, where the regime is prepared to accept one account for its simplicity, whereas a more complex account also exists which contradicts the first one.

Though not critical to the question of control, we may briefly also consider what we know about the CDM's impact on sustainable development. The CDM Executive Board seems genuinely to believe that the Kyoto Protocol has created a mechanism that both reduces greenhouse gas emissions and locally improves other environmental and social values.[77] Again, Fearnside's studies support a different conclusion. He highlights some of the impacts of CDM-supported dams in the Amazon: flooding and sediment movements;[78] deforestation and population displacement;[79] depletion of fish resources, especially through an impact on catfish migration and spawning, which affects the livelihoods of the local population in addition to biodiversity itself;[80] and releases of methylated mercury from the reservoirs, affecting livelihoods downstream.[81]

Returning for an instant to the book's main theme, I should add that implementation of a global-budget approach to mitigation would minimize the additionality requirements of mitigation mechanisms. The problem of additionality and the extensive discussion it generates result from the fact that current policies do not reflect the logic of the climate change problem. Once a global and regularly reviewed emission budget is set, the additionality of any given emission-reduction project is not relevant to the ultimate aim of achieving a global reduction in emissions, because emissions in the country hosting the project would be aggregated and debited to the global budget.[82]

5.3 Conclusion

This book has provided an epistemological exploration of the limits of (our knowledge of) climate finance that also critiques various asserted or implied positions (myths) about climate finance, its objectives, and benefits. It has addressed a range of questions, e.g. about whether we can know how much finance is mobilized and spent, under what conditions, pursuant to what obligations, and to what effect (impacts). Evidence from project implementation (e.g. the CDM) shows that our knowledge is ambiguous and does not allow for reliable conclusions about mitigation or sustainable development.

In addition, the analysis of climate finance presented in this book's chapters points to ways in which states could regulate climate finance rationally and comprehensively – even if presently, as I have argued, they do not do so in fact. Improved regulation is needed, in any case, to make state practice on climate finance legally compliant with the law that the states themselves have developed under the FCCC. The urgency of a solution to the climate change problem suggests that a fully developed legal approach to climate finance is desirable as a way of accelerating implementation of a solution.

To recap, the international law on climate finance implies the existence of a global emission budget, to be allocated equitably among states, with climate finance playing an important role in realizing the equitable allocation. Because such an

The philosophy of the control of nature 131

arrangement does not presently exist, the current implementation of international legal obligations on climate finance does not correspond to the logic of the climate change problem or to the legal obligations implied by the FCCC. Climate finance as it is now practised lacks a coherent rationale. In this, it is equivalent to the ill-defined general mitigation obligation of the FCCC's parties, which for more than two decades they have failed to particularize into state-level obligations.

The imposition and maintenance of a global emission budget, informed by science, and periodically revised by states, is necessary to raise climate finance in meaningful quantities. Current problems with climate finance are attributable to the non-implementation of a top-down approach and to an ongoing reliance on voluntary, ad-hoc contributions. Under a fully implemented top-down approach, there would be no conceptually separate programme of climate finance because the finance would be raised and distributed as part of a burden-setting mechanism to oversee the global emission budget. Still, an equitable burden-setting mechanism implies the possibility of ongoing revision. There can be no unvarying and permanent solution to burden allocation.

As the need for action against climate change becomes ever more urgent, states can be expected to converge, of necessity, on a burden-sharing formula. The fact that all state mitigation action to date has consisted of bottom-up pledges does not exclude the emergence of a top-down formula, as pressure to act increases. Under the pledging system developed for the Paris Agreement era, ongoing scrutiny of NDCs could be expected eventually to lead to the development of a formula for adequate and fair effort. However, it might also be that action is delayed for so long that the burden to be shared among states is largely made up of the cost of extreme geoengineering technologies.

This book acknowledges and works within the dominant ethic of control of nature. However, it has not been my intention to endorse that ethic. I doubt that we can control nature at a global scale. Perhaps the best we can hope for is that the international legal system does not pretend that no arrogant philosophy of control underlies it. We should demand of it that it makes explicit the fact that, if we are to continue in the current manner of almost decadal reassessment of our actions, there is a high risk of overshooting the temperature target. An honest law lays bare its philosophical assumptions. It is a kind of improvement.

An alternative to the ethic of control is the belief that sustainable human life is only possible within nature, as part of it, subordinate rather than superior to it. Under this ecocentric ethic, the same rules that we perceive as applying to ourselves would also apply to nature, and the rules which we think of as applying to nature would also apply to ourselves. Predictability would not be assumed of nature, just as it is not assumed of ourselves. Under this ethic, subordination of nature would not be conceivable. Environmental pollution through nature-altering amounts of greenhouse gases for short-term gain would be impermissible.

The ecocentric ethic is, for the moment, beyond reach. International climate law positively implies its origins in an ethic of control. The law of the FCCC is committed to the 2°C target and all the risks that it entails.

132 *The philosophy of the control of nature*

Notes

1   See John McPhee (1989), *The Control of Nature*, New York: Farrar, Straus, Giroux.
2   Methmann uses the notion of 'carbon governmentality' in a similar way to my ethic of control: Chris Methmann (2013), 'The Sky is the Limit: Global Warming as Global Governmentality', 19 (1) *European Journal of International Relations* 69, pp. 81–82.
3   Rive *et al.* refer to 'the cascading uncertainty along the climate change causal chain', namely the chain of greenhouse gas emissions, radiative forcing, increased temperatures, climate change impacts, and damage: Nathan Rive *et al.* (2007), 'To What Extent Can a Long-Term Temperature Target Guide Near-Term Climate Change Commitments?', 82 (3–4) *Climatic Change* 373, p. 386.
4   Intergovernmental Panel on Climate Change (2014b), *Climate Change 2014: Mitigation of Climate Change: Contribution of Working Group III to the Fifth Assessment Report of the Intergovernmental Panel on Climate Change*, New York: Cambridge University Press, p. 1149 (*5AR WG3*).
5   UN Environment Programme (2014), *The Emissions Gap Report 2014: A UNEP Synthesis Report*, Nairobi: UNEP, p. 9.
6   Ibid., p. 9.
7   Rive *et al.*, 'Long-Term Temperature Target', p. 377 ('the targets are no more than educated guesses').
8   UN Environment Programme (2015), *The Emissions Gap Report 2015: Executive Summary*, Nairobi: UNEP, p. 3.
9   Ibid., p. 2.
10   Ibid., p. 4; and see ibid., p. 3: 'A significant number of models are not able to produce 2°C scenarios consistent with global emission levels in 2030 above 55 GtCO2e'.
11   UNEP, *Emissions Gap Report 2014*, p. 17; and UNEP, *Emissions Gap Report 2015*, p. 2.
12   UNEP, *Emissions Gap Report 2014*, p. 13.
13   IPCC, *5AR WG3*, p. 1217.
14   Jeff Tollefson (2015b), 'The 2°C Dream', 527 *Nature* 436, p. 437; and UNEP, *Emissions Gap Report 2015*, p. 3.
15   Oliver Geden (2015b), 'The Dubious Carbon Budget', *New York Times* (1 December).
16   David G. Victor (2015), 'Embed the Social Sciences in Climate Policy', 520 *Nature* 27, p. 28; and see Tollefson, 'The 2°C Dream', p. 438.
17   Oliver Geden (2015a), 'Climate Advisers Must Maintain Integrity', 521 *Nature* 27, p. 28.
18   Victor, 'Climate Policy', p. 29; and Geden, 'Climate Advisers Must Maintain Integrity', p. 28 ('The climate policy mantra—that time is running out for 2°C but we can still make it . . . is a scientific nonsense').
19   See www.worldbank.org/projects/P116410/eskom-investment-support-project?lang=en&tab=overview.
20   Kemal Derviş and Sarah Puritz Milsom (2011), 'Development Aid and Global Public Goods: The Example of Climate Protection', in *Catalyzing Development: A New Vision for Aid*, edited by Homi Kharas, Koji Makino, and Woojin Jung, Washington, DC: Brookings Institution Press, p. 169.
21   Smita Nakhooda, Charlene Watson, and Liane Schalatek (2013), *The Global Climate Finance Architecture*, Washington, DC: Heinrich Böll Stiftung, p. 2.
22   Robert L. Hicks *et al.* (2008), *Greening Aid? Understanding the Environmental Impact of Development Assistance*, New York: Oxford University Press, pp. 27, 198; see also Christa S. Clapp *et al.* (2015), 'Influence of Climate Science on Financial Decisions', 5 *Nature Climate Change* 84, p. 85.
23   James Surowiecki (2015), 'Money to Burn', *The New Yorker* (7 December), p. 28.
24   Ibid.

The philosophy of the control of nature   133

25 Michael Forsythe (2015), 'China's Emissions Pledges are Undercut by Boom in Coal Projects Abroad', *New York Times* (11 December).

26 Kiran Stacey (2015), 'UK Turns to Diesel to Meet Power Supply Crunch', *Financial Times*, https://next.ft.com/content/0f664c78–821b–11e5–8095–ed1a37d1e096.

27 The global totals for public investment in fossil-fuel production are a measure of the profits still expected from this sector: Barbara Buchner *et al.* (2013), *The Global Landscape of Climate Finance 2013*, Climate Policy Initiative, p. 34 ('public support for fossil fuel production and use outweighs public investment in low-carbon alternatives by vast amounts'); IPCC, *5AR WG3*, p. 1160 (public support for fossil-fuel subsidies exceeded $489.1 billion globally in 2008 and $469.5 billion in 2011); Standing Committee on Finance (2014a), *Biennial Assessment and Overview of Climate Finance Flows Report*, p. 55 ('The resources devoted to increasing GHG emissions . . . are almost double the global resources devoted to addressing climate change'); David Coady *et al.* (2015), *How Large are Global Energy Subsidies?*, IMF working paper, p. 6; and Michael Jakob *et al.* (2015), 'Development Incentives for Fossil Fuel Subsidy Reform', 5 *Nature Climate Change* 709, p. 709.

28 Mattia Romani and Nicholas Stern (2013), 'Sources of Finance for Climate Action: Principles and Options for Implementation Mechanisms in this Decade', in *International Climate Finance*, edited by Erik Haites, Abingdon: Routledge, p. 121; and David Coady *et al.*, *Global Energy Subsidies*, pp. 6–7.

29 Some FCCC parties (including Denmark, Finland, Iceland, Norway, Sweden, the United Kingdom, and the United States) acknowledge the problem and have promised to mend their ways; however, there is no timetable and the promises do not come under the purview of the climate change regime; see United States (2014), *United States Climate Action Report 2014*, Washington, DC: US Department of State, p. 177. Japan and Australia, by contrast, argue that their finance for certain 'high-efficiency' coal plants in developing countries (of which Japan provided $3.2 billion in 2013–2014) should be counted as climate finance: Organization for Economic Cooperation and Development and Climate Policy Initiative (2015), *Climate Finance in 2013–14 and the USD 100 Billion Goal*, Paris: OECD and CPI, p. 10.

30 Government of Norway (2013), *Norwegian Climate Finance 2012*, p. 7.

31 Annalisa Savaresi (2015), *The Legal Status and Role of Safeguards*, Research Paper Series No. 2015/24, p. 3 ('safeguards [in the aid context] are typically part of conditions imposed upon countries receiving aid, and their fulfilment is a prerequisite for the provision of funding. Safeguards are often coupled with arrangements to monitor and verify their implementation').

32 Liane Schalatek (2010), *A Matter of Principle(s): A Normative Framework for a Global Compact on Public Climate Finance*, Berlin: Heinrich Böll Foundation, p. 20.

33 Hicks *et al.*, *Greening Aid*, p. 20.

34 Ibid., p. 247.

35 Axel Michaelowa and Katharina Michaelowa (2007), 'Climate or Development: Is ODA Diverted from Its Original Purpose?', 84 *Climatic Change* 5, pp. 14–15.

36 Ibid., pp. 14–15; Philip M. Fearnside (2014b), 'Impacts of Brazil's Madeira River Dams: Unlearned Lessons for Hydroelectric Development in Amazonia', 38 *Environmental Science and Policy* 164.

37 Meera Subramanian (2012), 'An Ill Wind', 486 *Nature* 310, p. 310.

38 Carrie Lee and Michael Lazarus (2013), 'Bioenergy Projects and Sustainable Development: Which Project Types Offer the Greatest Benefits?', 5 (4) *Climate and Development* 305.

39 Massimo Tavoni and Robert Socolow (2013), 'Modeling Meets Science and Technology: An Introduction to a Special Issue on Negative Emissions', 118 (1) *Climatic Change* 1, pp. 9–10; and ibid., p. 13.

134 *The philosophy of the control of nature*

40   Herbert Docena (2010), *The Clean Development Mechanism Projects in the Philippines: Costly Dirty Money-Making Schemes*, Quezon City: Focus on the Global South, p. 33; and Carrie Mitchell and Jati Kusumowati (2013), 'Is Carbon Financing Trashing Integrated Waste Management? Experience from Indonesia', 5 (4) *Climate and Development* 268.

41   Joel B. Smith *et al.* (2013), 'Development and Climate Change Adaptation Funding: Coordination and Integration', in *International Climate Finance*, edited by Erik Haites, Abingdon: Routledge, p. 63.

42   Hicks *et al.*, *Greening Aid*, p. 26; and Standing Committee on Finance, *Biennial Assessment 2014*, p. 59.

43   UNEP, *Emissions Gap Report 2015*, p. 8.

44   J. Phelps, D. A. Friess, and E. L. Webb (2012), 'Win–Win REDD+ Approaches Belie Carbon–Biodiversity Trade-Offs', 154 *Biological Conservation* 53.

45   Michaelowa and Michaelowa, 'Climate or Development?', p. 8.

46   Praise is also found in scholarly works; e.g. Charlotte Streck (2009), 'Expectations and Reality of the Clean Development Mechanism: A Climate Finance Instrument between Accusation and Aspirations', in *Climate Finance: Regulatory and Funding Strategies for Climate Change and Global Development*, edited by Richard B. Stewart, Benedict Kingsbury, and Bryce Rudyk, New York: New York University Press, pp. 67–68 ('the Clean Development Mechanism offers a story of unprecedented success').

47   CDM Executive Board (2012b), *Benefits of the Clean Development Mechanism 2012*, p. 9.

48   Ibid., p. 8.

49   FCCC (2015), *Paris Agreement (Annex to Decision 1/CP.21)*, FCCC/CP/2015/10/Add.1, article 6(4).

50   CDM Executive Board (12 November 2015), *Annual Report*, FCCC/KP/CMP/2015/5, paras 7–9.

51   Annalisa Savaresi, *Safeguards*, p. 4.

52   Constance L. McDermott *et al.* (2012), 'Operationalizing Social Safeguards in REDD+: Actors, Interests and Ideas', 21 *Environmental Science and Policy* 63, p. 64; Ingrid J. Visseren-Hamakers *et al.* (2012), 'Trade-Offs, Co-Benefits and Safeguards: Current Debates on the Breadth of REDD+', 4 (6) *Current Opinion in Environmental Sustainability* 646, p. 647; and Savaresi, *Safeguards*, pp. 4–5.

53   Ashwini Chhatre *et al.* (2012), 'Social Safeguards and Co-Benefits in REDD+: A Review of the Adjacent Possible', 4 (6) *Current Opinion in Environmental Sustainability* 654, p. 658.

54   Axel Michaelowa (2005), 'Determination of Baselines and Additionality for the CDM: A Crucial Element of Credibility of the Climate Regime', in *Climate Change and Carbon Markets: A Handbook of Emission Reduction Mechanisms*, edited by Farhana Yamin, London: Earthscan, p. 302.

55   Axel Michaelowa and Jorund Buen (2012), 'The Clean Development Mechanism Gold Rush', in *Carbon Markets or Climate Finance? Low Carbon and Adaptation Investment Choices for the Developing World*, edited by Axel Michaelowa, Abingdon: Routledge, p. 20.

56   Fearnside, 'Unlearned Lessons', p. 164.

57   Approximately 10 per cent of global CERs have been issued to dam projects, of which there were almost 2,000 in July 2013: Philip M. Fearnside (2015), 'Tropical Hydropower in the Clean Development Mechanism: Brazil's Santo Antônio Dam as an Example of the Need for Change', 131 (4) *Climatic Change* 575, p. 576.

58   Ibid., p. 585.

59   Ibid., p. 576.

60   Ibid., p. 576.

The philosophy of the control of nature 135

61 Intergovernmental Panel on Climate Change (2013a), *Climate Change 2013: The Physical Science Basis: Working Group I Contribution to the Fifth Assessment Report of the Intergovernmental Panel on Climate Change*, New York: Cambridge University Press, p. 714.

62 Philip M. Fearnside (2013), 'Carbon Credit for Hydroelectric Dams as a Source of Greenhouse-Gas Emissions: The Example of Brazil's Teles Pires Dam', 18 (5) *Mitigation and Adaptation Strategies for Global Change* 691, p. 692.

63 Fearnside, 'Santo Antônio Dam', p. 577.

64 Ibid., p. 582.

65 Ibid., p. 582.

66 Ibid., p. 583.

67 Fearnside, 'Teles Pires Dam', p. 691.

68 Ibid., p. 692. On the CDM's 'capture' by a pro-deforestation, large-scale agribusiness, see John C. Cole and J. Timmons Roberts (2011), 'Lost Opportunities? A Comparative Assessment of Social Development Elements of Six Hydroelectricity CDM Projects in Brazil and Peru', 3 (4) *Climate and Development* 361, p. 370.

69 Fearnside, 'Santo Antônio Dam', p. 581; see also Philip M. Fearnside (2014a), 'Brazil's Madeira River Dams: A Setback for Environmental Policy in Amazonian Development', 7 (1) *Water Alternatives* 256, pp. 260–261.

70 Fearnside, 'Teles Pires Dam', p. 692.

71 Fearnside, 'Santo Antônio Dam', p. 579.

72 Ibid., p. 584.

73 The Executive Board has attempted to answer Fearnside's line of criticism: CDM Executive Board (2012b), *Benefits of the CDM 2012*, p. 53. Neither of the reasons given in this brief passage manage to refute Fearnside's carefully developed argument on the dams' lack of financial additionality.

74 Fearnside, 'Teles Pires Dam', p. 692.

75 Ibid., p. 695.

76 Doubt has recently been cast on biofuel projects, many of which also enjoy CDM registration, whose mitigation benefits can vanish when production-chain emissions are factored in. For example, it has been found that where gasoline emissions are 99 g CO_2 eq/MJ, ethanol produces 69 g CO_2 eq/MJ from fossil fuels just from the growing and refining of the crops; ethanol production leads to an additional 42 g CO_2 eq/MJ from new cropland created to maintain food production: T. Searchinger *et al.* (2015), 'Do Biofuel Policies Seek to Cut Emissions by Cutting Food?', 347 (6229) *Science* 1420, p. 1421 (table). It is another case of filling in the big picture, which unfortunately is not the way of climate finance at the moment.

77 CDM Executive Board, *Benefits of the CDM 2012*, p. 25 ('Despite the lack of precision in the definition and understanding of sustainable development, it can be concluded that the occurrence of certain claims that include environmental and social considerations . . . are almost always solely attributed to the CDM project and would not have occurred in its absence'); see also CDM Executive Board (12 November 2015), *Annual Report*, para. 66.

78 Fearnside, 'Santo Antônio Dam', p. 581.

79 Fearnside, 'Setback', pp. 264–265.

80 Fearnside, 'Santo Antônio Dam', pp. 584–585; and Fearnside, 'Unlearned Lessons', p. 167.

81 Fearnside, 'Santo Antônio Dam', p. 585; see also Cole and Roberts, 'Lost Opportunities', p. 370.

82 It would be more like the Kyoto Protocol's Joint Implementation programme than the CDM.

Bibliography

A General works

Adeyemi, Adebola (2014). 'Changing the Face of Sustainable Development in Developing Countries: The Role of the International Finance Corporation'. 16 (2) *Environmental Law Review* 91–106.

Adger, Neil W., and Andrew Jordan (2009). 'Sustainability: Exploring the Processes and Outcomes of Governance'. In *Governing Sustainability*, edited by W. Neil Adger and Andrew Jordan. Cambridge: Cambridge University Press, 3–31.

Aggarwal, Ashish (2014). 'How Sustainable are Forestry Clean Development Mechanism Projects? A Review of Selected Projects From India'. 19 (1) *Mitigation and Adaptation Strategies for Global Change* 73–91.

Aguilar, Soledad, and Eugenia Recio (2013). 'Climate Law in Latin American Countries'. In *Climate Change and the Law*, edited by Erkki J. Hollo, Kati Kulovesi, and Michael Mehling. Dordrecht: Springer, 653–678.

Aicher, Christoph (2014). 'Discourse Practices in Environmental Governance: Social and Ecological Safeguards of REDD'. 23 *Biodiversity and Conservation* 3543–3560.

Aldy, Joseph E. (2015). 'Pricing Climate Risk Mitigation'. 5 *Nature Climate Change* 396–398.

Alexeew, Johannes, Linda Bergset, Kristin Meyer, Juliane Petersen, Lambert Schneider, and Charlotte Unger (2010). 'An Analysis of the Relationship Between the Additionality of CDM Projects and their Contribution to Sustainable Development'. 10 *International Environmental Agreements* 233–248.

Andresen, Steinar (2014). 'The Climate Regime: A Few Achievements, but Many Challenges'. 4 (1–2) *Climate Law* 21–29.

Anton, Donald K. (2013) 'The "Thirty-Percent Solution" and the Future of International Environmental Law'. 10 *Santa Clara Journal of International Law* 209–219.

Arhin, Albert Abraham (2014). 'Safeguards and Dangerguards: A Framework for Unpacking the Black Box of Safeguards for REDD+'. 45 *Forest Policy and Economics* 24–31.

Audoly, Richard, Adrien Vogt-Schilb, and Céline Guivarch (2014). *Pathways Toward Zero-Carbon Electricity Required for Climate Stabilization*. World Bank, Policy Research Working Paper No. 7075.

Baker, Shalanda H. (2015). 'Project Finance and Sustainable Development in the Global South'. In *International Environmental Law and the Global South*, edited by Shawkat Alam, Sumudu Atapattu, Carmen G. Gonzalez, and Jona Razzaque. Cambridge: Cambridge University Press, 338–355.

138 *Bibliography*

Bakker, Stefan, Constanze Haug, Harro van Asselt, Joyeeta Gupta, and Raouf Saïdi (2011). 'The Future of the CDM: Same Same, But Differentiated?' 11 *Climate Policy* 752–767.

Ballesteros, Athena, Smita Nakhooda, Jacob Werksman, and Kaija Hurlburt (2010). *Power, Responsibility, and Accountability: Rethinking the Legitimacy of Institutions for Climate Finance.* World Resources Institute.

Barrett, Sam (2013). 'Local Level Climate Justice? Adaptation Finance and Vulnerability Reduction'. 23 (6) *Global Environmental Change* 1819–1829.

Benjamin, Antonio, Michael Gerrard, Toon Huydecoper, Michael Kirby, M. C. Mehta, Thomas Pogge, Qin Tianbao, Dinah Shelton, James Silk, Jessica Simor, Jaap Spier, Elisabeth Steiner, and Philip Sutherland (2015a). *Oslo Principles on Global Climate Change Obligations.* Expert Group on Global Climate Obligations. Available at www.osloprinciples.org.

Benjamin, Antonio, Michael Gerrard, Toon Huydecoper, Michael Kirby, M. C. Mehta, Thomas Pogge, Qin Tianbao, Dinah Shelton, James Silk, Jessica Simor, Jaap Spier, Elisabeth Steiner, and Philip Sutherland (2015b). *Oslo Principles on Global Climate Change Obligations: Commentary.* Expert Group on Global Climate Obligations. Available at www.osloprinciples.org.

Bernauer, Thomas, Robert Gampfer, and Florian Landis (2014). 'Burden Sharing in Global Climate Governance'. In *Toward a New Climate Agreement: Conflict, Resolution and Governance*, edited by Todd L. Cherry, Jon Hovi, and David M. McEvoy. Abingdon: Routledge, 46–60.

Birnie, Patricia W., Alan E. Boyle, and Catherine Redgwell (2009). *International Law and the Environment.* Oxford: Oxford University Press.

Bodansky, Daniel (2010). *The Art and Craft of International Environmental Law.* Cambridge, MA: Harvard University Press.

Böhringer, Christoph, and Carsten Helm (2008). 'On the Fair Division of Greenhouse Gas Abatement Cost'. 30 (2) *Resource and Energy Economics* 260–276.

Boisson de Chazournes, Laurence (2005). 'The Global Environment Facility: A Unique and Crucial Institution'. 14 (3) *Review of European Community and International Environmental Law* 193–201.

Boisson de Chazournes, Laurence (2007). 'Technical and Financial Assistance'. In *The Oxford Handbook of International Environmental Law*, edited by Daniel Bodansky, Jutta Brunnée, and Ellen Hey. Oxford: Oxford University Press, 945–973.

Borges da Cunha, Kamyla, Arnaldo Walter, and Fernando Rei (2007). 'CDM Implementation in Brazil's Rural and Isolated Regions: The Amazonian Case'. 84 (1) *Climatic Change* 111–129.

Bowen, Alex (2013). 'Raising Climate Finance to Support Developing Country Action: Some Economic Considerations'. In *International Climate Finance*, edited by Erik Haites. Abingdon: Routledge, 96–116.

Boyd, Emily, and Michael K. Goodman (2011). 'The Clean Development Mechanism as Ethical Development? Reconciling Emissions Trading and Local Development'. 23 (6) *Journal of International Development* 836–854.

Boyd, Emily, Nate Hultman, Timmons Roberts, Esteve Corbera, John Cole, Alex Bozmoski, Johannes Ebeling, Robert Tippman, Philip Mann, Katrina Brown, and Diana M. Liverman (2009). 'Reforming the CDM for Sustainable Development: Lessons Learned and Policy Futures'. 12 (7) *Environmental Science and Policy* 820–831.

Boyle, Alan E. (2005). 'Globalising Environmental Liability: The Interplay of National and International Law'. 17 (1) *Journal of Environmental Law* 3–26.

Bibliography   139

Bozmoski, Alexander, Maria Carmen Lemos, and Emily Boyd (2008). 'Prosperous Negligence: Governing the Clean Development Mechanism for Markets and Development'. 50 (3) *Environment: Science and Policy for Sustainable Development* 18–30.

Brahmbhatt, Milan, and Andrew Steer (2013). 'Mobilizing Climate Finance'. In *International Climate Finance*, edited by Erik Haites. Abingdon: Routledge, 135–150.

Brohé, Arnaud (2014). 'Whither the CDM? Investment Outcomes and Future Prospects'. 16 *Environment, Development and Sustainability* 305–322.

Brown, Katrina (2009). 'Human Development and Environmental Governance: A Reality Check'. In *Governing Sustainability*, edited by W. Neil Adger and Andrew Jordan. Cambridge: Cambridge University Press, 32–51.

Brown, Katrina, W. Neil Adger, Emily Boyd, Esteve Corbera-Elizalde, and Simon Shackley (2004). *How do CDM Projects Contribute to Sustainable Development?* Tyndall Centre for Climate Change Research.

Brown, Sandra, and Daniel Zarin (2013). 'What does Zero Deforestation Mean?' 342 *Science* 805–807.

Brunnée, Jutta, and Charlotte Streck (2013). 'The UNFCCC as a Negotiation Forum: Towards Common but More Differentiated Responsibilities'. 13 (5) *Climate Policy* 589–607.

Buchner, Barbara, Morgan Hervé-Mignucci, Chiara Trabacchi, Jane Wilkinson, Martin Stadelmann, Rodney Boyd, Federico Mazza, and Valerio Micale (2013). *The Global Landscape of Climate Finance 2013*. Climate Policy Initiative.

Buchner, Barbara, Martin Stadelmann, Jane Wilkinson, Federico Mazza, Anja Rosenberg, and Dario Abramskiehn (2014). *The Global Landscape of Climate Finance 2014*. Climate Policy Initiative.

Buckley, Chris (2015). 'China Burns Much More Coal than Reported, Complicating Climate Talks'. *New York Times* (3 November).

Cameron, Edward, Tara Shine, and Wendi Bevins (2013). *Climate Justice: Equity and Justice Informing a New Climate Agreement*. Working paper. World Resources Institute and Mary Robinson Foundation.

Caney, Simon (2005). 'Cosmopolitan Justice, Responsibility, and Global Climate Change'. 18 *Leiden Journal of International Law* 747–775.

Caney, Simon (2010). 'Climate Change and the Duties of the Advantaged'. 13 (1) *Critical Review of International Social and Political Philosophy* 203–228.

Caravani, Alice, Smita Nakhooda, Charlene Watson, Will McFarland, and Liane Schalatek (2013). *Climate Finance Thematic Briefing: REDD+ Finance*. Heinrich Böll Stiftung.

Carlarne, Cinnamon (2014). 'Delinking International Environmental Law and Climate Change'. 4 (1) *Michigan Journal of Environmental and Administrative Law* 1–60.

Chhatre, Ashwini, Shikha Lakhanpal, Anne M. Larson, Fred Nelson, Hemant Ojha, and Jagdeesh Rao (2012). 'Social Safeguards and Co-Benefits in REDD+: A Review of the Adjacent Possible'. 4 (6) *Current Opinion in Environmental Sustainability* 654–660.

Clapp, Christa S., Knut H. Alfsen, Asbjørn Torvanger, and Harald Francke Lund (2015). 'Influence of Climate Science on Financial Decisions'. 5 *Nature Climate Change* 84–85.

Clémençon, Raymond (2006). 'What Future for the Global Environment Facility?' 15 (1) *The Journal of Environment and Development* 50–74.

Clémençon, Raymond (2012). 'Welcome to the Anthropocene: Rio+20 and the Meaning of Sustainable Development'. 21 (3) *The Journal of Environment and Development* 311–338.

Coady, David, Ian Parry, Louis Sears, and Baoping Shang (2015). *How Large Are Global Energy Subsidies?* IMF Working Paper.

140 *Bibliography*

Cole, Daniel H. (2015). 'Advantages of a Polycentric Approach to Climate Change Policy'. 5 *Nature Climate Change* 114–118.

Cole, John C. (2012). 'Genesis of the CDM: The Original Policymaking Goals of the 1997 Brazilian Proposal and their Evolution in the Kyoto Protocol Negotiations into the CDM'. 12 (1) *International Environmental Agreements* 41–61.

Cole, John C., and Diana M. Liverman (2011). 'Brazil's Clean Development Mechanism Governance in the Context of Brazil's Historical Environment-Development Discourses'. 2 (2) *Carbon Management* 145–160.

Cole, John C. and J. Timmons Roberts (2011). 'Lost Opportunities? A Comparative Assessment of Social Development Elements of Six Hydroelectricity CDM Projects in Brazil and Peru'. 3 (4) *Climate and Development* 361–379.

Collier, Paul, and David Dollar (2002). 'Aid Allocation and Poverty Reduction'. 46 *European Economic Review* 1475–1500.

Commonwealth of Australia (2011). *Australia's Fast-Start Finance: Progress Report.* Canberra.

Commonwealth of Australia (2013). *Australia's Sixth National Communication on Climate Change: A Report Under the United Nations Framework Convention on Climate Change.* Canberra.

Cosbey, Aaron, Jo-Ellen Parry, Jodi Browne, Yuvaraj Dinesh Babu, Preety Bhandari, John Drexhage, and Deborah Murphy (2005). *Realizing the Development Dividend: Making the CDM Work for Developing Countries.* Winnipeg: International Institute for Sustainable Development.

Das, Dipankar, and Partha P. Sengupta (2011). 'Social Cost of Environmental Pollution and Application of Counter Measures through the Clean Development Mechanism in the Context of Developing Countries'. 13 *Environment, Development and Sustainability* 833–844.

Das, Kasturi (2011). *Technology Transfer under the Clean Development Mechanism: An Empirical Study of 1000 CDM Projects.* The Governance of Clean Development Working Paper Series No. 14. School of International Development, University of East Anglia.

Dechezleprêtre, Antoine, Matthieu Glachant, and Yann Ménière (2008). 'The Clean Development Mechanism and the International Diffusion of Technologies: An Empirical Study'. 36 (4) *Energy Policy* 1273–1283.

Dellink, Rob, Michel den Elzen, Harry Aiking, Emmy Bergsma, Frans Berkhout, Thijs Dekker, and Joyeeta Gupta (2009). 'Sharing the Burden of Financing Adaptation to Climate Change'. 19 *Global Environmental Change* 411–421.

Derviş, Kemal, and Sarah Puritz Milsom (2011). 'Development Aid and Global Public Goods: The Example of Climate Protection'. In *Catalyzing Development: A New Vision for Aid*, edited by Homi Kharas, Koji Makino, and Woojin Jung. Washington, DC: Brookings Institution Press, 155–178.

DeSombre, Elizabeth R., and Joanne Kauffman (1996). 'The Montreal Protocol Multilateral Fund: Partial Success Story'. In *Institutions for Environmental Aid: Pitfalls and Promise*, edited by Robert O. Keohane and Marc A. Levy. Cambridge, MA: MIT Press, 89–126.

Disch, David (2010). 'A Comparative Analysis of the "Development Dividend" of Clean Development Mechanism Projects in Six Host Countries'. 2 *Climate and Development* 50–64.

Docena, Herbert (2010). *The Clean Development Mechanism Projects in the Philippines: Costly Dirty Money-Making Schemes.* Quezon City: Focus on the Global South.

Doelle, Meinhard (2016). 'The Paris Agreement: Historic Breakthrough or High Stakes Experiment?' 6 (1–2) *Climate Law* 1–20.

Bibliography 141

Dubash, Navroz K. (2009). 'Climate Change and Development: A Bottom-Up Approach to Mitigation for Developing Countries?' In *Climate Finance: Regulatory and Funding Strategies for Climate Change and Global Development*, edited by Richard B. Stewart, Benedict Kingsbury, and Bryce Rudyk. New York: New York University Press, 172–178.

Eliasch, Johan (2008). *Climate Change: Financing Global Forests – The Eliasch Review*. London: Earthscan.

Ellis, Jane, Harald Winkler, Jan Corfee-Morlot, and Frédéric Gagnon-Lebrun (2007). 'CDM: Taking Stock and Looking Forward'. 35 (1) *Energy Policy* 15–28.

Energy and Resources Institute (TERI) (2012). *Assessing the Impact of the Clean Development Mechanism on Sustainable Development and Technology Transfer*. New Delhi: TERI.

EU–China CDM Facilitation Project (2009). *Assessment of the Impact of China's CDM Projects on Sustainable Development*. Policy Research Center for Environment and Economy, Ministry of Environmental Protection, China.

Falconer, Angela, and Martin Stadelmann (2014). *What is Climate Finance? Definitions to Improve Tracking and Scale Up Climate Finance*. Climate Policy Initiative.

Fearnside, Philip M. (2005). 'Do Hydroelectric Dams Mitigate Global Warming? The Case of Brazil's Curuá-Una Dam'. 10 (4) *Mitigation and Adaptation Strategies for Global Change* 675–691.

Fearnside, Philip M. (2013). 'Carbon Credit for Hydroelectric Dams as a Source of Greenhouse-Gas Emissions: The Example of Brazil's Teles Pires Dam'. 18 (5) *Mitigation and Adaptation Strategies for Global Change* 691–699.

Fearnside, Philip M. (2014a). 'Brazil's Madeira River Dams: A Setback for Environmental Policy in Amazonian Development'. 7 (1) *Water Alternatives* 256–269.

Fearnside, Philip M. (2014b). 'Impacts of Brazil's Madeira River Dams: Unlearned Lessons for Hydroelectric Development in Amazonia'. 38 *Environmental Science and Policy* 164–172.

Fearnside, Philip M. (2015). 'Tropical Hydropower in the Clean Development Mechanism: Brazil's Santo Antônio Dam as an Example of the Need for Change'. 131 (4) *Climatic Change* 575–589.

Feng, Lin, and Jason Buhi (2010–2011). 'The Copenhagen Accord and the Silent Incorporation of the Polluter Pays Principle in International Climate Law: An Analysis of Sino-American Diplomacy at Copenhagen and Beyond'. 18 *Buffalo Environmental Law Journal* 1–74.

Fenhann, Jørgen, and Miriam Hinostroza (2011). *CDM Information and Guidebook*. 3rd edition. Roskilde: UNEP Risø Centre.

Figueres, Christiana, and Charlotte Streck (2009). *Enhanced Financial Mechanisms for Post-2012 Mitigation*. World Bank, Policy Research Working Paper 5008.

Finland (2015). *Finland's Second Biennial Report under the UNFCCC*. Helsinki: Statistics Finland and Finnish Ministry of the Environment.

Fisher, Robert, and Rosemary Lyster (2013). 'Land and Resource Tenure: The Rights of Indigenous Peoples and Forest Dwellers'. In *Law, Tropical Forests and Carbon: The Case of REDD+*, edited by Rosemary Lyster, Catherine MacKenzie, and Constance McDermott. Cambridge: Cambridge University Press, 187–206.

Flournoy, Alyson C. (2003). 'In Search of an Environmental Ethic'. 28 (1) *Columbia Journal of Environmental Law* 63–118.

Forsythe, Michael (2015). 'China's Emissions Pledges are Undercut by Boom in Coal Projects Abroad'. *New York Times* (11 December).

142 Bibliography

Fransen, Taryn (2009). *Enhancing Today's MRV Framework to Meet Tomorrow's Needs: The Role of National Communications and Inventories*. Washington, DC: World Resources Institute.

Freestone, David (1994). 'The Road from Rio: International Environmental Law After the Earth Summit'. 6 (2) *Journal of Environmental Law* 193–218.

Freestone, David (2010). 'The World Bank and Sustainable Development'. In Research Handbook on International Environmental Law, edited by Malgosia Fitzmaurice, David M. Ong, and Panos Merkouris. Cheltenham: Edward Elgar, 138–160.

Friberg, Lars (2009). 'Varieties of Carbon Governance: The Clean Development Mechanism in Brazil – A Success Story Challenged'. 18 (4) *The Journal of Environment and Development* 395–424.

Gampfer, Robert (2014). 'Do Individuals Care About Fairness in Burden Sharing for Climate Change Mitigation? Evidence from a Lab Experiment'. 124 (1) *Climatic Change* 65–77.

Garnaut, Ross (2011). *The Garnaut Review 2011: Australia in the Global Response to Climate Change*. Port Melbourne, Victoria: Cambridge University Press.

Geden, Oliver (2015a). 'Climate Advisers Must Maintain Integrity'. 521 *Nature* 27–28.

Geden, Oliver (2015b). 'The Dubious Carbon Budget'. *New York Times* (1 December).

George, Clive (2007). 'Sustainable Development and Global Governance'. 16 (1) *The Journal of Environment and Development* 102–125.

Gibson, Clark C., Krister Andersson, Elinor Ostrom, and Sujai Shivakumar (2005). *The Samaritan's Dilemma: The Political Economy of Development Aid*. New York: Oxford University Press.

Gibson, Robert B. (2005). *Sustainability Assessment: Criteria and Processes*. London: Earthscan.

Gillenwater, Michael, and Stephen Seres (2011). *The Clean Development Mechanism: A Review of the First International Offset Program*. Arlington, VA: Pew Center on Global Climate Change.

Glemarec, Yannick (2011). *Catalyzing Climate Finance: A Guidebook on Policy and Financing Options to Support Green, Low-Emission and Climate-Resilient Development*. New York: UNDP.

Goldin, Ian, and Kenneth Reinert (2012). *Globalization for Development: Meeting New Challenges*. Oxford: Oxford University Press.

Goldsmith, Arthur A. (2007). 'Is Governance Reform a Catalyst for Development?' 20 (2) *Governance* 165–186.

Gomez-Echeverri, Luis (2013). 'The Changing Geopolitics of Climate Change Finance'. 13 (5) *Climate Policy* 632–648.

Government of Norway (2013). *Norwegian Climate Finance 2012*.

Government of Norway (2014). *Norway's Sixth National Communication Under the Framework Convention on Climate Change*.

Green, Jessica F., Thomas Sterner, and Gernot Wagner (2014). 'A Balance of Bottom-Up and Top-Down in Linking Climate Policies'. 4 *Nature Climate Change* 1064–1067.

Grindle, Merilee S. (2004). 'Good Enough Governance: Poverty Reduction and Reform in Developing Countries'. 17 (4) *Governance* 525–548.

Grist, Natasha (2008). 'Positioning Climate Change in Sustainable Development Discourse'. 20 *Journal of International Development* 783–803.

Group of 18 States and the European Commission Providing Bilateral Climate Finance (2015). *Joint Statement on Tracking Progress Towards the $100 billion Goal*. Paris. Available at www.state.gov/documents/organization/246878.pdf.

Bibliography 143

Guan, Dabo, Zhu Liu, Yong Geng, Sören Lindner, and Klaus Hubacek (2012). 'The Gigatonne Gap in China's Carbon Dioxide Inventories'. 2 *Nature Climate Change* 672–675.

Haites, Erik (2011). 'Climate Change Finance'. 11 (3) *Climate Policy* 963–969.

Haites, Erik, and Carol Mwape (2013). 'Sources of Long-Term Climate Change Finance'. In *International Climate Finance*, edited by Erik Haites. Abingdon: Routledge, 162–177.

Halimanjaya, Aidy, Smita Nakhooda, Sam Barnard, Alice Caravani, and Liane Schalatek (2013). *Climate Finance Thematic Briefing: Mitigation Finance*. Heinrich Böll Stiftung.

Halsnaes, Kirsten (2002). 'A Review of the Literature on Climate Change and Sustainable Development'. In *Climate Change and Sustainable Development: Prospects for Developing Countries*, edited by Anil Markandya and Kirsten Halsnaes. London: Earthscan, 49–72.

Halsnaes, Kirsten, and Priyadarshi Shukla (2008). 'Sustainable Development as a Framework for Developing Country Participation in International Climate Change Policies'. 13 (2) *Mitigation and Adaptation Strategies for Global Change* 105–130.

Hayashi, Daisuke, and Stefan Wehner (2012). 'Mobilizing Mitigation Policies in the South Through a Financing Mix'. In *Carbon Markets or Climate Finance? Low Carbon and Adaptation Investment Choices for the Developing World*, edited by Axel Michaelowa. Abingdon: Routledge, 168–187.

Headon, Sam (2009). 'Whose Sustainable Development? Sustainable Development Under the Kyoto Protocol, the "Coldplay Effect", and the CDM Gold Standard'. 20 (2) *Colorado Journal of International Environmental Law and Policy* 127–156.

Heuberger, Renat, Alan Brent, Luis Santos, Christoph Sutter, and Dieter Imboden (2007). 'CDM Projects Under the Kyoto Protocol: A Methodology for Sustainability Assessment – Experiences from South Africa and Uruguay'. 9 *Environment, Development and Sustainability* 33–48.

Heyward, Madeleine (2007). 'Equity and International Climate Change Negotiations: A Matter of Perspective'. 7 *Climate Policy* 518–534.

Hickmann, Thomas (2013). 'Private Authority in Global Climate Governance: The Case of the Clean Development Mechanism'. 5 (1) *Climate and Development* 46–54.

Hicks, Robert L., Bradley C. Parks, J. Timmons Roberts, and Michael J. Tierney (2008). *Greening Aid? Understanding the Environmental Impact of Development Assistance*. New York: Oxford University Press.

Hope, Kempe Ronald (2005). 'Toward Good Governance and Sustainable Development: The African Peer Review Mechanism'. 18 (2) *Governance* 283–311.

Horstmann, Britta (2011). 'Operationalizing the Adaptation Fund: Challenges in Allocating Funds to the Vulnerable'. 11 (4) *Climate Policy* 1086–1096.

Hugé, Jean, Hai Le Trinh, Pham Hoang Hai, Jan Kuilman, and Luc Hens (2010). 'Sustainability Indicators for Clean Development Mechanism Projects in Vietnam'. 12 *Environment, Development and Sustainability* 561–571.

Huggins, Anna (2015). 'The Desirability of Depoliticization: Compliance in the International Climate Regime'. 4 (1) *Transnational Environmental Law* 101–124.

Hultman, Nathan E., E. Boyd, J. T. Roberts, J. Cole, E. Corbera, J. Ebeling, K. Brown, D. M. Liverman (2009). 'How Can the Clean Development Mechanism Better Contribute to Sustainable Development?' 38 (2) *Ambio* 120–122.

Huq, Saleemul (2002). *Applying Sustainable Development Criteria to CDM Projects: PCF Experience*. Washington, DC: World Bank, Prototype Carbon Fund.

Intergovernmental Panel on Climate Change (2013a). *Climate Change 2013: The Physical Science Basis: Working Group I Contribution to the Fifth Assessment Report of the Intergovernmental Panel on Climate Change*. New York: Cambridge University Press.

144 *Bibliography*

Intergovernmental Panel on Climate Change (2013b). *Climate Change 2013: The Physical Science Basis: Working Group I Contribution to the Fifth Assessment Report of the Intergovernmental Panel on Climate Change: Summary for Policymakers.* New York: Cambridge University Press

Intergovernmental Panel on Climate Change (2014a). *Climate Change 2014: Impacts, Adaptation, and Vulnerability: Working Group II Contribution to the Fifth Assessment Report of the Intergovernmental Panel on Climate Change: Summary for Policymakers.* New York: Cambridge University Press

Intergovernmental Panel on Climate Change (2014b). *Climate Change 2014: Mitigation of Climate Change: Contribution of Working Group III to the Fifth Assessment Report of the Intergovernmental Panel on Climate Change.* New York: Cambridge University Press.

Intergovernmental Panel on Climate Change (2014c). *Climate Change 2014: Mitigation of Climate Change: Working Group III Contribution to the Fifth Assessment Report of the Intergovernmental Panel on Climate Change: Summary for Policymakers.* New York: Cambridge University Press

Jabareen, Yosef (2008). 'A New Conceptual Framework for Sustainable Development'. 10 *Environment, Development and Sustainability* 179–192.

Jakob, Michael, Claudine Chen, Sabine Fuss, Annika Marxen, and Ottmar Edenhofer (2015). 'Development Incentives for Fossil Fuel Subsidy Reform'. 5 *Nature Climate Change* 709–712.

Jia, Ruiyue, Xiumei Guo, and Dora Marinova (2013). 'The Role of the Clean Development Mechanism in Achieving China's Goal of a Resource-Efficient and Environmentally Friendly Society'. 15 *Environment, Development and Sustainability* 133–148.

Kallbekken, Steffen, Håkon Sælen, and Arild Underdal (2014). *Equity and Spectrum of Mitigation Commitments in the 2015 Agreement.* Copenhagen: Nordic Council of Ministers.

Karani, Patrick, and Mandla Gantsho (2007). 'The Role of Development Finance Institutions in Promoting the Clean Development Mechanism in Africa'. 9 *Environment, Development and Sustainability* 203–228.

Kaufmann, Daniel, Aart Kraay, and Pablo Zoido-Lobatón (2000). 'Governance Matters: From Measurement to Action'. 37 (2) *Finance and Development* 10–13.

Khatun, Kaysara, Paul J. Valdes, Wolfgang Knorr, and Monowar Alam Khalid (2010). 'Exploring Synergies Between the Clean Development Mechanism and National Forest Policies in India to Advance Sustainable Development for a Post-2012 Climate Policy'. 2 (3) *Climate and Development* 207–220.

Kidd, Michael, and Ed Couzens (2013). 'Climate Change Responses in South Africa'. In *Climate Change and the Law*, edited by Erkki J. Hollo, Kati Kulovesi, and Michael Mehling. Dordrecht: Springer, 619–638.

Kim, Joy A. (2004). 'Sustainable Development and the Clean Development Mechanism: A South African Case Study'. 13 (3) *The Journal of Environment and Development* 201–219.

Kim, Joy A., Jane Ellis, and Sara Moarif (2009). *Matching Mitigation Actions with Support: Key Issues for Channelling International Public Finance.* OECD and IEA.

Kim, Jung Eun, David Popp, and Andrew Prag (2013). 'The Clean Development Mechanism and Neglected Environmental Technologies'. 55 *Energy Policy* 165–179.

Kishor, Nalin, and Arati Belle (2004). 'Does Improved Governance Contribute to Sustainable Forest Management?' 19 (1–3) *Journal of Sustainable Forestry* 55–79.

Klinsky, Sonja, and Hadi Dowlatabadi (2009). 'Conceptualizations of Justice in Climate Policy'. 9 (1) *Climate Policy* 88–108.

Bibliography 145

Krause, Torsten, and Tobias Dan Nielsen (2014). 'The Legitimacy of Incentive-Based Conservation and a Critical Account of Social Safeguards'. 41 *Environmental Science and Policy* 44–51.

Krey, Matthias, and Heike Santen (2009). 'Trying to Catch Up with the Executive Board: Regulatory Decision-Making and its Impact on CDM Performance'. In *Legal Aspects of Carbon Trading*, edited by David Freestone and Charlotte Streck. New York: Oxford University Press, 231–247.

Kumar, Sanjay (2015). 'Green Climate Fund Faces Slew of Criticism'. 527 *Nature* 419–420.

Lange, Andreas, Andreas Löschel, Carsten Vogt, and Andreas Ziegler (2010). 'On the Self-Interested Use of Equity in International Climate Negotiations'. 54 *European Economic Review* 359–375.

Lee, Carrie, and Michael Lazarus (2011). *Bioenergy Projects and Sustainable Development: Which Project Types Offer the Greatest Benefits?* Stockholm: Stockholm Environment Institute.

Lee, Carrie, and Michael Lazarus (2013). 'Bioenergy Projects and Sustainable Development: Which Project Types Offer the Greatest Benefits?' 5 (4) *Climate and Development* 305–317.

Lee, Yong-Shik (2006) *Reclaiming Development in the World Trading System*. Cambridge: Cambridge University Press.

Lewis, Simon L., and Mark A. Maslin (2015). 'Defining the Anthropocene'. 519 *Nature* 171–180.

Lin, Jolene (2014). 'Litigating Climate Change in Asia'. 4 (1) *Climate Law* 140–149.

Lin, Jolene, and Charlotte Streck (2009). 'Mobilising Finance for Climate Change Mitigation: Private Sector Involvement in International Carbon Finance Mechanisms'. 10 (1) *Melbourne Journal of International Law* 70–101.

Lowe, Vaughan (1999). 'Sustainable Development and Unsustainable Arguments'. In *International Law and Sustainable Development*, edited by Alan Boyle and David Freestone. Oxford: Oxford University Press, 19–37.

Ludwinski, Daniel, Kent Moriarty, and Bruce Wydick (2011). 'Environmental and Health Impacts from the Introduction of Improved Wood Stoves: Evidence From a Field Experiment in Guatemala'. 13 *Environment, Development and Sustainability* 657–676.

Lund, Emma (2010). 'Dysfunctional Delegation: Why the Design of the CDM's Supervisory System is Fundamentally Flawed'. 10 *Climate Policy* 277–288.

Luppi, Barbara, Francesco Parisi, and Shruti Rajagopalan (2012). 'The Rise and Fall of the Polluter-Pays Principle in Developing Countries'. 32 *International Review of Law and Economics* 135–144.

Lütken, Søren Ender, and Axel Michaelowa (2008). *Corporate Strategies and the Clean Development Mechanism: Developing-Country Financing for Developed-Country Commitments?* Cheltenham: Edward Elgar.

Mace, M. J. (2005). 'Funding for Adaptation to Climate Change: UNFCCC and GEF Developments since COP-7'. 14 (3) *Review of European Community and International Environmental Law* 225–246.

Machado-Filho, Haroldo (2012). 'Financial Mechanisms Under the Climate Regime'. In *Promoting Compliance in an Evolving Climate Regime*, edited by Jutta Brunnée, Meinhard Doelle, and Lavanya Rajamani. Cambridge: Cambridge University Press, 216–239.

Machado-Filho, Haroldo (2013). 'Climate Change Policy and Legislation in Brazil'. In *Climate Change and the Law*, edited by Erkki J. Hollo, Kati Kulovesi, and Michael Mehling. Dordrecht: Springer, 639–651.

146 *Bibliography*

MacKay, David J. C., Peter Cramton, Axel Ockenfels, and Steven Stoft (2015). 'Price Carbon: I Will if You Will'. 526 *Nature* 315–316.

Magraw, Daniel Barstow, and Lisa D. Hawke (2007). 'Sustainable Development'. In *The Oxford Handbook of International Environmental Law*, edited by Daniel Bodansky, Jutta Brunnée, and Ellen Hey. Oxford: Oxford University Press, 613–638.

Mamlyuk, Boris N. (2009). 'Analyzing the Polluter Pays Principle Through Law and Economics'. 18 (1) *Southeastern Environmental Law Journal* 39–79.

Matthews, Robin B., Meine van Noordwijk, Eric Lambin, Patrick Meyfroidt, Joyeeta Gupta, Louis Verchot, Kristell Hergoualc'h, and Edzo Veldkamp (2014). 'Implementing REDD: Evidence on Governance, Evaluation and Impacts from the REDD-ALERT Project'. 19 (6) *Mitigation and Adaptation Strategies for Global Change* 907–925.

Matz, Nele (2002). 'Environmental Financing: Function and Coherence of Financial Mechanisms in International Environmental Agreements'. 6 *Max Planck Yearbook of United Nations Law* 473–534.

Matz, Nele (2005). 'Financial Institutions Between Effectiveness and Legitimacy: A Legal Analysis of the World Bank, Global Environment Facility and Prototype Carbon Fund'. 5 *International Environmental Agreements* 265–302.

May, Peter H., Emily Boyd, Fernando Veiga, and Manyu Chang (2004). *Local Sustainable Development Effects of Forest Carbon Projects in Brazil and Bolivia: A View From the Field*. London: International Institute for Environment and Development.

Mayer, Benoit (2014). 'State Responsibility and Climate Change Governance: A Light through the Storm'. 13 *Chinese Journal of International Law* 539–575.

Mayer, Benoit (2015a). 'Conceiving the Rationale for International Climate Law'. 130 (3) *Climatic Change* 371–382.

Mayer, Benoit (2015b). 'The Applicability of the Principle of Prevention to Climate Change: A Response to Zahar'. 5 (1) *Climate Law* 1–24.

McDermott, Constance L., Lauren Coad, Ariella Helfgott, and Heike Schroeder (2012). 'Operationalizing Social Safeguards in REDD+: Actors, Interests and Ideas'. 21 *Environmental Science and Policy* 63–72.

McGee, Jeffrey, and Jens Steffek (2016). 'The Copenhagen Turn in Global Climate Governance and the Contentious History of Differentiation in International Law'. 28 *Journal of Environmental Law* 37–63.

McNutt, Marcia (2015). 'The Beyond-Two-Degree Inferno'. 349 (6243) *Science* 7.

McPhee, John (1989). *The Control of Nature*. New York: Farrar, Straus, Giroux.

Mee, Laurence D., Holly T. Dublin, and Anton A. Eberhard (2008). 'Evaluating the Global Environment Facility: A Goodwill Gesture or a Serious Attempt to Deliver Global Benefits?' 18 (4) *Global Environmental Change* 800–810.

Methmann, Chris (2013). 'The Sky is the Limit: Global Warming as Global Governmentality'. 19 (1) *European Journal of International Relations* 69–91.

Metz, Bert, Marcel Berk, Michel den Elzen, Bert de Vries, and Detlef van Vuuren (2002). 'Towards an Equitable Global Climate Change Regime: Compatibility with Article 2 of the Climate Change Convention and the Link with Sustainable Development'. 2 *Climate Policy* 211–230.

Meyer, Lukas H., and Dominic Roser (2010). 'Climate Justice and Historical Emissions'. 13 (1) *Critical Review of International Social and Political Philosophy* 229–253.

Meyer, Timothy (2014). 'From Contract to Legislation: The Logic of Modern International Lawmaking'. 14 (2) *Chicago Journal of International Law* 559–624.

Meyers, Stephen (1999). *Additionality of Emissions Reductions from Clean Development Mechanism Projects: Issues and Options for Project-Level Assessment*. Lawrence Berkeley National Laboratory, Research Paper LBNL-43704.

Bibliography 147

Michaelowa, Axel (2003). 'CDM Host Country Institution Building'. 8 *Mitigation and Adaptation Strategies for Global Change* 201–220.

Michaelowa, Axel (2005). 'Determination of Baselines and Additionality for the CDM: A Crucial Element of Credibility of the Climate Regime'. In *Climate Change and Carbon Markets: A Handbook of Emission Reduction Mechanisms*, edited by Farhana Yamin. London: Earthscan, 289–303.

Michaelowa, Axel (2012). 'Manoeuvring Climate Finance Around the Pitfalls: Finding the Right Policy Mix'. In *Carbon Markets or Climate Finance? Low Carbon and Adaptation Investment Choices for the Developing World*, edited by Axel Michaelowa. Abingdon: Routledge, 255–265.

Michaelowa, Axel, and Jorund Buen (2012). 'The Clean Development Mechanism Gold Rush'. In *Carbon Markets or Climate Finance? Low Carbon and Adaptation Investment Choices for the Developing World*, edited by Axel Michaelowa. Abingdon: Routledge, 1–38.

Michaelowa, Axel, and Katharina Michaelowa (2007). 'Climate or Development: Is ODA Diverted from its Original Purpose?' 84 *Climatic Change* 5–21.

Michaelowa, Axel, and Pallav Purohit (2007). *Additionality Determination of Indian CDM Projects: Can Indian CDM Project Developers Outwit the CDM Executive Board?* University of Zurich, Institute for Political Science, Discussion Paper CDM-1.

Mickwitz, Per (2003). 'A Framework for Evaluating Environmental Policy Instruments'. 9 (4) *Evaluation* 415–436.

Miller, Mark (2012). *Climate Public Expenditure and Institutional Reviews in the Asia-Pacific Region: What Have We Learnt?* Bangkok: UNDP.

Miller, Russell A. (2006). 'Surprising Parallels Between *Trail Smelter* and the Global Climate Change Regime'. In *Transboundary Harm in International Law: Lessons from the Trail Smelter Arbitration*, edited by Rebecca M. Bratspies and Russell A. Miller. Cambridge: Cambridge University Press, 167–180.

Mitchell, Carrie, and Jati Kusumowati (2013). 'Is Carbon Financing Trashing Integrated Waste Management? Experience from Indonesia'. 5 (4) *Climate and Development* 268–276.

Müller, Benito (2001). 'Varieties of Distributive Justice in Climate Change'. 48 (2) *Climatic Change* 273–288.

Müller, Benito, Niklas Höhne, and Christian Ellermann (2009). 'Differentiating (Historic) Responsibilities for Climate Change'. 9 (6) *Climate Policy* 593–611.

Multilateral Development Bank Group (2015). *2014 Joint Report on Multilateral Development Banks' Climate Finance.* Available at: www.worldbank.org/climate/MDB climatefinance2014.

Murase, Shinya, et al. (2014). *Legal Principles Relating to Climate Change: Report and Draft Declaration for Consideration at the 2014 Washington Conference.* London: International Law Association.

Murdiyarso, Daniel, Maria Brockhaus, William D. Sunderlin, and Lou Verchot (2012). 'Some Lessons Learned from the First Generation of REDD+ Activities'. 4 *Current Opinion in Environmental Sustainability* 678–685.

Nachmany, Michal, Sam Fankhauser, Terry Townshend, Murray Collins, Tucker Landesman, Adam Matthews, Carolina Pavese, Katharina Rietig, Philip Schleifer, and Joana Setzer (2014). *The GLOBE Climate Legislation Study: A Review of Climate Change Legislation in 66 Countries*, 4th edition. London: GLOBE International and Grantham Research Institute.

148 *Bibliography*

Nagle, John Copeland (2009). 'Discounting China's CDM Dams'. 7 (1) *Loyola University Chicago International Law Review* 9–30.

Nagle, John Copeland (2010). 'Climate Exceptionalism'. 40 *Environmental Law* 53–88.

Nakhooda, Smita (2013). *The Effectiveness of Climate Finance: A Review of the Global Environment Facility*. London: Overseas Development Institute.

Nakhooda, Smita, and Marigold Norman (2014). *Climate Finance: Is it Making a Difference? A Review of the Effectiveness of Multilateral Climate Funds*. London: Overseas Development Institute.

Nakhooda, Smita, Taryn Fransen, Takeshi Kuramochi, Alice Caravani, Annalisa Prizzon, Noriko Shimizu, Helen Tilley, Aidy Halimanjaya, and Bryn Welham (2013). *Mobilising International Climate Finance: Lessons from the Fast-Start Finance Period*. Washington, DC: World Resources Institute.

Narain, Urvashi, Sergio Margulis, and Timothy Essam (2013). 'Estimating Costs of Adaptation to Climate Change'. In *International Climate Finance*, edited by Erik Haites. Abingdon: Routledge, 72–95.

Nash, Jonathan Remy (2000). 'Too Much Market? Conflict Between Tradable Pollution Allowances and the "Polluter Pays" Principle'. 24 *Harvard Environmental Law Review* 466–535.

Neeff, Till, and Francisco Ascui (2009). 'Lessons from Carbon Markets for Designing an Effective REDD Architecture'. 9 *Climate Policy* 306–315.

Neeff, Till, Daniela Göhler, and Francisco Ascui (2014). 'Finding a Path for REDD+ Between ODA and the CDM'. 14 (2) *Climate Policy* 149–166.

Neilson, Jeff, and Beria Leimona (2013). 'Payments for Ecosystem Services and Environmental Governance in Indonesia'. In *Law, Tropical Forests and Carbon: The Case of REDD+*, edited by Rosemary Lyster, Catherine MacKenzie, and Constance McDermott. Cambridge: Cambridge University Press, 207–229.

Neuhoff, Karsten, Sam Fankhauser, Emmanuel Guerin, Jean-Charles Hourcade, Helen Jackson, Ranjita Rajan, and John Ward (2009). *Structuring International Financial Support to Support Domestic Climate Change Mitigation in Developing Countries*. Cambridge: Climate Strategies.

Newell, Peter, Nicky Jenner, and Lucy Baker (2009). 'Governing Clean Development: A Framework for Analysis'. 27 (6) *Development Policy Review* 717–739.

Nguyen, Nhan T., Minh Ha-Duong, Sandra Greiner, and Michael Mehling (2010). 'Improving the Clean Development Mechanism Post-2012: A Developing Country Perspective'. 1 (1) *Carbon and Climate Law Review* 76–85.

NOAA National Climatic Data Center (2015). *State of the Climate: Global Analysis for March 2015*. Available from www.ncdc.noaa.gov/sotc/global/2015/3.

Nordhaus, William D. (2015a). 'A New Solution: The Climate Club'. 62 (10) *The New York Review of Books* 36–39.

Nordhaus, William D. (2015b). 'The Pope and the Market'. 62 (15) *The New York Review of Books* 26–27.

Nussbaumer, Patrick (2009). 'On the Contribution of Labelled Certified Emission Reductions to Sustainable Development: A Multi-Criteria Evaluation of CDM Projects'. 37 (1) *Energy Policy* 91–101.

Olbrisch, Susanne, Erik Haites, Matthew Savage, Pradeep Dadhich, and Manish Kumar Shrivastava (2013). 'Estimates of Incremental Investment for, and Cost of, Mitigation Measures in Developing Countries'. In *International Climate Finance*, edited by Erik Haites. Abingdon: Routledge, 32–53.

Bibliography 149

Olsen, Karen Holm (2007). 'The Clean Development Mechanism's Contribution to Sustainable Development: A Review of the Literature'. 84 *Climatic Change* 59–73.

Olsen, Karen Holm, and Jørgen Fenhann (2008). 'Sustainable Development Benefits of Clean Development Mechanism Projects: A New Methodology for Sustainability Assessment Based on Text Analysis of the Project Design Documents Submitted for Validation'. 36 (8) *Energy Policy* 2819–2830.

Organization for Economic Cooperation and Development (1992). *The Polluter-Pays Principle: OECD Analyses and Recommendations*. Paris: OECD.

Organization for Economic Cooperation and Development and Climate Policy Initiative (2015). *Climate Finance in 2013–14 and the USD 100 Billion Goal*. Paris: OECD and CPI.

Page, Edward A. (2008). 'Distributing the Burdens of Climate Change'. 17 (4) *Environmental Politics* 556–575.

Pallemaerts, Marc (2003a). 'International Law and Sustainable Development: Any Progress in Johannesburg?' 12 (1) *Review of European Community and International Environmental Law* 1–11.

Pallemaerts, Marc (2003b). 'Is Multilateralism the Future? Sustainable Development or Globalisation as "A Comprehensive Vision of the Future of Humanity"'. 5 (1–2) *Environment, Development and Sustainability* 275–295.

Palmujoki, Eero (2006). 'Public–Private Governance Patterns and Environmental Sustainability'. 8 *Environment, Development and Sustainability* 1–17.

Parry, Martin (2009). 'Climate Change is a Development Issue, and Only Sustainable Development Can Confront the Challenge'. 1 (1) *Climate and Development* 5–9.

Paulsson, Emma (2009). 'A Review of the CDM Literature: From Fine-Tuning to Critical Scrutiny?' 9 (1) *International Environmental Agreements* 63–80.

Peskett, Leo (2013). 'REDD+ and Development'. In *Law, Tropical Forests and Carbon: The Case of REDD+*, edited by Rosemary Lyster, Catherine MacKenzie, and Constance McDermott. Cambridge: Cambridge University Press, 230–250.

Pettit, Marguerite (2012). 'Reducing Emissions from Deforestation and Degradation: Human Rights and the Commodification of Carbon'. 14 (1–2) *Asia-Pacific Journal of Environmental Law* 87–103.

Phelps, J., D. A. Friess, and E. L. Webb (2012). 'Win–Win REDD+ Approaches Belie Carbon–Biodiversity Trade-Offs'. 154 *Biological Conservation* 53–60.

Pittock, Jamie (2010), 'A Pale Reflection of Political Reality: Integration of Global Climate, Wetland, and Biodiversity Agreements'. 1 (3) *Climate Law* 343–373.

Polycarp, Clifford, Louise Brown, and Xing Fu-Bertaux (2013). *Mobilizing Climate Investment: The Role of International Climate Finance in Creating Readiness for Scaled-up Low-Carbon Energy*. Washington, DC: World Resources Institute.

Purdon, Mark (2010). 'The Clean Development Mechanism and Community Forests in Sub-Saharan Africa: Reconsidering Kyoto's "Moral Position" on Biocarbon Sinks in the Carbon Market'. 12 *Environment, Development and Sustainability* 1025–1050.

Qin Tianbao and Zhou Chen (2015). 'Introduction'. In *Research Handbook on Chinese Environmental Law*, edited by Qin Tianbao. Cheltenham: Edward Elgar, 1–22.

Rastogi, Patodia (2013). 'India's Evolving Climate Change Strategy'. In *Climate Change and the Law*, edited by Erkki J. Hollo, Kati Kulovesi, and Michael Mehling. Dordrecht: Springer, 605–618.

Richardson, Benjamin J. (2009). 'Climate Finance and its Governance: Moving to a Low Carbon Economy Through Socially Responsible Financing?' 58 *International and Comparative Law Quarterly* 597–626.

150 Bibliography

Ringius, Lasse, Asbjørn Torvanger, and Arild Underdal (2002). 'Burden Sharing and Fairness Principles in International Climate Policy'. 2 *International Environmental Agreements* 1–22.

Rive, Nathan, Asbjørn Torvanger, Terje Berntsen, and Steffen Kallbekken (2007). 'To What Extent can a Long-Term Temperature Target Guide Near-Term Climate Change Commitments?' 82 (3–4) *Climatic Change* 373–391.

Rivera-Batiz, Francisco L. (2002). 'Democracy, Governance, and Economic Growth: Theory and Evidence'. 6 (2) *Review of Development Economics* 225–247.

Romani, Mattia, and Nicholas Stern (2013). 'Sources of Finance for Climate Action: Principles and Options for Implementation Mechanisms in this Decade'. In *International Climate Finance*, edited by Erik Haites. Abingdon: Routledge, 117–134.

Romijn, Erika, Martin Herold, Lammert Kooistra, Daniel Murdiyarso, and Louis Verchot (2012). 'Assessing Capacities of Non-Annex I Countries for National Forest Monitoring in the Context of REDD+'. 19–20 *Environmental Science and Policy* 33–48.

Rosenberg, Anja, and Jane Wilkinson (2013). *Demonstrating Approaches to REDD+ Lessons from the Kalimantan Forests and Climate Partnership*. Climate Policy Initiative.

Sands, Philippe, and Jacqueline Peel (2012). *Principles of International Environmental Law*, 3rd edition. Cambridge: Cambridge University Press.

Sanwal, Mukul (2012). 'Rio+20, Climate Change and Development: The Evolution of Sustainable Development (1972–2012)'. 4 (2) *Climate and Development* 157–166.

Savaresi, Annalisa (2015). *The Legal Status and Role of Safeguards*. University of Edinburgh, School of Law. Research Paper Series No. 2015/24.

Schalatek, Liane (2010). *A Matter of Principle(s): A Normative Framework for a Global Compact on Public Climate Finance*. Berlin: Heinrich Böll Stiftung.

Schalatek, Liane, and Neil Bird (2013). *The Principles and Criteria of Public Climate Finance: A Normative Framework*. Washington, DC: Heinrich Böll Stiftung.

Schalatek, Liane, and Smita Nakhooda (2013). *The Green Climate Fund*. Washington, DC: Heinrich Böll Stiftung.

Schneider, Lambert (2007). *Is the CDM Fulfilling its Environmental and Sustainable Development Objectives? An Evaluation of the CDM and Options for Improvement*. Freiburg: Öko-Institut.

Schneider, Lambert (2009). 'Assessing the Additionality of CDM Projects: Practical Experience and Lessons Learned'. 9 *Climate Policy* 242–254.

Schneider, Lambert (2011). 'Perverse Incentives Under the CDM: An Evaluation of HFC-23 Destruction Projects'. 11 *Climate Policy* 851–864.

Searchinger, T., R. Edwards, D. Mulligan, R. Heimlich, and R. Plevin (2015). 'Do Biofuel Policies Seek to Cut Emissions by Cutting Food?' 347 (6229) *Science* 1420–1422.

Shelton, Dinah (2007). 'Equity'. In *The Oxford Handbook of International Environmental Law*, edited by Daniel Bodansky, Jutta Brunnée, and Ellen Hey. Oxford: Oxford University Press, 639–662.

Sirohi, Smita (2007). 'CDM: Is it a "Win–Win" Strategy for Rural Poverty Alleviation in India?' 84 *Climatic Change* 91–110.

Smith, Joel B., Thea Dickinson, Joseph D. B. Donahue, Ian Burton, Erik Haites, Richard J. T. Klein, and Anand Patwardhan (2013). 'Development and Climate Change Adaptation Funding: Coordination and Integration'. In *International Climate Finance*, edited by Erik Haites. Abingdon: Routledge, 54–71.

Soltau, Friedrich (2009). *Fairness in International Climate Change Law and Policy*. Cambridge: Cambridge University Press.

Bibliography 151

Spalding-Fecher, Randall, Amrita Narayan Achanta, Pete Erickson, Erik Haites, Michael Lazarus, Neha Pahuja, Nimisha Pandey, Stephen Seres, and Ritika Tewari (2012). *Assessing the Impact of the Clean Development Mechanism (Report Commissioned by the High-Level Panel on the CDM Policy Dialogue)*. UNFCCC.

Spratt, Stephen (2009). *Development Finance: Debates, Dogmas and New Directions*. Abingdon: Routledge.

Stadelmann, Martin, Jessica Brown, and Lena Hörnlein (2012). 'Fast-Start Finance: Scattered Governance, Information and Programmes'. In *Carbon Markets or Climate Finance? Low Carbon and Adaptation Investment Choices for the Developing World*, edited by Axel Michaelowa. Abingdon: Routledge, 117–145.

Stern, Nicholas (2007). *Stern Review Report on the Economics of Climate Change*. UK Treasury.

Stewart, Richard B., Benedict Kingsbury, and Bryce Rudyk (2009). 'Climate Finance for Limiting Emissions and Promoting Green Development'. In *Climate Finance: Regulatory and Funding Strategies for Climate Change and Global Development*, edited by Richard B. Stewart, Benedict Kingsbury, and Bryce Rudyk. New York: New York University Press, 3–34.

Streck, Charlotte (2001). 'The Global Environment Facility: A Role Model for International Governance?' 1 *Global Environmental Politics* 71–94.

Streck, Charlotte (2006). 'Financial Instruments and Cooperation in Implementing Agreements for the Global Environment'. In *Multilevel Governance of Global Environmental Change: Perspectives from Science, Sociology and the Law*, edited by Gerd Winter. Cambridge: Cambridge University Press, 493–516.

Streck, Charlotte (2007). 'The Governance of the Clean Development Mechanism: The Case for Strength and Stability'. 15 (2) *Environmental Liability* 91–100.

Streck, Charlotte (2009). 'Expectations and Reality of the Clean Development Mechanism: A Climate Finance Instrument Between Accusation and Aspirations'. In *Climate Finance: Regulatory and Funding Strategies for Climate Change and Global Development*, edited by Richard B. Stewart, Benedict Kingsbury, and Bryce Rudyk. New York: New York University Press, 67–75.

Streck, Charlotte (2011). 'Ensuring New Finance and Real Emission Reduction: A Critical Review of the Additionality Concept'. 5 (2) *Carbon and Climate Law Review* 158–168.

Streck, Charlotte (2013). 'The Financial Aspects of REDD+: Assessing Costs, Mobilizing and Disbursing Funds'. In *Law, Tropical Forests and Carbon: The Case of REDD+*, edited by Rosemary Lyster, Catherine MacKenzie, and Constance McDermott. Cambridge: Cambridge University Press, 105–127.

Streck, Charlotte, and John Costenbader (2012). *Standards for Results-Based REDD+ Finance: Overview and Design Parameters*. Climate Focus.

Streck, Charlotte, and Charlie Parker (2012). 'Financing REDD+'. In *Analysing REDD+: Challenges and Choices*, edited by Arild Angelsen, Maria Brockhaus, William D. Sunderlin, and Louis V. Verchot. Center for International Forestry Research, 111–127.

Subbarao, Srikanth, and Bob Lloyd (2011). 'Can the Clean Development Mechanism Deliver?' 39 (3) *Energy Policy* 1600–1611.

Subramanian, Meera (2012). 'An Ill Wind'. 486 *Nature* 310–311.

Sugiyama, Taishi, and Axel Michaelowa (2001). 'Reconciling the Design of CDM with Inborn Paradox of Additionality Concept'. 1 (1) *Climate Policy* 75–83.

Sullivan, Sian (2013). 'Banking Nature? The Spectacular Financialisation of Environmental Conservation'. 45 (1) *Antipode* 198–217.

Surowiecki, James (2015). 'Money to Burn'. *The New Yorker* (7 December).

152   Bibliography

Sutter, Christoph, and Juan Carlos Parreño (2007). 'Does the Current Clean Development Mechanism Deliver its Sustainable Development Claim? An Analysis of Officially Registered CDM Projects'. 84 *Climatic Change* 75–90.

Tatrallyay, Nicholas, and Martin Stadelmann (2013). 'Climate Change Mitigation and International Finance: The Effectiveness of the Clean Development Mechanism and the Global Environment Facility in India and Brazil'. 18 (7) *Mitigation and Adaptation Strategies for Global Change* 903–919.

Tavoni, Massimo, and Robert Socolow (2013). 'Modeling Meets Science and Technology: An Introduction to a Special Issue on Negative Emissions'. 118 (1) *Climatic Change* 1–14.

Timilsina, Govinda R., Christophe de Gouvello, Massamba Thioye, and Felix B. Dayo (2010). 'Clean Development Mechanism Potential and Challenges in Sub-Saharan Africa'. 15 (1) *Mitigation and Adaptation Strategies for Global Change* 93–111.

Tollefson, Jeff (2015a). 'Fossil-Fuel Divestment Campaign Hits Resistance'. 521 *Nature* 16–17.

Tollefson, Jeff (2015b). 'The 2°C Dream'. 527 *Nature* 436–438.

Tonami, Aki, and Akihisa Mori (2007). 'Sustainable Development in Thailand: Lessons from Implementing Local Agenda 21 in Three Cities'. 16 (3) *The Journal of Environment and Development* 269–289.

Torvanger, Asbjørn, Manish Kumar Shrivastava, Nimisha Pandey, and Silje H. Tørnblad (2013). 'A Two-Track CDM: Improved Incentives for Sustainable Development and Offset Production'. 13 (4) *Climate Policy* 471–489.

Tung, Christopher (2013). 'Sustainable Development and Climate Policy and Law in China'. In *Climate Change and the Law*, edited by Erkki J. Hollo, Kati Kulovesi, and Michael Mehling. Dordrecht: Springer, 597–603.

Ulfstein, Geir, and Christina Voigt (2014). 'Rethinking the Legal Form and Principles of a New Climate Agreement'. In *Toward a New Climate Agreement: Conflict, Resolution and Governance*, edited by Todd L. Cherry, Jon Hovi, and David M. McEvoy. Abingdon: Routledge, 183–198.

UN Environment Programme (2013). *The Emissions Gap Report 2013: A UNEP Synthesis Report*. Nairobi: UNEP.

UN Environment Programme (2014). *The Emissions Gap Report 2014: A UNEP Synthesis Report*. Nairobi: UNEP.

UN Environment Programme (2016). *The Adaptation Finance Gap Report 2016*. Nairobi: UNEP.

United States (2011). *Meeting the Fast Start Commitment: US Climate Finance in Fiscal Year 2011*. Washington, DC: US Department of State.

United States (2014). *United States Climate Action Report 2014*. Washington, DC: US Department of State.

United States (2016). *Second Biennial Report of the United States of America Under the United Nations Framework Convention on Climate Change*. Washington, DC: US Department of State.

van Asselt, Harro, Michael Mehling, and Clarisse Kehler Siebert (2015). 'The Changing Architecture of International Climate Change Law'. In *Research Handbook on Climate Change Mitigation Law*, edited by Geert van Calster, Wim Vandenberghe, and Leonie Reins. Cheltenham: Edward Elgar, 1–30.

van Klink, Bart (2008). 'Can There be Law Without the State? The Ehrlich–Kelsen Debate Revisited in a Globalizing Setting'. In *International Governance and Law: State Regulation and Non-State Law*, edited by Hanneke van Schooten and Jonathan Verschuuren. Cheltenham: Edward Elgar, 74–93.

Bibliography   153

van Melle, Timme, Niklas Höhne, and Murray Ward (2011). *International Climate Financing: From Cancun to a 2°C Stabilisation Pathway*. Utrecht: Ecofys.

van Renssen, Sonja (2015). 'Coal Resists Pressure'. 5 *Nature Climate Change* 96–97.

van Vliet, Oscar, André Faaij, and Carel Dieperink (2003). 'Forestry Projects Under the Clean Development Mechanism?' 61 *Climatic Change* 123–156.

Verschuuren, Jonathan (ed.) (2013). *Research Handbook on Climate Change Adaptation Law*. Cheltenham: Edward Elgar.

Victor, David G. (2015). 'Embed the Social Sciences in Climate Policy'. 520 *Nature* 27–29.

Virgilio, Nicole R., Sarene Marshall, Olaf Zerbock, and Christopher Holmes (2010). *Reducing Emissions from Deforestation and Degradation (REDD): A Casebook of On-the-Ground Experience*. Arlington, VA: The Nature Conservancy.

Visseren-Hamakers, Ingrid J., Constance McDermott, Marjanneke J. Vijge, and Benjamin Cashore (2012). 'Trade-Offs, Co-Benefits and Safeguards: Current Debates on the Breadth of REDD+'. 4 (6) *Current Opinion in Environmental Sustainability* 646–653.

Voigt, Christina (2009). 'The Deadlock of the Clean Development Mechanism: Caught Between Sustainability, Environmental Integrity and Economic Efficiency'. In *Climate Law and Developing Countries: Legal and Policy Changes for the World Economy*, edited by Benjamin J. Richardson, Yves Le Bouthillier, Heather McLeod-Kilmurray, and Stepan Wood. Cheltenham: Edward Elgar, 235–261.

Voigt, Christina, and Felipe Ferreira (2016). 'Differentiation in the Paris Agreement'. 6 (1–2) *Climate Law* 58–74.

Wagner, Gernot (2015). 'Push Renewables to Spur Carbon Pricing'. 525 *Nature* 27–29.

Wang, Mingyuan (2008). 'Supervision of Clean Development Mechanism Projects in China: Illusory Rules of Law and Real Government Intervention'. 11 (1–2) *Asia-Pacific Journal of Environmental Law* 121–130.

Wara, Michael W., and David G. Victor (2008). *A Realistic Policy on International Carbon Offsets*. Program on Energy and Sustainable Development, Stanford University, Working Paper No. 74.

Weisslitz, Michael (2002). 'Rethinking the Equitable Principle of Common but Differentiated Responsibility: Differential Versus Absolute Norms of Compliance and Contribution in the Global Climate Change Context'. 13 (2) *Colorado Journal of International Environmental Law and Policy* 473–509.

Winkler, Harald (2004). 'National Policies and the CDM: Avoiding Perverse Incentives'. 15 (4) *Journal of Energy in Southern Africa* 118–122.

World Bank (2010). *World Development Report 2010: Development and Climate Change*. Washington, DC: World Bank.

Yamin, Farhana, and Joanna Depledge (2004). *The International Climate Change Regime: A Guide to Rules, Institutions and Procedures*. Cambridge: Cambridge University Press.

Yamineva, Yulia, and Kati Kulovesi (2013). 'The New Framework for Climate Finance Under the United Nations Framework Convention on Climate Change: A Breakthrough or an Empty Promise?' In *Climate Change and the Law*, edited by Erkki J. Hollo, Kati Kulovesi, and Michael Mehling. Dordrecht: Springer, 191–223.

Yan, Qishe, Chang-Bo Zhou, Peng Qu, and Rui-qin Zhang (2009). 'The Promotion of the Clean Development Mechanism to the Cement Industry for Capturing Waste Heat for Power Generation in China'. 14 (8) *Mitigation and Adaptation Strategies for Global Change* 793–804.

154 *Bibliography*

Young, Oran R. (2014). 'Does Fairness Matter in International Environmental Governance? Creating an Effective and Equitable Climate Regime'. In *Toward a New Climate Agreement: Conflict, Resolution and Governance*, edited by Todd L. Cherry, Jon Hovi, and David M. McEvoy. Abingdon: Routledge, 16–27.

Zahar, Alexander (2012), 'The Climate Change Regime'. In *The Routledge Handbook of International Environmental Law*, edited by Shawkat Alam, Jahid Hossain Bhuiyan, Tareq M. R. Chowdhury, and Erika J. Techera. Oxford: Routledge, 349–373.

Zahar, Alexander (2014a). 'International Environmental Institutions'. In *Oxford Bibliographies in International Law*, edited by Tony Carty. New York: Oxford University Press (online chapter).

Zahar, Alexander (2014b). 'Mediated Versus Cumulative Environmental Damage and the International Law Association's Legal Principles on Climate Change'. 4 (3–4) *Climate Law* 217–233.

Zahar, Alexander (2015a). *International Climate Change Law and State Compliance*. Abingdon: Routledge.

Zahar, Alexander (2015b). 'Methodological Issues in Climate Law'. 5 (1) *Climate Law* 25–34.

Zahar, Alexander (2016). 'The Paris Agreement and the Gradual Development of a Law on Climate Finance'. 6 (1–2) *Climate Law* 75–90.

Zahar, Alexander, Jacqueline Peel, and Lee Godden (2012). *Australian Climate Law in Global Context*. Cambridge: Cambridge University Press.

Zarnetske, Phoebe L., David K. Skelly, and Mark C. Urban (2012). 'Biotic Multipliers of Climate Change'. 336 *Science* 1516–1518.

Zhang, Junjie, and Can Wang (2011). 'Co-Benefits and Additionality of the Clean Development Mechanism: An Empirical Analysis'. 62 *Journal of Environmental Economics and Management* 140–154.

B Reports of FCCC-related bodies (including FCCC reporting guidelines)

CDM (2014). *Voluntary Tool for Describing Sustainable Development Co-Benefits of CDM Project Activities or Programmes of Activities (v. 1.1)*. SD-TOOL01.

CDM Executive Board (2007). *Thirty-Fifth Meeting Report*. CDM-EB-35.

CDM Executive Board (2009). *Annual Report 2009*. FCCC/KP/CMP/2009/16.

CDM Executive Board (2011a). *Annual Report 2011*. FCCC/KP/CMP/2011/3 (Part I).

CDM Executive Board (2011b). *Benefits of the Clean Development Mechanism 2011*.

CDM Executive Board (2012a). *Annual Report 2012*. FCCC/KP/CMP/2012/3 (Part I).

CDM Executive Board (2012b). *Benefits of the Clean Development Mechanism 2012*.

CDM Executive Board (2013). *Annual Report 2013*. FCCC/KP/CMP/2013/5 (Part I).

CDM Executive Board (2015). *Annual Report 2015*. FCCC/KP/CMP/2015/5.

FCCC (1999a). *Guidelines for the Preparation of National Communications by Parties Included in Annex I to the Convention, Part I: UNFCCC Reporting Guidelines on Annual Inventories*. FCCC/CP/1999/7 (annex to Decision 3/CP.5), pp. 3–79.

FCCC (1999b). *Guidelines for the Preparation of National Communications by Parties Included in Annex I to the Convention, Part II: UNFCCC Reporting Guidelines on National Communications*. FCCC/CP/1999/7 (annex to Decision 4/CP.5), pp. 80–100.

FCCC (1999c). *Guidelines for the Technical Review of Greenhouse Gas Inventories from Parties Included in Annex I to the Convention*. FCCC/CP/1999/7 (annex to Decision 6/CP.5), pp. 109–114.

Bibliography   155

FCCC (2011). *UNFCCC Biennial Reporting Guidelines for Developed Country Parties.* FCCC/CP/2011/9/Add.1 (annex to Decision 2/CP.17), pp. 31–35.

FCCC (2013). *Guidelines for the Technical Review of Information Reported Under the Convention Related to Greenhouse Gas Inventories, Biennial Reports and National Communications by Parties Included in Annex I to the Convention.* FCCC/CP/2013/10/Add.2 (annex to Decision 23/CP.19), pp. 20–30.

FCCC Secretariat (2007). *Investment and Financial Flows to Address Climate Change.* Bonn: UNFCCC.

FCCC Secretariat (2008). *Investment and Financial Flows to Address Climate Change: An Update.* FCCC/TP/2008/7.

FCCC Secretariat (2011). *Compilation of Information on Nationally Appropriate Mitigation Actions to be Implemented by Parties not Included in Annex I to the Convention.* FCCC/AWGLCA/2011/INF.1.

Global Environment Facility (2013a). *Final Report of the Fifth Overall Performance Study of the GEF: At Crossroads for Higher Impact.* GEF/R.6/17.

Global Environment Facility (2013b). *Report of the Global Environment Facility to the Nineteenth Session of the Conference of the Parties to the United Nations Framework Convention on Climate Change.* FCCC/CP/2013/3.

Global Environment Facility (2014). *Report of the Global Environment Facility to the Twentieth Session of the Conference of the Parties to the United Nations Framework Convention on Climate Change.* FCCC/CP/2014/2.

Global Environment Facility (2015). *Report of the Global Environment Facility to the Twenty-First Session of the Conference of the Parties to the United Nations Framework Convention on Climate Change.* FCCC/CP/2015/4.

Green Climate Fund (2013). *Report of the Green Climate Fund to the Conference of the Parties.* FCCC/CP/2013/6.

Green Climate Fund (2014). *Report of the Green Climate Fund to the Conference of the Parties.* FCCC/CP/2014/8.

Green Climate Fund (2015). *Report of the Green Climate Fund to the Conference of the Parties.* FCCC/CP/2015/3.

High-Level Panel on the CDM Policy Dialogue (2012). *Climate Change, Carbon Markets and the CDM: A Call to Action.* CDM Policy Dialogue Final Report.

Standing Committee on Finance (2013). *Report of the Standing Committee on Finance to the Conference of the Parties.* FCCC/CP/2013/8.

Standing Committee on Finance (2014a). *Biennial Assessment and Overview of Climate Finance Flows Report.* FCCC.

Standing Committee on Finance (2014b). *Report of the Standing Committee on Finance to the Conference of the Parties.* FCCC/CP/2014/5.

Standing Committee on Finance (2015). *Report of the Standing Committee on Finance to the Conference of the Parties.* FCCC/CP/2015/8.

Subsidiary Body for Implementation (2007). *An Assessment of the Funding Necessary to Assist Developing Countries in Meeting Their Commitments Relating to the Global Environment Facility Replenishment Cycle.* FCCC/SBI/2007/21.

Subsidiary Body for Implementation (2013). *Compilation of Information on Nationally Appropriate Mitigation Actions to be Implemented by Developing Country Parties.* FCCC/SBI/2013/INF.12/Rev.2.

Subsidiary Body for Implementation (2014). *Compilation and Synthesis of Sixth National Communications and First Biennial Reports from Parties Included in Annex I to the Convention: Executive Summary.* FCCC/SBI/2014/INF.20.

156 *Bibliography*

Subsidiary Body for Scientific and Technical Advice (2004). *Guidelines for the Preparation of National Communications by Parties Included in Annex I to the Convention, Part I: UNFCCC Reporting Guidelines on Annual Inventories (Following Incorporation of the Provisions of Decision 13/CP.9)*. FCCC/SBSTA/2004/8.

Subsidiary Body for Scientific and Technical Advice (2006). *Updated UNFCCC Reporting Guidelines on Annual Inventories Following Incorporation of the Provisions of Decision 14/CP.11*. FCCC/SBSTA/2006/9.

Subsidiary Body for Scientific and Technical Advice (2011). *Report on the Expert Meeting on Forest Reference Emission Levels and Forest Reference Levels for Implementation of REDD-Plus Activities*. FCCC/SBSTA/2011/INF.18.

Work Programme on Long-Term Finance (2013). *Report on the Outcomes of the Extended Work Programme on Long-Term Finance*. FCCC/CP/2013/7.

C FCCC and Kyoto Protocol decisions

COP 7 (Marrakesh)

Decision 7/CP.7 (2001). *Funding Under the Convention*. FCCC/CP/2001/13/Add.1.

Decision 10/CP.7 (2001). *Funding Under the Kyoto Protocol*. FCCC/CP/2001/13/Add.1.

Decision 27/CP.7 (2001). *Guidance to an Entity Entrusted with the Operation of the Financial Mechanism of the Convention, for the Operation of the Least Developed Countries Fund*. FCCC/CP/2001/13/Add.4.

COP 8 (New Delhi)

Decision 5/CP.8 (2002). *Review of the Financial Mechanism*. FCCC/CP/2002/7/Add.1.

Decision 7/CP.8 (2002). *Initial Guidance to an Entity Entrusted with the Operation of the Financial Mechanism of the Convention, for the Operation of the Special Climate Change Fund*. FCCC/CP/2002/7/Add.1.

Decision 8/CP.8 (2002). *Guidance to an Entity Entrusted with the Operation of the Financial Mechanism of the Convention, for the Operation of the Least Developed Countries Fund*. FCCC/CP/2002/7/Add.1.

Decision 17/CP.8 (2002). *Guidelines for the Preparation of National Communications from Parties not Included in Annex I to the Convention*. FCCC/CP/2002/7/Add.2.

Decision 18/CP.8 (2002). *Guidelines for the Preparation of National Communications by Parties Included in Annex I to the Convention, Part I: UNFCCC Reporting Guidelines on Annual Inventories*. FCCC/CP/2002/7/Add.2.

Decision 19/CP.8 (2002). *Guidelines for the Technical Review of Greenhouse Gas Inventories from Parties Included in Annex I to the Convention*. FCCC/CP/2002/7/Add.2.

COP 9 (Milan)

Decision 3/CP.9 (2003). *Report of the Global Environment Facility to the Conference of the Parties*. FCCC/CP/2003/6/Add.1.

Decision 4/CP.9 (2003). *Additional Guidance to an Operating Entity of the Financial Mechanism*. FCCC/CP/2003/6/Add.1.

Bibliography   157

COP 10 (Buenos Aires)

Decision 9/CP.10 (2004). *Assessment of Funding to Assist Developing Countries in Fulfilling Their Commitments Under the Convention*. FCCC/CP/2004/10/Add.1.

COP 11/MOP 1 (Montreal)

Decision 2/CMP.1 (2005). *Principles, Nature and Scope of the Mechanisms Pursuant to Articles 6, 12 and 17 of the Kyoto Protocol*. FCCC/KP/CMP/2005/8/Add.1.

Decision 3/CMP.1 (2005). *Modalities and Procedures for a Clean Development Mechanism as Defined in Article 12 of the Kyoto Protocol*. FCCC/KP/CMP/2005/8/Add.1.

Decision 5/CMP.1 (2005). *Modalities and Procedures for Afforestation and Reforestation Project Activities under the Clean Development Mechanism in the First Commitment Period of the Kyoto Protocol*. FCCC/KP/CMP/2005/8/Add.1.

Decision 28/CMP.1 (2005). *Initial Guidance to an Entity Entrusted with the Operation of the Financial Mechanism of the Convention, for the Operation of the Adaptation Fund*. FCCC/KP/CMP/2005/8/Add.4.

COP 12/MOP 2 (Nairobi)

Decision 2/CP.12 (2006). *Review of the Financial Mechanism*. FCCC/CP/2006/5/Add.1.

Decision 3/CP.12 (2006). *Additional Guidance to the Global Environment Facility*. FCCC/CP/2006/5/Add.1.

COP 13/MOP 3 (Bali)

Decision 1/CP.13 (2007). *Bali Action Plan*. FCCC/CP/2007/6/Add.1.

Decision 2/CP.13 (2007). *Reducing Emissions from Deforestation in Developing Countries: Approaches to Stimulate Action*. FCCC/CP/2007/6/Add.1.

COP 14/MOP 4 (Poznan)

Decision 3/CP.14 (2008). *Financial Mechanism of the Convention: Fourth Review of the Financial Mechanism*. FCCC/CP/2008/7/Add.1.

Decision 4/CP.14 (2008). *Additional Guidance to the Global Environment Facility*. FCCC/CP/2008/7/Add.1.

Decision 5/CP.14 (2008). *Further Guidance for the Operation of the Least Developed Countries Fund*. FCCC/CP/2008/7/Add.1.

Decision 1/CMP.4 (2008). *Adaptation Fund*. FCCC/KP/CMP/2008/11/Add.2.

COP 15/MOP 5 (Copenhagen)

Decision 2/CP.15 (2009). *Copenhagen Accord*. FCCC/CP/2009/11/Add.1.

Decision 4/CP.15 (2009). *Methodological Guidance for Activities Relating to Reducing Emissions from Deforestation and Forest Degradation and the Role of Conservation, Sustainable Management of Forests and Enhancement of Forest Carbon Stocks in Developing Countries*. FCCC/CP/2009/11/Add.1.

158   *Bibliography*

Decision 6/CP.15 (2009). *Fourth Review of the Financial Mechanism.* FCCC/CP/2009/11/Add.1.

Decision 7/CP.15 (2009). *Additional Guidance to the Global Environment Facility.* FCCC/CP/2009/11/Add.1.

COP 16/MOP 6 (Cancun)

Decision 1/CP.16 (2010). *The Cancun Agreements: Outcome of the Work of the Ad Hoc Working Group on Long-Term Cooperative Action under the Convention.* FCCC/CP/2010/7/Add.1.

Decision 2/CP.16 (2010). *Fourth Review of the Financial Mechanism.* FCCC/CP/2010/7/Add.2.

Decision 3/CP.16 (2010). *Additional Guidance to the Global Environment Facility.* FCCC/CP/2010/7/Add.2.

Decision 4/CP.16 (2010). *Assessment of the Special Climate Change Fund.* FCCC/CP/2010/7/Add.2.

Decision 5/CP.16 (2010). *Further Guidance for the Operation of the Least Developed Countries Fund.* FCCC/CP/2010/7/Add.2.

COP 17/MOP 7 (Durban)

Decision 2/CP.17 (2011). *Outcome of the Work of the Ad Hoc Working Group on Long-Term Cooperative Action Under the Convention.* FCCC/CP/2011/9/Add.1.

Decision 3/CP.17 (2011). *Launching the Green Climate Fund.* FCCC/CP/2011/9/Add.1.

Decision 11/CP.17 (2011). *Report of the Global Environment Facility to the Conference of the Parties and Additional Guidance to the Global Environment Facility.* FCCC/CP/2011/9/Add.2.

Decision 12/CP.17 (2011). *Guidance on Systems for Providing Information on How Safeguards are Addressed and Respected and Modalities Relating to Forest Reference Emission Levels and Forest Reference Levels as Referred to in Decision 1/CP.16, Appendix I.* FCCC/CP/2011/9/Add.2.

Decision 8/CMP.7 (2011). *Further Guidance Relating to the Clean Development Mechanism.* FCCC/KP/CMP/2011/10/Add.2.

COP 18/MOP 8 (Doha)

Decision 1/CP.18 (2012). *Agreed Outcome Pursuant to the Bali Action Plan.* FCCC/CP/2012/8/Add.1.

Decision 4/CP.18 (2012). *Work Programme on Long-Term Finance.* FCCC/CP/2012/8/Add.1.

Decision 5/CP.18 (2012). *Report of the Standing Committee.* FCCC/CP/2012/8/Add.1.

Decision 6/CP.18 (2012). *Report of the Green Climate Fund to the Conference of the Parties and Guidance to the Green Climate Fund.* FCCC/CP/2012/8/Add.1.

Decision 7/CP.18 (2012). *Arrangements Between the Conference of the Parties and the Green Climate Fund.* FCCC/CP/2012/8/Add.1.

Decision 8/CP.18 (2012). *Review of the Financial Mechanism.* FCCC/CP/2012/8/Add.1.

Decision 9/CP.18 (2012). *Report of the Global Environment Facility to the Conference of the Parties and Additional Guidance to the Global Environment Facility.* FCCC/CP/2012/8/Add.1.

Bibliography 159

Decision 10/CP.18 (2012). *Further Guidance to the Least Developed Countries Fund.* FCCC/CP/2012/8/Add.1.

Decision 19/CP.18 (2012). *Common Tabular Format for 'UNFCCC Biennial Reporting Guidelines for Developed Country Parties'.* FCCC/CP/2012/8/Add.3.

Decision 1/CMP.8 (2012). *Amendment to the Kyoto Protocol Pursuant to its Article 3, Paragraph 9 (the Doha Amendment).* FCCC/KP/CMP/2012/13/Add.1.

COP 19/MOP 9 (Warsaw)

Decision 3/CP.19 (2013). *Long-Term Climate Finance.* FCCC/CP/2013/10/Add.1.

Decision 4/CP.19 (2013). *Report of the Green Climate Fund to the Conference of the Parties and Guidance to the Green Climate Fund.* FCCC/CP/2013/10/Add.1.

Decision 5/CP.19 (2013). *Arrangements between the Conference of the Parties and the Green Climate Fund.* FCCC/CP/2013/10/Add.1.

Decision 6/CP.19 (2013). *Report of the Global Environment Facility to the Conference of the Parties and Guidance to the Global Environment Facility.* FCCC/CP/2013/10/Add.1.

Decision 7/CP.19 (2013). *Report of the Standing Committee on Finance to the Conference of the Parties.* FCCC/CP/2013/10/Add.1.

Decision 9/CP.19 (2013). *Work Programme on Results-Based Finance to Progress the Full Implementation of the Activities Referred to in Decision 1/CP.16, Paragraph 70.* FCCC/CP/2013/10/Add.1.

Decision 11/CP.19 (2013). *Modalities for National Forest Monitoring Systems.* FCCC/CP/2013/10/Add.1.

Decision 13/CP.19 (2013). *Guidelines and Procedures for the Technical Assessment of Submissions from Parties on Proposed Forest Reference Emission Levels and/or Forest Reference Levels.* FCCC/CP/2013/10/Add.1.

Decision 21/CP.19 (2013). *General Guidelines for Domestic Measurement, Reporting and Verification of Domestically Supported Nationally Appropriate Mitigation Actions by Developing Country Parties.* FCCC/CP/2013/10/Add.2.

Decision 23/CP.19 (2013). *Work Programme on the Revision of the Guidelines for the Review of Biennial Reports and National Communications, Including National Inventory Reviews, for Developed Country Parties.* FCCC/CP/2013/10/Add.2.

Decision 24/CP.19 (2013). *Revision of the UNFCCC Reporting Guidelines on Annual Inventories for Parties Included in Annex I to the Convention.* FCCC/CP/2013/10/Add.3.

Decision 3/CMP.9 (2013). *Guidance Relating to the Clean Development Mechanism.* FCCC/KP/CMP/2013/9/Add.1.

COP 20/MOP 10 (Lima)

Decision 1/CP.20 (2014). *Lima Call for Climate Action.* FCCC/CP/2014/10/Add.1.

Decision 5/CP.20 (2014). *Long-Term Climate Finance.* FCCC/CP/2014/10/Add.2.

Decision 6/CP.20 (2014). *Report of the Standing Committee on Finance.* FCCC/CP/2014/10/Add.2.

Decision 7/CP.20 (2014). *Report of the Green Climate Fund to the Conference of the Parties and Guidance to the Green Climate Fund.* FCCC/CP/2014/10/Add.2.

Decision 8/CP.20 (2014). *Report of the Global Environment Facility to the Conference of the Parties and Guidance to the Global Environment Facility.* FCCC/CP/2014/10/Add.2.

Decision 9/CP.20 (2014). *Fifth Review of the Financial Mechanism.* FCCC/CP/2014/10/Add.2.

160   *Bibliography*

Decision 11/CP.20 (2014). *Methodologies for the Reporting of Financial Information by Parties Included in Annex I to the Convention*. FCCC/CP/2014/10/Add.2.

Decision 13/CP.20 (2014). *Guidelines for the Technical Review of Information Reported Under the Convention Related to Greenhouse Gas Inventories, Biennial Reports and National Communications by Parties Included in Annex I to the Convention.* FCCC/CP/2014/10/Add.3.

COP 21/MOP 11 (Paris)

Decision 1/CP.21 (2015). *Adoption of the Paris Agreement.*

Decision 7/CP.21 (2015). *Report of the Green Climate Fund to the Conference of the Parties and Guidance to the Green Climate Fund.*

Decision 8/CP.21 (2015). *Report of the Global Environment Facility to the Conference of the Parties and Guidance to the Global Environment Facility.*

Decision 9/CP.21 (2015). *Methodologies for the Reporting of Financial Information by Parties Included in Annex I to the Convention.*

Index

$100 billion goal (for 2020) 6, 17, 73, 77, 104, 109–10, 122

1.5°C limit 13, 121
2°C limit 5–6, 11, 13, 14, 16, 18–19, 21n23, 39, 41, 58–9, 64, 71, 73–4, 77, 81–3, 88, 90–3, 101–4, 110, 112, 119–24, 131

access to climate finance *see* climate finance, access to
accountable reporting rule 15, 77, 91, 93
adaptation: incremental cost of 27, 102
adaptation costs, irreducibility of 5
adaptation finance 102; distinguished from mitigation finance 5–8, 34, 38, 70, 91, 101–2, 120–1; estimates of need for 105–6; for emission-intensive projects 126; supply of 106–11
Adaptation Fund 40
adequacy and predictability (of climate finance) 25, 28–9
Ad Hoc Working Group on Long-Term Cooperative Action (AWG-LCA) 40
Ad Hoc Working Group on the Durban Platform for Enhanced Action (ADP) 22n39, 86, 110
agreed full incremental costs *see* incremental cost
aid *see* Official Development Assistance
Annex I/non-Annex I differentiation *see* developed vs developing countries, differentiation
Annex II states 4, 30–1, 73, 75, 77, 108
Anton, D.K. 82
'alternative' sources of climate finance *see* climate finance, innovative sources of
Asian Development Bank 39
Australia: and fast-start finance 111

'balance' between mitigation and adaptation finance 18, 35, 41, 70, 74, 91, 102, 120
Bali COP (COP 13) 8–9, 86
baseline (for additionality) 26
Biennial Reports (and Biennial Update Reports) 28, 31, 75–7, 95n31, 107, 111, 123
Biennial Review *see* Biennial Reports
biofuels 83, 123, 126, 135n76
Bird, N. 64
Birnie, P.W. *et al.* 63, 78, 80
Bodansky, D. 62
bottom-up vs top-down approaches to mitigation commitments 15–16, 131
Brazil 30, 127–30
Brunnée, J. 85–6
budget *see* emission budget, global
Buchner, B. 24, 103
Buhi, J. 21n14
burden-sharing of emission reductions or climate finance 16–17, 25, 29–30, 33, 57, 71, 73, 77, 86–90, 131

Cancun COP (COP 16) 4–5, 13, 71, 73, 76–7, 86, 101
capacity building 20n6
carbon capture and storage (CCS) 83, 123
CBDR mitigation model 7–9, 12–13, 16, 18, 39, 92–3, 119; and its arbitrary approach to the quantification of climate finance 17–18, 41, 63, 104, 109
CBDR principle *see* common but differentiated responsibility, principle of
China 31, 100n100, 124–5, 127; greenhouse gas emissions 25
clarification of international law, legal scholarship's role in 3, 9–10, 13, 16–17, 58, 62, 69–70

162 *Index*

Clean Development Mechanism (CDM) 31, 35–6, 39–40, 93, 108, 126–30; and additionality 127–30; Executive Board 40, 61, 111, 126–30; and hydropower projects 127–30; and sustainable development 125, 130
Clean Technology Fund 37–38
climate change law, content of 2, 18, 51–60, 90–3, 121–2; defined 51
climate finance: access to 34–5; as mechanism of equity 11, 14, 92; definition of 2, 20n1, 23–5, 32, 34, 45n63, 77; conceptual history of 3; gap 29; as grant or concessional loan 32, 39, 45n55, 71; impact of 19, 35, 75–6, 93, 111–12, 127–30; innovative sources of 36; and its insignificant role within the CBDR mitigation model 9, 12–13, 86, 92, 120; 'need' for 29, 74, 102–6; 'pillars' of 5; reporting of *see* Biennial Reports; supply of 29, 30–1, 73, 75–7, 101, 106–11; *see also* compliance of states with climate finance obligations; new and additional climate finance
climate finance law 12, 18, 90–3, 119–22; integral to climate law 2–3, 12, 69; meaning of 1–2; procedural aspects of 19, 74–7, 120, 123; sources of 69; substantive aspects of 71–4, 77
Climate Investment Funds 39
common but differentiated responsibility (CBDR), principle of 8–9, 11–12, 16, 22n39, 56, 63–4, 84–6
compliance of states with climate finance obligations 18–19
concessional loan *see* climate finance, as grant or concessional loan
containment rule 90
control philosophy 19, 121–31
Copenhagen Accord 61, 76; mitigation model 6–9, 10–11, 14, 16, 41, 86; and polluter-pays principle 10–11; provisions on climate finance 3–8, 17–18, 62, 75, 108–9, 120
Copenhagen COP (COP 15) 1, 3, 16, 18–19, 70–2, 119

dams *see* Clean Development Mechanism, and hydropower projects
Depledge, J. 28, 30
developed countries: obligation to supply climate finance 6–7, 30–1, 72–3
developed vs developing countries: differentiation 4, 6–7, 74, 77, 85–6; and reciprocal obligations on climate finance 4–6, 20n12, 30, 60, 72, 76–7, 86, 92, 119–20; and weak vs strong notions of differentiation 20n11
developing countries: increased emissions from 6, 22n35; obligation to use available climate finance 6–7, 30, 60, 77, 92, 119–20
development aid *see* Official Development Assistance
differentiation *see* developed vs developing countries, differentiation
Durban COP (COP 17) 86

'early' climate finance 108
ecocentric ethic 131
effort-sharing *see* burden-sharing of emission reductions or climate finance
emission budget, global 12, 14–15, 21n25, 33, 59, 72–3, 111, 120, 122–3, 130–1
emission gap 29
emission pricing *see* polluter-pays principle
emissions *see* greenhouse gas emissions
emissions from hydropower projects *see* Clean Development Mechanism, and hydropower projects
emission trading 31
energy demand, growth of 21n27
enhanced transparency framework for action and support (ETF) 76
Environmental Impact Assessment (EIA) 81–2
equity, principle of 11, 14, 56, 84–6, 90, 92, 119
equitable burden-sharing *see* burden-sharing of emission reductions or climate finance
equivalence rule 91, 119
Eskom power plant 124
ethic of control of nature *see* control philosophy
Expert Review Teams (ERTs) 76–7, 107
Export-Import Bank of the United States 37

Fast-Start Finance (FSF) 20n9, 101; supply of 108–9
FCCC mitigation model *see* CBDR mitigation model
FCCC study on climate finance need 103, 105, 110
Fearnside, P. 127–30
Feng, L. 21n14

Index 163

Fifth Assessment Report (of the IPCC) *see* Intergovernmental Panel on Climate Change Fifth Assessment Report

financing gap *see* climate finance gap

Forest Investment Program 37

fossil fuels, legal and economic support for 124–5, 133n27

GCF *see* Green Climate Fund

GEF *see* Global Environment Facility

general mitigation rule 15, 120, 131

geoengineering 83, 119, 121, 131

good-faith obligation/principle/rule 15, 56, 84–5, 91

global emission budget *see* emission budget, global

Global Environment Facility (GEF) 30, 32, 37–8, 75, 106, 108, 110, 112

global stocktake 76, 122

grant *see* climate finance, as grant or concessional loan

Green Climate Fund (GCF) 14, 32, 37, 41, 76, 110

greenhouse gas emissions: growth of 14, 22n32; as pollution 10–11; pricing of *see* polluter-pays principle; reporting of 74–5, 77, 111, 123

Haites, E. 103

Hicks, R.L. *et al.* 108, 124

hydropower CDM projects *see* Clean Development Mechanism, and hydropower projects

ILA Principles 55–60, 80

impact and effectiveness of climate finance *see* climate finance, impact of

incremental cost 25–8, 102–3; defined 27

INDC *see* Intended Nationally Determined Contribution

India 104–6, 127

individualization rule 15, 120, 131

Initiative for Sustainable Forest Landscapes 37

innovative sources of climate finance *see* climate finance, innovative sources of

Intended Nationally Determined Contribution (INDC) 104–6, 110

Inter-American Development Bank 39

Intergovernmental Panel on Climate Change (IPCC) 31, 83, 91, 103, 122–3, 128; and climate finance 24–5; Fifth Assessment Report 3

International Assessment and Review (IAR) 76–7

international climate finance law *see* climate finance law

International Consultation and Analysis (ICA) 76–7

International Energy Agency (IEA) 103

International Law Association (ILA) 55–8, 63, 70, 78

IPPC *see* Intergovernmental Panel on Climate Change

Japan 108

Joint Implementation 31

Kerry, J. (US Secretary of State) 20n12

Kulovesi, K. 61–2

Kyoto Protocol 8–9, 15–16, 31, 36, 40, 60, 64, 69, 71, 85, 88–9, 111

law *see* climate change law; climate finance law

LDC Fund 37, 40, 106, 108

Least Developed Countries (LDCs) 7, 92, 106

Lin, J. 61–2

long-term finance 101

Mayer, B. 52–5

Mehling, M. 52

methodology, legal *see* clarification of international law, legal scholarship's role in

mid-term finance 101, 109–10

mitigation obligations, and their convertibility into climate finance obligations 14, 19

mitigation finance 102; distinguished from adaptation finance 5, 34, 70, 91; estimates of need for 103–5; and mal-adaptive effects 126; supply of 106–11

'modified' polluter-pays principle 11, 13–14, 17, 18, 58, 86, 89, 91–3, 101, 112, 119–20, 122

Multilateral Development Banks (MDBs) 32, 37–9, 108, 124, 126

Nakhooda, S. 24

NAMA *see* nationally appropriate mitigation action

NAPA *see* National Adaptation Programme of Action

National Adaptation Programme of Action (NAPA) 105–6, 114n24

164   *Index*

National Communications 75, 123
nationally appropriate mitigation action (NAMA) 104
Nationally Determined Contribution (NDC) 15, 90, 104, 110–11, 120, 122–3, 131
need for climate finance *see* climate finance, 'need' for
new and additional climate finance 18, 25–6, 36, 75, 107, 109
no-harm principle 52–7, 62, 78–9
Norway 32, 40
nuclear energy 83

OECD Development Assistance Committee 108
Official Development Assistance (ODA) 25–6, 33–4, 108, 126
Olbrisch, S. *et al.* 27, 104, 108
'original' mitigation model *see* CBDR mitigation model
Oslo Principles 58–60
Other Official Flows 109
outcomes of climate finance *see* climate finance, impact of
Overseas Private Investment Corporation 37

Papua New Guinea 104
Paris Agreement 5, 11, 13, 16, 40–1, 69, 76–7, 80, 102, 104, 120, 122–3; and climate finance 15, 25, 30–1, 72–4, 106–7, 110–11; and emission pricing 36; and offset trading 40, 127; *see also* Nationally Determined Contribution
Paris COP (COP 21) 8, 17, 90
Peel, J. 62–3
per-capita emissions 56, 60–1, 89, 92
Philippines 129
Pilot Program for Climate Resilience 37
pledge period (2013–2020) 6, 18, 71–2, 74–6, 101, 109–10
philosophy of the control of nature *see* control philosophy
polluter-pays principle 19, 31, 62–4, 70, 87–93, 99n93; as a manifestation of the principle of equity 11–12, 88; definition of 10; in domestic systems 35, 63, 87; in international law 10, 63–4, 87–8; pre-2009 neglect of 12; rationale for 11, 90; top-down logic of 16, 90
precautionary principle 59, 62, 79–80
prevention principle *see* no-harm principle

principle of common but differentiated responsibility *see* common but differentiated responsibility, principle of
principle of environmental sovereignty *see* no-harm principle
principle of equity *see* equity, principle of
principle of good-faith cooperation *see* good-faith obligation/principle/rule
principle of precaution *see* precautionary principle
prioritization rule 91
private (climate) finance 23–4, 45n63
public (climate) finance 32, 108–10

re-assessment and re-negotiation rule 91
REDD 5, 40, 61, 125–7
regime finance *see* climate finance
renewable energy, project costs 28
reporting, by states (on climate finance etc.) *see* Biennial Reports; National Communications
review of state reports 76; see also International Assessment and Review; International Consultation and Analysis
Rio Declaration 64, 79–81, 84, 87–8
rule against transboundary harm *see* no-harm principle

Sands, P. 62–3
Santo Antônio dam 128–9
Scaling-Up Renewable Energy Program in Low Income Countries 38
Schalatek, L. 63–4, 82
Small-Island Developing States (SIDS) 7
Smith, J.B. *et al.* 105
South Africa 104, 124
Special Climate Change Fund 38, 108
specific mitigation rule 15
Stadelmann, M. *et al.* 109
Standing Committee on Finance 106–7, 112
state compliance *see* compliance of states with climate finance obligations
state finance 24, 33, 36; defined 23, 32
state-leveraged finance 24, 33; defined 23; *see also* private (climate) finance
Stockholm Declaration 78
Strategic Climate Fund 39
Streck, C. 38, 61–2, 85–6
Subsidiary Body for Implementation (SBI) 76
subsidies for fossil fuels *see* fossil fuels, legal and economic support for

Index 165

supply of climate finance *see* climate finance, supply of

sustainable development, principle of 57–8, 80–4

technical analysis (of Biennial Update Report) 76

technical review report (on Biennial Report) 76

Technical Team of Experts (TTEs) 76, 96n34

technology transfer 20n6, 25, 71

top down vs bottom up *see* bottom-up vs top-down approaches to mitigation commitments

transnational finance *see* climate finance

transparency rule *see* accountable reporting rule

treaty finance *see* climate finance

Ulfstein, G. 86

UNEP 29; study on climate finance need 105

United Kingdom 125

United Nations Framework Convention on Climate Change *see* FCCC

United States 37–8, 108, 124–5

USAID 37

van Asselt, H. 52

Vietnam 129

Voigt, C. 86

'voluntarism' in climate finance 21n18, 60, 63, 71–2, 77, 119–20, 131

World Bank 39; study on climate finance need 103, 105

Yamin, F. 28, 30

Yamineva, Y. 61–2

Taylor & Francis eBooks

Helping you to choose the right eBooks for your Library

Add Routledge titles to your library's digital collection today. Taylor and Francis ebooks contains over 50,000 titles in the Humanities, Social Sciences, Behavioural Sciences, Built Environment and Law.

Choose from a range of subject packages or create your own!

Benefits for you
- Free MARC records
- COUNTER-compliant usage statistics
- Flexible purchase and pricing options
- All titles DRM-free.

Benefits for your user
- Off-site, anytime access via Athens or referring URL
- Print or copy pages or chapters
- Full content search
- Bookmark, highlight and annotate text
- Access to thousands of pages of quality research at the click of a button.

REQUEST YOUR FREE INSTITUTIONAL TRIAL TODAY

Free Trials Available
We offer free trials to qualifying academic, corporate and government customers.

eCollections – Choose from over 30 subject eCollections, including:

Archaeology	Language Learning
Architecture	Law
Asian Studies	Literature
Business & Management	Media & Communication
Classical Studies	Middle East Studies
Construction	Music
Creative & Media Arts	Philosophy
Criminology & Criminal Justice	Planning
Economics	Politics
Education	Psychology & Mental Health
Energy	Religion
Engineering	Security
English Language & Linguistics	Social Work
Environment & Sustainability	Sociology
Geography	Sport
Health Studies	Theatre & Performance
History	Tourism, Hospitality & Events

For more information, pricing enquiries or to order a free trial, please contact your local sales team:
www.tandfebooks.com/page/sales

 | The home of Routledge books

www.tandfebooks.com